Principles of Peace

Finney's Lessons on Romans

Volume II

C. G. Finney

Books by L.G. Parkhurst, Jr.

Principles of Righteousness:
Finney's Lessons on Romans, Volume I
Compiled and edited from the works of Charles G. Finney
Edmond: Agion Press, 2006

Prayer Steps to Serenity: The Twelve Steps Journey:
New Serenity Prayer Edition
Edmond: Agion Press, 2006

Prayer Steps to Serenity:
Daily Quiet Time Edition
Edmond: Agion Press, 2005

How God Teaches Us to Pray:
Lessons from the Lives of Francis and Edith Schaeffer
Milton Keynes, England: Nelson Word Ltd. 1993

How to Pray in the Spirit
Compiled and edited from the works of John Bunyan
Grand Rapids: Kregel Publications, 1993, 1998

Principles of Prayer
Compiled and edited from the works of Charles Finney
Minneapolis: Bethany House Publishers, 1980, 2001

Finney's Systematic Theology:
New Expanded Edition
Compiled and edited from the works of Charles G. Finney
Minneapolis: Bethany House Publishers, 1994

Principles of Devotion
Compiled and edited from the works of Charles Finney
Minneapolis: Bethany House Publishers, 1987

Principles of Peace

Finney's Lessons on Romans
Volume II

Charles Grandison Finney

With Commentary from Henry Cowles
The Longer Epistles of Paul

Compiled and Newly Edited for Today by
L.G. Parkhurst, Jr.

"For the kingdom of God is not a matter of eating and drinking, but of righteousness, peace and joy in the Holy Spirit."—Romans 14:17

Agion Press
AgionPress.com

Principles of Peace: Finney's Lessons on Romans: Volume II:
   The Biblical Companion to Finney's Systematic Theology
Copyright © 2010 Louis Gifford Parkhurst, Jr. All Rights Reserved.

Published by Agion Press, P.O. Box 1052, Edmond, OK 73083-1052

No part of this book may be reproduced or transmitted in any form or by any means, graphic, electronic, or mechanical, including photocopying, recording, taping, or by any information storage retrieval system, without the prior written permission of the copyright owners.

All Scripture quotations in this book are from the *King James Version of the Bible* or *The Holy Bible: New International Version*, copyright 1973, 1978, 1984, by the International Bible Society. Used by permission of Zondervan Bible Publishers.

Cover Photo and Cover Design
Copyright © 2010 by Kathryn Winterscheidt: Used by Permission

The Charles G. Finney Lessons on Romans
    Volume I: *Principles of Righteousness*
    Volume II: *Principles of Peace*
    Volume III: *Principles of Joy in the Holy Spirit*

Publisher's Cataloging-in-Publication Data

Finney, Charles Grandison, 1792-1875.
    Principles of Peace: Finney's Lessons on Romans, Volume II /
Charles G. Finney ; compiled and edited by Louis Gifford Parkhurst, Jr.
    267 p. : port. ; 23 cm.
    1, Bible. N.T. Romans—Sermons. 2. Sermons, American.
I. Parkhurst, Louis Gifford, 1946- . II. Title
BS2665.4.F58   2010   227'.106
ISBN 978-0-9778053-2-7 (pbk.):   LCCN 2006922106
P 10 9 8 7 6 5 4 3 2 1

Principles of Righteousness
Volume I

Preface

1. The Wrath of God Against Those Who Withstand His Truth
    Romans 1:18-19—1857 11
2. God's Wrath Against Those Who Withstand His Truth
    Romans 1:18-19—1858 23
3. Holding the Truth in Unrighteousness
    Romans 1:18-19—1861 35
4. On the Atonement
    Romans 3:25-26—1856 53
5. Sanctification by Faith
    Romans 3:31—1837 67
6. The Foundation, Conditions, Relations, and Results of Faith
    Romans 4:1-5—1850 79
7. The Rationality of Faith
    Romans 4:20-21—1851 93
8. God's Love Commended to Us
    Romans 5:8—1858 105
9. The Nature of Death to Sin
    Romans 6:7—1840 105
10. Death to Sin through Christ
    Romans 6:11—1853 125
11. Sanctification under Grace
    Romans 6:14—1839 141
12. The Wages of Sin
    Romans 6:23—1854 153
Study Questions for Individuals and Groups 171
Henry Cowles Commentary on Key Verses from Romans 185
About Agion Press 207

Principles of Peace
Volume II

Preface

1. Legal Experience
   Romans 7:1, 22-23—1837 1
2. Christ the Husband of the Church
   Romans 7:4—1837 17
3. Revival of Sin and the Law
   Romans 7:9—1853 31
4. Thanks for the Gospel Victory
   Romans 7:25—1856 45
5. Justification
   Romans 8:1—1843 59
6. Total Depravity
   Romans 8:7—1836 73
7. Moral Depravity
   Romans 8:7—1862 117
8. License, Bondage and Liberty
   Romans 8:15—1854 131
9. Spirit of Prayer
   Romans 8:26-27—1835 145
10. All Things for Good to Those That Love God
    Romans 8:28—1847 167
11. All Events Ruinous to the Sinner
    Romans 8:28—1847 179
12. All Things for Good to Those That Love God
    Romans 8:28—1852 193
13. Religion of the Law and the Gospel
    Romans 9:30-33—1837 205

Study Questions for Individuals and Groups 217
Henry Cowles Commentary on Key Verses from Romans 235

Principles of Joy in the Holy Spirit
Volume III

Preface

1. Men, Ignorant of God's Righteousness Would Establish Own
    Romans 10:3—1855
2. The Way to be Holy
    Romans 10:4—1843
3. On Believing with the Heart
    Romans 10:10—1856
4. Conformity to the World
    Romans 12:2—1837
5. How to Prevent Our Employments from Injuring Our Souls
    Romans 12:11—1839
6. Being in Debt
    Romans 13:8—1839
7. Nature of True Virtue
    Romans 13:8-10—1843
8. Love Is the Whole of Religion
    Romans 13:10—1837
9. Love Worketh No Ill
    Romans 13:10—1841
10. Putting on Christ
    Romans 13:14—1843
11. The Kingdom of God in Consciousness
    Romans 14:17—1861
12. Total Abstinence A Christian Duty
    Romans 14:21—1850
13. Doubtful Actions are Sinful
    Romans 14:23—1837

Study Questions for Individuals and Groups
Henry Cowles Commentary on Key Verses from Romans

Charles Grandison Finney
Revivalist, Pastor, and Theologian
1792-1875

"*The writer is inclined to regard Charles G. Finney as the greatest evangelist and theologian since the days of the apostles. Over eighty-five in every hundred persons professing conversion to Christ in Finney's meetings remained true to God. Finney seems to have had the power of impressing the conscience with the necessity of holy living in such a manner as to procure the most lasting results.*"

From *Deeper Experiences of Famous Christians* by James Gilcrist Lawson, Anderson, Indiana: The Warner Press, 1978, page 175.

Preface

After a delay much longer than I anticipated, Charles G. Finney's *Principles of Peace* has finally been published by Agion Press. One of the reasons I intend to complete this three volume set of Finney's *Lessons on Romans* is because I believe students of the Bible, evangelists, ministers, and revivalists need a comprehensive Biblical companion to *Finney's Systematic Theology*. Finney's sermons or lessons on Romans show how he drew his theological teachings from the Bible, and how he related his theology to his preaching in a very effective manner. His sermons reached the average person in the pew; while *Finney's Systematic Theology* primarily reached college students and professors, ministers and preachers.

In Finney's publication of his *Systematic Theology*, he never completed the first volume, which would have revealed the main points of historic, Biblical Christianity that all true Christians believed in his day. He intended to publish the first volume last, because he believed that he would only be publishing what everyone already knew and believed. Because his intention to publish the first volume last (which he did not live long enough to do) has not been widely understood (and in some cases purposely ignored), Finney's Christian and ethical ideas have been misunderstood and sometimes purposely misrepresented. For example, he has been accused of legalism, of preaching a religion of works, of perfectionism, and of not giving enough honor to the work of the Holy Spirit in the conversion of sinners. I believe the first volume of his *Systematic Theology* would have refuted these criticisms. In any event, if Finney's *Lessons on Romans* are carefully studied the reader will see many of the ways Finney's critics have been in error. I believe the proposed three volume work of Finney's *Lessons on Romans* will partially answer many questions about Finney's true beliefs, and hopefully muffle some of his critics.

Preface

Charles G. Finney's *Principles of Righteousness: Finney's Lessons on Romans,* Volume I, resumed the "Finney's Principles" series, which I began with the first book in the series, *Principles of Prayer*, published by Bethany House Publishers in 1980. *Principles of Peace*, Volume II, will be followed, God-willing, by *Principles of Joy in the Holy Spirit*, Volume III. Unlike the first series, Finney's *Lessons on Romans* include study questions for each lesson that can be used by the individual student for review or in a class study on Romans. Each volume includes 12 to 13 lessons for study during 3 quarters of the year. In addition, Finney's *Lessons on Romans* includes extensive excerpts from the commentary on Romans by Henry Cowles, a contemporary and colleague of Finney's at Oberlin College; therefore, in the new *Finney's Principles Series* you have a variety of tools to use in your study of the Bible.

From time to time during the last thirty years, since the beginning of this series, some have asked me how I have used what I have learned from Finney in my preaching. The best way to learn the answer to this question is to read the many weekly Bible Lessons that I have published in *The Oklahoman* newspaper for more than twenty years. For the last few years, I have published these lessons on the *International Bible Lessons* web site at internationalbiblelessons.com. These Bible Lessons are based on the Uniform Lesson Series and are used by teachers and students in many different Christian denominations around the world. To learn how Finney's ethical and life-transforming teachings can be applied today, see my books, *Prayer Steps to Serenity The Twelve Steps Journey: New Serenity Prayer Edition* or *Prayer Steps to Serenity: Daily Quiet Time Edition*.

May God bless your continuing study of His word!

Love in the Lamb of God
L.G. Parkhurst, Jr.
November 8, 2009

1

Legal Experience
1837

Know ye not, brethren, (for I speak to them that know the law,) how that the law hath dominion over a man as long as he liveth?.... For I delight in the law of God after the inward man: But I see another law in my members, warring against the law of my mind, and bringing me into captivity to the law of sin which is in my members.—Romans 7:1, 22-23—KJV

Do you not know, brothers—for I am speaking to men who know the law—that the law has authority over a man only as long as he lives?.... For in my inner being I delight in God's law; but I see another law at work in the members of my body, waging war against the law of my mind and making me a prisoner of the law of sin at work within my members.—Romans 7:1, 22-23—NIV

In this lesson, I will give a summary and survey of Romans, Chapter Seven. Different opinions have prevailed in the church concerning this chapter and I shall simplify the subject as much as possible so as to bring it within the compass of a single lecture. Otherwise, I might make a volume; so much has been written to show the meaning of the seventh chapter.

The principal opinions concerning the application of this chapter.

One opinion that has extensively prevailed and still prevails is that the latter part of the chapter is an epitome [a typical or ideal example] of Christian experience. Some suppose it describes the situation and exercises of a Christian, and is designed to exhibit the Christian warfare with indwelling sin. This is, comparatively, a modern opinion. For centuries after the Apostle Paul wrote Romans, no writer is known to have held this modern view of the chapter. According to Professor Stuart, who has examined the subject more thoroughly than any other man in America, Augustine was the first writer that exhibited this interpretation, and Augustine resorted to it in his controversy with Pelagius.*

The only other interpretation which prevailed in the first centuries, and which is still generally adopted on the continent of Europe as well as by a considerable number of writers in England and America, is that this passage describes the experience of a sinner under conviction, who was acting under the motives of the law, and not yet brought to the experience of the gospel. Unfortunately, in America, the most prevalent opinion is that the seventh chapter of Romans delineates the experience of a Christian.

The importance of rightly understanding this chapter.

A right understanding of this chapter must be fundamental. If this passage in fact describes a sinner under conviction (or a purely legal experience), and if a person supposing that it is a Christian experience finds his own experience corresponds with it, then his mistake is fatal. If Paul in chapter seven is in fact giving only the experience of a sinner under legal motives and considerations, it must be a fatal error to rest in his experience as the experience of a real Christian because his experience corresponds with the seventh chapter of Romans.

Legal Experience

Some principles and facts bearing on the elucidation of this subject.

People act in all cases, and from the nature of mind must always act, as on the whole they feel to be preferable. Or, in other words, the will governs the conduct. People never act against their will. The will governs the motion of the limbs. Voluntary beings cannot act contrary to their will.

People often desire what, on the whole, they do not choose. The desires and the will are often opposed to each other. The conduct is governed by the choice, not by the desires. The desires may be inconsistent with the choice. You may desire to go to some other place, and yet on the whole choose to remain where you are. Perhaps you desire very strongly to be somewhere else, and yet choose to remain in a meeting. For example, a man wishes to go on a journey. Perhaps he desires it strongly. It may be very important to his business or ambition. But his wife and children are sick, or some other situation requires him to stay at home; therefore, on the whole he chooses to remain. In all cases, the conduct follows the actual choice.

Regeneration, or conversion, involves a change in choice. It is a change in the supreme controlling choice of the mind. The regenerated or converted person prefers God's glory to everything else. He chooses God as his supreme object of affection. This is a change of heart. Before, he chose his own interest or happiness as his supreme end. Now, he chooses God's service in preference to his own interest. When a person is truly born again, his *choice is habitually right* and his *conduct is in the main right.*

The force of *temptation may produce an occasional wrong choice*, or even a succession of wrong choices, but his *habitual* course of action is right. The will, or choice, of a converted person is habitually right, and of course his conduct is too. If this is not true, in what sense does the converted person differ from the unconverted person? If it is not the character of the converted person that he habitually obeys the commandments of God, what is his character? But I presume this position will not be disputed by anyone who believes in the doctrine of regeneration.

Moral agents are so constituted that they naturally and necessarily approve of what is right. A moral agent is one who possesses understanding, will, and conscience. Conscience is the power of discerning the difference of moral objects. A moral agent can be led to see the difference between right and wrong, so that his moral nature shall approve of what is right. Otherwise, a sinner never can be brought under conviction of sin. If he does not have a moral nature that can see and highly approve of the law of God, and justify the penalty of disobedience, he cannot be convicted of sin. *This is conviction of sin:* to see the goodness of the law that he has broken and the justice of the penalty he has incurred. But in fact, there is not a moral agent in heaven, earth, or hell, that cannot be made to see that the law of God is right and whose conscience does not approve the law.

Some people may not only approve the law as right but may often, when it is viewed abstractly and without reference to its bearing on themselves, take real pleasure in contemplating it. This is one great source of self-deception. People view the law of God in the abstract and love it. When no selfish reason is present for opposing God's law, they take pleasure in viewing it. They approve of what is right and condemn wickedness in the abstract. All people do this when no selfish reason is pressing on them. Whoever found a person so wicked that he approved of evil in the abstract? Where was a moral being ever found that approved the character of the devil, or approved of other wicked people unconnected with himself? How often do you hear wicked people express the greatest abhorrence and detestation of enormous wickedness in others. If their passions are in no way enlisted in favor of error or wrong, they always stand up for what is right. And this merely constitutional approbation of what is right may amount even to delight, when they do not see the relations of right interfering in any manner with their own selfishness.

In this constitutional approbation of truth and the law of God, and the delight which naturally arises from it, there is no virtue. It is only what belongs to our moral nature. It arises naturally from the constitution of the mind. Mind is constitutionally capable of seeing the beauty of virtue. And so far from their being any virtue in it, it is in fact only a clearer proof of the strength of their depravity that when they know the right, and see its excellence, they do not obey it. Seeing the beauty of virtue does not mean that impenitent sinners have in them something that is holy. Instead, their wickedness is herein seen to be so much the greater. For the wickedness of sin is in proportion to the light (truth) that is enjoyed.

Legal Experience

When we find that people may not only see the excellence of the law of God, but even strongly approve of it and take delight in it, and yet not obey it, it shows how desperately wicked they are and makes sin appear exceeding sinful.

A common usage of language is for people to say, "I would do so and so, but cannot," when they only mean to be understood as desiring it, but not as actually choosing to do it. And so they say, "I *could not* do so," when they only mean that they *would not* do so. They could, if they would.

Recently, I asked a minister to preach for me the next Sunday. He answered, "I can't." I found out afterwards that he could, if he would. I asked a merchant to take a certain price for a piece of goods. He said, "I can't do it." What did he mean? That he did not have the power to accept such a price? Not at all. He could, if he would. He chose not to do it. You will see the bearing of these remarks as I proceed.

Some rules of interpretation and evidence.

There are certain rules of evidence which all people are bound to apply when ascertaining the meaning of testimony and writings.

First, we are always to put that construction on language which is required by the nature of the subject. We are obligated always to understand a person's language as it is applicable to the subject of discourse. Much of the language of common life may be tortured into anything, if you lose sight of the subject and take the liberty to interpret it without reference to what people are speaking about. How much injury has been done by interpreting separate passages and single expressions in the scriptures in violation of this principle! It is chiefly by overlooking this simple rule that the scriptures have been tortured into supporting errors and contradictions innumerable and absurd beyond all calculation. This rule is applicable to all statements. Courts of justice never would allow such perversions as have been committed upon the Bible.

Second, if a person's language will admit, we are bound always to construe it so as to make him consistent with himself. Unless you observe this rule, you can scarcely converse five minutes with any individual on any subject and not make him contradict himself. If you do not hold to this rule, how can one person ever communicate his ideas so that another person will understand him? How can a witness ever make known the facts to the jury if his language is to be tortured at pleasure without the restraints of this rule?

Third, when interpreting a person's language, we are always to keep in view the point to which he is speaking. We are to understand the scope of his argument, the object he has in view, and the point to which he is speaking. Otherwise, we shall naturally not understand his language. Suppose I were to take up a book, any book, and not keep my eye on the object the writer had in view in making it, and the point to which he is aiming. I never can understand that book. It is easy to see how endless errors have grown out of a practice of interpreting the scriptures in disregard of the first principles of interpretation.

Fourth, when you understand the point to which a person is speaking, you are to understand him as speaking to that point; and not to put a construction on his language unconnected with his object, or inconsistent with it. By losing sight of this rule, you may make nonsense of everything. You are always obligated to interpret language in the light of the subject to which it is applied or about which it is spoken.

In light of these rules and principles, I will now proceed to give my own view of the meaning of the disputed parts of this chapter and my reasons for it.

Whether the apostle was speaking of himself in this passage, or whether he was supposing a case, is not material to the right interpretation of the language. Many suppose that because he speaks in the first person, he is to be understood as referring to himself. But it is a common practise when we are discussing general principles or arguing a point to suppose a case by way of illustration or to establish a point. It is very natural to state it in the first person without at all intending to be understood, and in fact without ever being understood, as declaring an actual occurrence or an experience of our own. In this chapter, the Apostle Paul was pursuing a close train of argument, and he introduces this simply by way of illustration. It is no way material whether it is his own actual experience or a supposed case.

The Apostle James, in the third chapter of *The Letter of James*, speaks

Legal Experience

in the first person; even in administering reproof: "My brethren, be not many masters, knowing that we shall receive the greater condemnation. For in many things we offend all.... Therewith bless we God, even the Father; and therewith curse we men, which are made after the similitude of God" (James 3:1, 9). He did not mean *he himself* "cursed men."

The Apostle Paul often says "I," and uses the first person, when discussing and illustrating general principles: "All things are lawful unto me, but all things are not expedient: all things are lawful for me, but I will not be brought under the power of any" (1 Corinthians 6:12). And again, "Conscience, I say, not thine own, but of the other: for why is my liberty judged of another man's conscience? For if I by grace be a partaker, why am I evil spoken of for that for which I give thanks?" (1 Corinthians 10:29-30). And again, "For now we see through a glass, darkly; but then face to face: now I know in part; but then shall I know even as also I am known. And now abideth faith, hope, charity, these three; but the greatest of these is charity" (1 Corinthians 13:12-13). So also, "For if I build again the things which I destroyed, I make myself a transgressor" (Galatians 2:18). In his letter to the Corinthians, he explains exactly how he uses illustrations, "And these things, brethren, I have in a figure transferred to myself, and to Apollos, for your sakes: that ye might learn in us not to think of men above that which is written, that no one of you be puffed up for one against another" (1 Corinthians 4:6).

Much of the language which the Apostle Paul uses in Romans, chapter seven, is applicable to the case of a backslider; one who has lost all but the form of religion. He has left his first love, and has in fact fallen under the influence of legal motives, of hope and fear, just like an impenitent sinner. If there be such a character as a real backslider, one who has been a real convert, he is then actuated by the same motives as the sinner, and the same language may be equally applicable to both. Therefore, the fact that some of the language before us is applicable to a Christian who has become a backslider does not prove at all that the experience here described is Christian experience, but only that *a backslider and a sinner are in many respects alike*. I do not hesitate to say this much, at least; that *no one who was conscious that he was actuated by love to God could ever have thought of applying this chapter to himself*. If anyone is not in the exercise of love to God, this describes his character; and whether he is backslider or sinner, it is all the same thing in his experience.

Some of the expressions Paul used in Romans chapter seven are supposed to describe the case of a believer who is not an habitual backslider, but who is overcome by temptation and passion for a time, and speaks of himself as if he were all wrong. A person is tempted, we are told, when he is drawn away by his own lusts and enticed. And in that state, no doubt, he might find expressions here that would describe his own experience while under such an influence. But that proves nothing in regard to the design of the passage, for while he is in this state he is so far under a certain influence. The impenitent sinner is *all the time* under just such an influence. The same language, therefore, may be applicable to both without inconsistency.

Although some expressions may bear this plausible construction, yet a view of the whole chapter makes it evident that it cannot be a delineation of Christian experience. Therefore, my own opinion is that the Apostle Paul designed here to represent the experience of a sinner, not careless, but strongly convicted and yet not converted. My reasons are these:

First, because the apostle is here manifestly describing the *habitual character* of someone; and this one is wholly under the dominion of the flesh. It is not as a whole a description of one who, under the power of present temptation, is acting inconsistently with his general character, but his general character is so. It is one who uniformly falls into sin, notwithstanding his approval of the law.

Second, it would have been entirely irrelevant to Paul's purpose to state the experience of a Christian as an illustration of his argument. That was not what was needed. He was laboring to vindicate the law of God in its influence on a carnal mind. In a previous chapter, he had stated the fact that justification was only by faith, and not by works of law. In this seventh chapter, he maintains not only that justification is by faith, but also that sanctification is only by faith. "Know ye not brethren, (for I speak to them that know the law) how that the law hath dominion over a man as long as he liveth? . . . So then, if while her husband liveth, she be married to another man, she shall be called an adulteress: but if her husband be dead, she is free from that law; so that she is no adulteress, though she

Legal Experience

be married to another man" (Romans 7:1, 3). What is the use of all this? Why, this, "Wherefore, my brethren, ye also are become dead to the law by the body of Christ; that ye should be married to another, even to him who is raised from the dead, that we should bring forth fruit unto God" (Romans 7:4). While you were under the law you were bound to obey the law and hold to the terms of the law for justification. But, now being made free from the law as a rule of judgment, you are no longer influenced by legal considerations, of hope and fear, for Christ to whom you are married, has set aside the penalty, that by faith ye might be justified before God.

"For when we were in the flesh," that is, in an unconverted state, "the motions of sins, which were by the law, did work in our members to bring forth fruit unto death: But now we are delivered from the law, that being dead wherein we were held; that we should serve in newness of spirit, and not in the oldness of the letter" (Romans 7:5, 6). Paul is stating here *the real condition of a Christian*; he serves in newness of spirit and not in the oldness of the letter. He had found that the fruit of the law was only death, and by the gospel he had been brought into true subjection to Christ. What is the objection to this? "What shall we say then? Is the law sin? God forbid. Nay, I had not known sin, but by the law: for I had not known lust, except the law had said, Thou shalt not covet . . . And the commandment which was ordained to life, I found to be unto death" (Romans 7:7, 10). The law was enacted that people might live by it, if they would perfectly obey it; but when we were in the flesh, we found it unto death. "For sin, taking occasion by the commandment, deceived me, and by it slew me. Wherefore the law is holy, and the commandment holy, and just, and good" (Romans 7:11-12). Now he brings up the objection again. How can anything that is good be made death unto a person? "Was then that which is good made death unto me? God forbid. But sin, that it might appear sin, working death in me by that which is good; that sin by the commandment might be exceedingly sinful" (Romans 7:13). And he vindicates the law by showing that it is not the fault of the law, but the fault of sin, and that this very result shows at once the excellence of the law and the exceeding sinfulness of sin. Sin must be a horrible thing, if it can work such a perversion as to take the good law of God and make it the means of death.

"For we know that the law is spiritual; but I am carnal, sold under sin" (Romans 7:14). Here is the hinge on which the whole questions turns. Now notice: the apostle is here vindicating the law against the objection that if the law is the means of death to sinners it cannot be good. Against this objection he goes on to show that all its action on the mind of the sinner proves it to be good. Keeping his eye on this point, he argues that the law is good and that the evil comes from the motions of sin in our members. Then he comes to that part which is supposed to delineate a Christian experience, and which is the subject of controversy. He begins by saying, "the law is spiritual but I am carnal" (Romans 7:14). This word *carnal* he uses once and only once in reference to Christians, and then it was in reference to persons who were in a very low state in religion: "For ye are yet carnal; for whereas there is among you envying, and strife, and divisions, are ye not carnal, and walk as men" (1 Corinthians 3:3). These Christians had backslidden, and acted as if they were not converted persons, but were *carnal*. The term itself is generally used to signify *the worst of sinners*. Paul here defines it so: "carnal, sold under sin." Could that be said of Paul himself at the time he wrote the *Epistle to the Romans*? Was that his own experience? Was he "sold under sin?" Was that true of the great apostle? No; he was vindicating the law, and he uses an illustration by supposing a case. He goes on, "For that which I do, I allow not; for what I would, that I do not; but what I hate, that do I" (Romans 7:15).

Here you see the application of the principles I have laid down. In the interpretation of this word "would," we are not to understand it of the choice or will, but only a desire. Otherwise the apostle contradicts a plain matter of fact which everybody knows to be true, that *the will governs the conduct*. Professor Stuart has very properly rendered the word *desire*; *what I desire, I do not, but what I disapprove, that I do*.** Then comes the conclusion, "If, then, I do that which I would not, I consent unto the law, that it is good" (Romans 7:16). If I do that which I disapprove, if I disapprove of my own conduct, if I condemn myself, I thereby bear testimony that the law is good. Now, keep your eye on the object the apostle has in view, and read the next verse, "Now then it is no more that I do it, but sin that dwelleth in me" (Romans 7:17). Here he, as it were, divides

Legal Experience

himself against himself, or speaks of himself as possessing two natures, or, as some of the heathen philosophers taught, as having two souls, one which approves the good and another which loves and chooses evil. "For I know that in me (that is, in my flesh) dwelleth no good thing: for to will is present with me; but how to perform that which is good I find not" (Romans 7:18). Here "to will" means to approve, for if people really will to do a thing, they do it. Everybody knows this. Where the language will admit, we are bound to interpret it so as to make it consistent with known facts. If you understand "to will" literally, you involve the apostle in the absurdity of saying that he willed what he did not do, and so acted contrary to his own will, which contradicts a obvious fact. The meaning of "to will" here must be *desire*. Then it coincides with the experience of every convicted sinner. He knows what he ought to do, and he strongly approves it, but he is not ready to do it. Suppose I were to call on you to do some act. Suppose, for instance, I were to call on those of you who are impenitent to come forward and take that seat, that we might see who you are, and pray for you, and should show you your sins, and that it is your duty to submit to God; some of you would exclaim, "I know it is my duty, and I greatly desire to do it, but I cannot." What do you mean by it? Why, simply, that on the whole, the balance of your will is on the other side.

In the 20th verse Paul repeats what he said before, "Now if I do that I would not, it is no more I that do it, but sin that dwelleth in me" (Romans 7:20). Is that the *habitual character and experience* of a Christian? I admit that a Christian may fall so low that this language may apply to him; but if this is his general character how does it differ from that of an impenitent sinner? If this is the habitual character of a Christian, there is not a word of truth in the scripture representations that the *true Christians are those who really obey God*; for here is one called a Christian of whom it is said expressly that he never does obey God.

"I find then a law, that when I would do good, evil is present within me" (Romans 7:21). Here Paul speaks of the action of the carnal propensities as being so constant and so prevalent that he calls it a "law." "For I delight in the law of God after the inward man" (Romans 7:22). Here is the great stumbling-block. Can it be said of an impenitent sinner that he "delights" in the law of God? I answer, "Yes." I know the expression is a strong one, but the apostle was using strong language all along on both sides. It is no stronger language than the prophet Isaiah uses in Chapter 58. He was describing as wicked and rebellious a generation as ever lived. He says, "Cry aloud, spare not; lift up thy voice like a trumpet, and show my people their transgression, and the house of Jacob their sins" (Isaiah 58:1). Yet Isaiah goes on to say of this very people, "Yet they seek me daily, and delight to know my ways, as a nation that did righteousness, and forsook not the ordinance of their God; they ask of me the ordinances of justice; they TAKE DELIGHT in approaching to God" (Isaiah 58:2). Here is one instance of impenitent sinners manifestly delighting in approaching God. We find the same thing in Ezekiel: "And lo, thou art unto them as a very lovely song of one that hath a pleasant voice, and can play well on an instrument: for they hear thy words, but they do them not" (Ezekiel 33:32). The prophet had been telling how wicked they were. "And they come unto thee as the people cometh, and they sit before thee as my people, and they hear thy words, but they will not do them: for with their mouth they show much love, but their heart goeth after their covetousness" (Ezekiel 33:31). Ezekiel is speaking of unrepentant sinners, plainly enough, yet they loved to hear the eloquent prophet. How often do ungodly sinners delight in eloquent preaching or powerful reasoning by some able minister! It is to them an intellectual feast. And sometimes they are so pleased with it that they really think they love the word of God. This is consistent with entire depravity of heart and enmity against the true character of God. Moreover, it sets their depravity in a stronger light, because they know and approve the right and yet do the wrong.

So, notwithstanding this delight in the law, Paul writes, "But I see another law in my members, warring against the law of my mind, and bringing me into captivity to the law of sin which is in my members. O wretched man that I am! who shall deliver me from the body of this death?" (Romans 7:23, 24). These words are followed by, "I thank God, through Jesus Christ our Lord," and they are plainly a parenthesis, for they break in upon the train of thought. Then he sums up the whole matter, "So then, with the mind I myself serve the law of God, but with the flesh the law of sin" (Romans 7:25).

Legal Experience

It is as if Paul had said, "My better self, my unbiased judgment, my conscience, approves the law of God; but the law in my members, my passions, have such a control over me that I still disobey." Remember, the apostle was describing the habitual character of one who was wholly under the dominion of sin. It was irrelevant to his purpose to adduce the experience of a Christian. He was vindicating the law; therefore, it was necessary for him to take the case of one who was under the law. If Paul was writing about Christian experience, he was reasoning against himself; for if it was Christian experience this would prove not only that the law is inefficacious for the subduing of passion and the sanctification of believers but that the gospel also is inefficacious. Christians are under grace, and it is irrelevant in vindicating the law to adduce the experience of those who are not under the law but under grace.

Another conclusive reason is that Paul actually states the case of a believer as entirely different. In verses 4 and 6, he speaks of those who are not under law and not in the flesh, that is, *not carnal*, but delivered from the law, and actually serving, or obeying God, in spirit.

In beginning the eighth chapter, Paul goes on to say, "There is therefore now no condemnation to them which are in Christ Jesus, who walk not after the flesh, but after the Spirit. For the law of the Spirit of life in Christ Jesus, hath made me free from the law of sin and death" (Romans 8:1, 2). He had alluded to this in the parenthesis above, "I thank God, etc." "For what the law could not do, in that it was weak through the flesh, God sending his own Son in the flesh, and for sin, condemned sin in the flesh: that the righteousness of the law might be fulfilled in us, who walk not after the flesh, but after the Spirit" (Romans 8:3, 4). Of whom is he now speaking? If the person in chapter seven was one who had a Christian experience, whose experience is this in chapter eight? Here is something entirely different. The other was wholly under the power of sin, and under the law, and while he knew his duty, he never did it. In chapter eight we find one for whom what the law could not do, through the power of passion, the gospel has done, so that the righteousness of the law is fulfilled, or *what the law requires is obeyed*. "For they that are after the flesh, do mind the things of the flesh; but they that are after the Spirit, the things of the Spirit. For to be carnally minded is death; but to be spiritually minded is life and peace: because the carnal mind is enmity against God: for it is not subject to the law of God, neither indeed can be. So then they that are in the flesh cannot please God" (Romans 8:5-8). There it is. Those whom he had described in the seventh chapter as *being carnal, cannot please God*. "But ye are not in the flesh, but in the Spirit, if so be that the Spirit of God dwell in you. Now, if any man have not the Spirit of Christ, he is none of his. And if Christ be in you, the body is dead because of sin; but the Spirit is life because of righteousness" (Romans 8:9-10). But here is an individual whose body is dead. Before, the body had the control, and dragged him away from duty and from salvation; but now the power of passion is subdued.

In summary, take careful note of these six important points:

1. The strength of the apostle's language cannot decide this question, for he uses strong language on both sides. If it is objected that the individual he is describing is said to "delight in the law," he is also said to be "carnal, sold under sin." When a writer uses strong language, it must be so understood as not to make it irrelevant or inconsistent.

2. Whether he spoke of himself, or of some other person, or merely supposed a case by way of illustration, is wholly immaterial to the question.

3. It is plain that the point he wished to illustrate was the vindication of the law of God, as to its influence on a carnal mind.

4. The point required by way of illustration is the case of a convicted sinner, who saw the excellence of the law, but in whom the passions had the ascendency.

5. If this is spoken of Christian experience, it is not only irrelevant, but proves the reverse of what Paul intended. He intended to show that the law, though good, could not break the power of passion. But if this is Christian experience, then it proves that the gospel, instead of the law, cannot subdue passion and sanctify men.

6. The contrast between the state described in the seventh chapter and that described in the eighth chapter proves that the experience of the former was not that of a Christian.

Legal Experience

REMARKS

To apply the seventh chapter of Romans more personally, those who find their own experience written about in this chapter of Romans are not converted persons. If that is their habitual character, they are not regenerated. They are under conviction of sin, but not Christians.

From this chapter, you can see the great importance of using the law in dealing with sinners to make them prize the gospel, to lead them to justify God and condemn themselves. Sinners are never made truly to repent until they are convicted of sin by the law. At the same time, you see the entire insufficiency of the law to convert anyone. In this respect, the case of the devil illustrates the highest efficacy of the law.

Observe the danger of mistaking mere desires for piety. Desire that does not result in right choice has nothing good in it. The devil may have such desires. The most wicked people on earth may desire religion, and no doubt often do desire it, when they see that it is necessary to their salvation, or to control their passions.

Christ and the gospel present the only motives that can sanctify the mind. The law only convicts of sin and condemns sinners.

Those who are truly converted and brought into the liberty of the gospel do find deliverance from the bondage of their own corruptions. They do find the power of the body over the mind broken. They may have conflicts and trials, many and severe; but *as a habitual thing*, they are delivered from the thraldom of passion; *they get the victory over sin, and they find it easy to serve God*. His commandments are not grievous to them. His yoke is easy, and his burden light.

The true convert finds peace with God. He feels that he has it. He enjoys it. He has a sense of pardoned sin, and of victory over corruption.

Now, do you see from this subject the true position of a vast many church members? They are all the while struggling under the law. They approve of the law, both in its precept and its penalty; they feel condemned and desire relief. But still they are unhappy. They have no spirit of prayer, no communion with God, no evidence of adoption. They only refer to the seventh chapter of Romans as their evidence. Such a person will say, "There is my experience exactly!" Let me tell you, if this is your experience, you are yet in the gall of bitterness and the bonds of iniquity. You feel that you are in the bonds of guilt, and you are overcome by iniquity, and surely you know that it is bitter as gall. Now, don't cheat your soul by supposing that with such an experience as this you can go and sit down by the side of the Apostle Paul. You are yet carnal, sold under sin, and unless you embrace the gospel, you will be damned. ***

---

* Moses Stuart (1780-1852), *A Commentary on the Epistle to the Romans,* Andover: W.F. Draper, 1854. Stuart discusses Augustine in several places in his commentary, and says that not everyone will agree with his interpretations of Romans 5:12-19, Romans 7:5-25, or Romans 8:28ff. Finney is referring here to Stuart's "Excursus VII on Romans vii. 5-25" page 610: "The result of extensive and candid reading, in regard to the history of the doctrine in question, will be, as I must think, a full persuasion, that in the form and shape in which this doctrine was maintained by most of the Reformers, it was first introduced by Augustine in his dispute with Pelagius; from whose works, and those of his friends and followers, it came into the creeds of the Reformers, and thence has come down to us. The whole subject needs, in this country, an investigation and review *de novo* ["from the beginning," "afresh," "anew"], such as it has not yet received." Today, many contemporary commentators have adopted the views of Finney and Stuart: see *Principles of Victory*, page 98.

** See Stuart's *Commentary*, 328-334.

*** Charles G. Finney, *Lectures to Professing Christians* (Sermons delivered in New York in 1836-37), 320-338, *Principles of Victory*, 87–98. For Review: Answer the Study Questions on page 218, Cowles page 237.

Editor's Note: To assist your study, I have included some scripture quotations that use the word "peace" from the Psalms and Isaiah on pages 58 and 166 in this book. Rather than just include blank even numbered pages when I wanted the new chapter page to begin on the right hand (odd numbered) page, I chose to add these Bible verses in these locations. One way to discover the Bible's meaning of a word is to study how the Bible uses that word, in context, in several locations in the Bible. I hope these verses expand your Biblical understanding of the word "peace."

2

Christ the Husband of the Church
1837

> *Wherefore, my brethren, ye also are become dead to the law by the body of Christ; that ye should be married to another, even to him who is raised from the dead, that we should bring forth fruit unto God.* —Romans 7:4—KJV
>
> *So, my brothers, you also died to the law through the body of Christ, that you might belong to another, to him who was raised from the dead, in order that we might bear fruit to God.* —Romans 7:4—NIV

The marriage state is abundantly set forth in the Bible as describing the relationship between Christ and His church. I intend to show what is implied in this relationship, the reason for the existence of this relationship, the great guilt of the church in acting toward Christ as she does, and the forbearance of Christ toward the church.

Marriage and the relationship between Christ and His church.

The Bible describes Christ as the husband of the church. "For thy Maker is thy husband, the Lord of Hosts is his name" (Isaiah 54:5). "Turn, O backsliding children, saith the Lord, for I am married unto you" (Jeremiah 3:14). The church is spoken of as the bride, the Lamb's wife. "The Spirit and the Bride say, Come" (Revelation 22:17). That is, Christ and the church say, "Come." The Apostle Paul says, "For I am jealous over you with godly jealously: for I have espoused you to one husband, that I may present you as a chaste virgin to Christ" (2 Corinthians 11:2) I can merely refer to these passages. Those acquainted with their Bibles will not need me to take up time showing that this relation is often adverted to in the Bible in a great variety of forms.

What the marriage state implies for the Church.

The wife gives up her own name and assumes that of her husband. This is universally true in the marriage state. Likewise, the church assumes the name of Christ, and when united with Him is baptized into His name.

In marriage, the wife's separate interest is merged in that of her husband's. A married woman has no separate interest and no right to have any. Likewise, the church has no right to have a separate interest from the Lord Jesus Christ. If a wife has property, it goes to her husband. If it is real estate, the life interest passes to him, and if it is personal estate, the whole merges in him.

The reputation of the wife is wholly united to that of her husband, so that his reputation is hers and her reputation is his. What affects her character affects his. What affects his character affects hers. Their reputation is one and their interests are one. Likewise with the church, whatever concerns the church is just as much the interest of Christ as if it were personally His own matter. As the husband of the church, Christ is just as much pledged to do everything that is needful to promote the interest of the church; just as the husband is pledged to promote the welfare of his wife. As a faithful husband gives up his time, his labor, and his talents to promote the interest and happiness of his wife, so Jesus Christ gives himself up to promote the welfare of His church. He is as jealous of the reputation of His church as ever a husband was of the reputation of his wife. Never was a human being so pledged and so devoted to the interest of his wife, or felt so keenly an injury, as Jesus Christ feels when His church has her reputation or her feelings injured. He declares that it would be better for someone to have a millstone hanged about his neck, and be cast into the depths of the sea, than for him to offend one of these little ones that believe in Him (see Matthew 18:6).

The relationship between a husband and a wife is such that if anything is the matter with one, the other is full of sympathy.

Likewise, Christ feels for all the sufferings of the church, and the church feels for all the sufferings of Christ. When a believer has any realizing view of the sufferings of Christ, there is nothing in the universe that so affects and dissolves the mind with sorrow. A wife does not feel as much distress, as much broken-hearted grief, over the suffering or death of her husband that she might have caused, as the Christian feels when he views his sins as the cause of the death of Jesus Christ. Let me ask a married woman, "How would you feel if your husband, to redeem you from merited ignominy and death, had volunteered the greatest suffering, pain, and death for you? When you saw his face, how would that affect you? To be reminded of it by any circumstance, how would it melt you down in broken-hearted grief?" Now, do you understand that your sins caused the death of Christ? He died for you just as absolutely as if you had been the only sinner in all God's world! He suffered pain, contempt, and death for you. He loved His church, and gave himself for her. She is called the Church of God, which He purchased with His own blood.

A wife pledges herself to yield her will to the will of her husband, and to yield obedience to his will. She has no separate interest, and ought to have no separate will. The Bible enjoins this and makes it a Christian duty for the wife to conform in all things to the will of her husband. The will of the husband becomes to the faithful wife the mainspring of her activity. Her entire life is only carrying out the will of her husband. The relation of the church to Christ is precisely the same. The church is governed by Christ's will. When believers exercise faith, they choose the will of Christ as the moving influence for all their conduct.

The wife recognizes her husband as her head. The Bible declares that he is so. In a similar manner, as from the head proceed those influences that govern the body, so from Christ proceed those influences that govern the church.

The wife looks to her husband as her support, her protector, and her guide. Every believer places himself as absolutely under the protection of Christ, as a married woman is under the protection of her husband. The woman naturally looks to her husband to preserve her from injury, from insult, and from want. She hangs her happiness on him and expects him to protect her; and he is obligated to do it. Likewise, Christ is pledged to protect His church from every foe. How often have the powers of hell tried to put down the church, but Christ, her husband, has never abandoned her. No weapon formed against the church has ever been allowed to prosper, or ever shall. Never will the Lord Jesus Christ so far forget His relation to the church as to leave His bride unprotected. Let all earth and all hell conspire against His church, and it is just as certain as Christ has power to protect her; His church is safe. And every individual believer is just as safe as if he were the only believer on earth; Christ has truly pledged to preserve him. The devil can no more put down a single believer to final destruction than he can put down God Almighty. He may murder him, but that is no injury. Overcoming a believer by taking his life affords Satan no triumph. He put Christ to death, but what did he gain by it? The grave had no power over Jesus Christ to retain Him. So with a believer; neither the grave nor hell has any more power to injure one of Christ's little ones that believe in Him than they have to injure Christ himself. He says, "Because I live, ye shall live also" (John 14:19). And, "He that believeth in me, though he were dead, yet shall he live; and whosoever liveth, and believeth in me, shall never die" (John 11:25, 26). No power in the universe can prevail against a single believer to destroy him. Jesus Christ is the Head of the church, and Head over all things to the church; therefore, the church is safe.

The legal existence of the wife is so merged in that of her husband that she is not known in law as a separate person. If any actions or civil liability come against the wife, the husband is responsible. If the wife has committed a trespass, the husband is answerable. It is his business to guide

Christ the Husband of the Church

and govern her, and her business to obey. If he does not restrain her from breaking the laws, he is responsible. And if the wife does not obey her husband, she has it in her power to bring him into great trouble, disgrace, and expense. In a similar way, Jesus Christ is Lord over His church, and if He does not actually restrain His church from sin, He has it to answer for, and is brought into great trouble and reproach by the misconduct of His people. By human laws, the husband is not liable for capital crimes committed by his wife, but the law so far recognizes her separate existence as to punish her. But Christ has assumed the responsibility for His church and for all her conduct. He took the place of His people when they were convicted of capital crimes and sentenced to eternal damnation. This is answering in good earnest. And now it is His business to take care of the church and control her and keep her from sin; and for every sin of every member, Jesus Christ is responsible and must answer. And He does answer for them. He has made an atonement to cover all this and ever liveth to make intercession for His people. Jesus Christ holds himself responsible before God for all the conduct of His church. Every believer is so a part of Jesus Christ, and so perfectly united to Him, that whatever sins any of them may be guilty of, Jesus Christ takes upon himself to answer for. This is abundantly taught in the Bible.

What an amazing relationship! Christ has assumed the responsibility, not only for the civil conduct of His church, but even for the capital crime of rebellion against God. There is a sense, therefore, in which the church is lost in Christ, and has no separate existence known in law. God has so given up the church to Christ, by the covenant of grace, that strictly speaking the church is not known in law. I do not mean that crimes committed by believers against the moral law are not sin, but that the law cannot get hold of them to condemn them. There is now no condemnation to them that are in Christ Jesus (see Romans 8:1). The penalty of the law is for ever remitted. The crimes of the believer are not taken into account so as to bring him under condemnation; no, in no case whatever. Whatever is to be done falls upon Jesus Christ. He has assumed the responsibility of bringing them from under the power of sin, as well as from under the law, and He stands pledged to give them all the assistance they need to gain a complete victory.

Reasons for this relationship between Christ and His Church.

The first reason is given in the text, "that we should bring forth fruit unto God" (Romans 7:4). A principal design of the institution of marriage is the propagation of the species. So it is in regard to the church. Through the instrumentality of the church, children are to be born to Christ, and He is to see His seed, and to see of the travail of His soul, and be satisfied by converts multiplied as the drops of morning dew. It is not only through the travail of the Redeemer's soul, but also through the travail of the church, that believers are born unto Jesus Christ. As soon as Zion travailed, she brought forth children.

Another object of the marriage institution is the protection and support of those who are naturally helpless and dependent. If the law of power prevailed in society, everybody knows that females, being the weaker sex, would be universally enslaved. The design of the institution of marriage is to secure protection and support to those who are so much more frail that by the law of force they would be continually enslaved. So Jesus Christ upholds His church; He gives her all the protection against her enemies, and all the powers of hell, that she needs.

The mutual happiness of the husband and wife is another end of the marriage institution. The same is true of the relationship between Christ and His church. Perhaps you will think it strange when I tell you that the happiness of Christ is increased by the love of the church. But what does the Bible say? "Who, for the joy set before him, endured the cross, despising the shame" (Hebrews 12:2). What was the joy set before Him if the love of the church was not part of it? It would be very strange to hear of a husband contributing to the happiness of his wife and not enjoy it himself. Jesus Christ enjoys the happiness of His church as much as He loves His church, and He loves His church much better than any husband loves his wife.

The alleviation of mutual sufferings and sorrows is one goal of marriage. Sharing each other's sorrow is a great alleviation. Who does not know this? In like manner, Christ and His church share each other's sorrows. The Apostle Paul says he was always bearing about in his body the dying of the Lord Jesus: "For as the sufferings of Christ abound in us, so our consolation also aboundeth by Christ" (2 Corinthians 1:5). And he declared that one purpose of all his toils and self-denials was that he might know the "fellowship of Christ's sufferings" (Philippians 3:10). Paul rejoiced in all his sufferings, that he might fill up that which was "behind of the afflictions of Christ" (Colossians 1:24). The church feels keenly every reproach cast upon Christ, and Christ feels keenly every injury inflicted on the church.

The primary reason for this union of Christ with His church is so He may sanctify the church. Read what Paul said in Ephesians 5: 22-27: "Wives, submit yourselves unto your own husbands, as unto the Lord. For the husband is the head of the wife, even as Christ is the head of the church: and he is the Savior of the body. Therefore as the church is subject unto Christ, so let the wives be to their own husbands in every thing. Husbands, love your wives, even as Christ also loved the church, and gave himself for it; that he might sanctify and cleanse it with the washing of water by the word. That he might present it to himself a glorious church, not having spot or wrinkle, or any such thing; but that it should be holy and without blemish." Here, Paul set forth the great design of Christ in marrying the church; that He might sanctify her and cleanse her, or that she should be perfectly holy and without blemish. John informs us that he saw those who had "washed their robes and made them white in the blood of the Lamb" (Revelation 7:14). See how beautifully the Bride, the Lamb's wife, is described as "coming down from God out of heaven, prepared as a bride adorned for her husband" (Revelation 21:2).

The wickedness of the church toward Christ.

Vast multitudes who profess to be a part of the church, the bride of Christ, really set up a separate interest. They have pretended to merge their self-interest in the interest of Christ, but manifestly they keep up a separate interest. And if you attempt to make them act on the principle that they have no separate interest, they will plainly show that they have no such design. What would you think of a wife keeping up a separate interest from her husband? You would say it was plain that she did not love her husband as she ought.

Principles of Peace — Finney's Lessons on Romans

Unfortunately, the church is not satisfied with Christ's love. Everybody knows what an abominable thing it is for a wife not to be satisfied with the love of her husband, but to be continually seeking other lovers, and always associating with other men. Yet, how plain it is that the church is not satisfied with the love of Christ, but is always seeking after other lovers. What are we to think of those members of the church who are not satisfied with the love of Christ for happiness, but must have the riches and pleasures and honors of the world to make them happy?

Still more horrible would be the conduct of a wife, who should select her lovers from the enemies of her husband, and should bring them home with her, and make them her chosen friends. Yet how many who profess to belong to Christ go away and give their affections to Christ's enemies. Some will even marry those whom they know to be haters of God and Christianity. Horrible! Is that the way a bride should act?

Everyone knows that it is a disgraceful thing for the wife to play the harlot. Yet God often speaks of His church as going astray and committing spiritual whoredom. And it is true! He does not make this charge as a man makes it against his wife, when he is determined to leave her and cast her off. He makes the charge with grief and tenderness, and accompanies it with the most moving expostulations, and the most melting entreaties that she would return.

What would you think of a married woman who expected at the very time of her marriage that if she got tired of her husband, she would leave him and play the harlot? Yet, how many there are in the church, people who profess to be Christians, who when they made a profession of faith had no more expectation of living without sin than they expected to have wings and fly. They have come into His house, and have pledged themselves to live entirely for Christ, and they have married Him in this public manner, covenanting to forsake all sin and to live for Christ alone and be satisfied with His love and have no other lovers. Yet, all the while they are doing it, they expect in their minds that they shall scatter their ways to strangers upon every high hill and commit sin and dishonor Christ.

What would we think of a woman who at the very time of her marriage expected to continue in her course of adultery as long as she lived in spite of all the commands and expostulations of her husband? Likewise, what should we think of those who profess to be Christians who deliberately expect to commit spiritual adultery and continue in it as long as they live? But the most abominable part of such a wife's wickedness is when she turns around and blames her conduct upon her faithful husband. Now, the church does this. In spite of what Christ has done, and all that He could do short of absolute force, to keep His church from sinning; yet, the church charges her sin upon Him, as if He had laid her under an absolute necessity of sinning by not making any adequate provision for preserving His people against temptation. And some of these people are horrified now at the very name of "Christian Perfection," as if it was really dishonoring Christ to believe that He is able to keep His people from committing sin and falling into the snare of the devil. And so it has been for hundreds of years that with the greater part of the church it has not been orthodox to teach that Jesus Christ really has made such provision that His people may live free from sin. And it is really considered a wonder that anyone should teach that the bride of the Lord Jesus Christ is expected to do as she pretends to do. Has He married a bride and made no provision adequate to protect her against the arts and seductions of the devil? Well done! That must be the ridicule of hell!

Suppose a wife should refuse to obey her husband and then make him responsible for her conduct. Yet, the church refuses to obey Jesus Christ, and then makes Him answer for her sins. This is the great difficulty with the church; she is continually blaming her Head for her delinquencies.

The church is continually dishonoring Christ. The reputation of husband and wife is one. Whatever dishonors one dishonors the other. Now, the church, instead of avoiding every appearance of evil, is continually causing the enemies of God to blaspheme by her conduct.

The forbearance of Christ toward His church.

In these horrid circumstances, what other husband would allow the connection to remain and bear what Christ bears? Yet He still offers to be reconciled and lays himself out to regain the affections of His bride. Sometimes a husband really loses his affection toward his wife and treats her so like a brute that although she once loved him she loves him no more. But where can anything be found in the character and conduct of Christ to justify the treatment He receives? He has laid himself out to the utmost to engross the affections of the church. What more could He have done? Where can any fault or any deficiency be found in Him? And even after all that the church has done against Him, what is He doing now? Suppose a husband should for years follow his wandering, guilty wife from city to city beseeching and entreating her with tears to return to his house and be reconciled; and after all, she should persist in going after her lovers, and yet he continues to cry after her and beg her to come back and live with him, and he will forgive and love her still. Is there any such forbearance and condescension known among men?

REMARKS

Christians ought to understand the consequences of their sins. Your sins dishonor Christ, and grieve Christ, and injure Christ, and then you make Christ responsible for them. You sustain such a relationship to Him that you ought to know the effect of your sin upon Him. How does a wife feel when she has disgraced her husband? How blushes cover her face and tears fill her eyes! When her guilty offended husband comes into her presence, how she falls down at his feet with a full heart and confesses her fault, and pours her penitential tears into his bosom. She is grieved and humbled, and though she loves him, his very presence is a grief until she breaks down before him, and feels that he has forgiven her.

Now, how can a Christian fail to recognise this? When he is betrayed into sin and has injured Christ, how can he sleep? How can you help realizing that your sins take hold of Jesus Christ and injure Him in all these tender relations?

One great difficulty of Christians is their expecting to live in sin, because this expectation insures their continuance in sin. If an individual expects to live in sin, he in fact means to live in sin; and of course, he will live in sin. It is very much to be feared that many who profess to be Christians never really mean to live without sin. The apostle insists that believers should reckon themselves dead to sin; they should henceforth have no more to do with it than if they were dead, and no more expect

Christ the Husband of the Church

to sin than a dead man should expect to walk. They should throw themselves upon Christ, and receive Him in all His relations, and expect to be preserved and sanctified and saved by Him. If they would do this, do you not suppose they would be kept from sin? Just as certainly as they believe in Christ for it. To believe in Christ that He will keep them insures the result that He will. And the reason why they do not receive preserving grace at all times as they need it and all they need is that they do not expect it, and do not trust in Jesus Christ to preserve them in perfect love. The person who tries to preserve himself instead of throwing himself upon Christ, he throws himself upon his own resources, and then in his weakness expects to sin, and of course he does sin. If he knew his own entire emptiness and threw himself upon Christ as absolutely and rest on Christ as confidently for sanctification as for justification, the one is just as certain as the other.

No one who trusted in God for anything He has promised ever failed to receive according to his faith the very thing for which he trusted. If you trust in God for what He has not promised, that is tempting God. If Peter had not been called by Christ to come to Him on the water, it would have been tempting God for him to get down out of the ship into the water, and he would have lost his life for his presumption and folly. But as soon as Christ told him to come, it was merely an act of sound and rational faith for him to do it. It was a pledge on the part of Christ that he would be sustained; and so he was sustained as long as he had faith. Now, if the Bible has promised that those who receive Christ as their sanctification shall be sanctified, then you who believe in Him for this purpose have just as much reason to expect it as Peter had to expect he should walk on the waves. It is true, we do not expect a miracle to be wrought to sustain the believer, as it was to sustain Peter. But God promises that the believer shall be sustained, and if miracles were necessary, no doubt they would be performed, for God would move the universe and turn the course of nature upside down sooner than let one of His promises fail those who put their trust in Him. If God is pledged to anything, a person who ventures on that pledge will find it redeemed just as certainly as God possesses almighty power. Has God promised sanctification to those who trust Him for it? If He has not, then to go to Him in faith for preservation from temptation and sin is tempting God. It is fanaticism. If God has left us to the dire necessity of getting along with our own watchfulness and our own firmness and strength, then we must submit to it and do the best we can. But if He has made any promises, He will redeem them to the uttermost, though all earth and all hell should oppose. And so it is in regard to the mistakes and errors which Christians fall into. If there is no promise that they shall be guided just as far as they need, and led into the truth, and in the way of duty and of peace; then for a Christian to look to God for knowledge, wisdom, guidance, and direction without any promise is tempting God. But if there are promises on this subject, depend on it, they will be fulfilled to the very last mite to the believer who trusts in them; and exercising confidence in such promises is only a sober and rational faith in the word of God.

I believe the great difficulty of the church on the subject of "Christian Perfection" lies here, that she has not fully understood how the Lord Jesus Christ is wholly pledged in all these relations, and that the church has just as much reason and is just as much bound to trust Him for sanctification as for justification.* What does the scripture teach? "Who of God is made unto us wisdom, and righteousness, and sanctification, and redemption" (1 Corinthians 1:30). How did the idea come to be taken up in the church that Jesus Christ is our Redemption, and has made himself responsible for the meanest individual who throws himself on Him for justification so that he shall infallibly obtain it? This has been universally admitted in the church in all ages. But that is no more plainly or more abundantly taught than that Jesus Christ is promised and pledged for Wisdom and for Sanctification to all that receive Him in these relations. Has He promised that if anyone lacks wisdom, he may ask of God, and if he asks in faith, God will give it to him? What then? Is there then no such thing as being preserved by Christ from falling into this and that delusion and error? God has made this broad promise, and Christ is as much pledged for our wisdom and our sanctification, if we only trust in Him, as He is for our justification. If the church would only renounce any expectation from herself, and die as absolutely to her own wisdom and strength as she does to her own righteousness or the expectation of being saved by her own works, Jesus Christ is as much pledged for one as for the other. The only reason why the church does not realize the same results is that Christ is trusted for justification, and as for wisdom and sanctification He is not trusted.

The truth is, the great body of believers having begun in the Spirit are now trying to be made perfect by the flesh. We have thrown ourselves on Christ for justification, and then have been attempting to sanctify ourselves. If it is true, as the apostle affirms, that Christ is to the church both wisdom and sanctification, what excuse have Christians for not being sanctified?

If individuals do not as much expect to live without sin against Christ, as they expect to live without open sins against others, such as murder or adultery, it must be for one of three reasons:

1. Either we love others better than we do Christ, and so are less willing to do them an injury.

2. Or we are restrained by a regard to our own reputation; and this proves that we love reputation more than Christ.

3. Or we think we can preserve ourselves better from these disgraceful crimes than we can from less heinous sins.

Suppose I were to ask any of you if you expect to commit murder or adultery? "Horrible," you say! But why not? Are you so virtuous that you can resist any temptation which the devil can offer? If you say so, you do not know yourself. If you have real power to keep yourself, so as to abstain from openly disgraceful sins in your own strength, you have power to abstain from all sins. But if your only reliance is on Jesus Christ to keep you from committing murder and adultery, how is it that you should get the idea that He is not equally able to keep you from all sin? If believers would only throw themselves wholly on Christ and make Him responsible by placing themselves entirely at His control, they would know His power to save and would live without sin.

What a horrible reproach the church is to Jesus Christ today! Do you see why converts are what they are? Degenerate plants of a strange vine sure enough! The church is in such a state that it is no wonder those who are brought in, with few exceptions, prove a disgrace to Christianity. How can it be otherwise? How can the church, living in such a manner, bring forth offspring that shall honor Christ? The church does not, and individual believers do not, in general, receive Christ in all His offices, as He is offered in the Bible.** If they did, it would be impossible for them to live like such loathsome harlots. ***

---

* See Charles G. Finney, *Principles of Holiness*, Minneapolis: Bethany House Publishers, 1984, for two of Finney's sermons specifically on "Christian Perfection." The entire book explains Finney's teaching on Christian Holiness and how his view differs from what has come to be known as Perfectionism. See Charles G. Finney, *Principles of Sanctification*, Minneapolis: Bethany House Publishers, 1986, for further studies on Biblical Sanctification.

** See Charles G. Finney, *Principles of Union with Christ*, Minneapolis: Bethany House Publishers, 1985, for 31 devotional meditations on the various relationships Jesus Christ has with His church and how believers can grow in grace and faith as they learn more about these offices and relationships and as they deepen these relationships with Christ, in union with Him.

*** Charles G. Finney, *Lectures to Professing Christians*, 453-468, *Principles of Victory*, 99–108. For Review: Answer the Study Questions on page 219, Cowles page 240.

3

Revival of Sin and the Law
1853

For I was alive without the law once: but when the commandment came, sin revived, and I died.—Romans 7:9—KJV

Once I was alive apart from law; but when the commandment came, sin sprang to life and I died.—Romans 7:9—NIV

We need to examine the sense in which Paul was without the law, the consequences of being "alive without the law," in what sense "the commandment came," and the consequences of the commandment coming.

The sense in which Paul was without the law.

Paul was thoroughly a Pharisee before he came to believe in Jesus Christ as his Lord and Savior. He had been brought up and instructed in the oracles of God according to the best teachings of his time; therefore, he could not have been "without law" in the sense of not having the letter of it in his hands and before his mind. He had the law as given to Moses, the whole of it, both moral and ceremonial. Indeed, he had given much of his life to the study of it, having been brought up at the feet of Gamaliel and enjoying the best advantages his country could afford for knowledge in the Jewish law.

Unfortunately, Paul was really ignorant of the true meaning and spirit of the law. His grand mistake was that he regarded the law only in its relations to his *outward life*. He assumed that the law had no other relationship and made no other demands. His moral and spiritual eyes were not open. I mean by this that he did not see his moral and spiritual relations to God and to others. He did not even seem to recognize the fact of the existence of any such relationships.

As to Paul's outward relationships, his course of life was objectively just; while subjectively unjust; his life was altogether unjust. By *subjectively just*, I mean a person who is just and right *at heart*; who is being and doing in reference to the law what the law requires from their *heart*. In the state of his heart, Paul was all wrong, for he was supremely selfish. Here lay the great error of his school of moralists. Their whole attention was directed to the *objective obedience* of the law and withdrawn from the *subjective obedience* that comes from the heart. In other words, they thought everything of the outside, but nothing of the heart. Exclusively regarding the letter of the law and the ceremony, they seemed never to ask if the heart is honest and pure before God. Thus the moral and spiritual eye was not trained to discern or even to notice the real meaning of the law. Consequently it is not strange that the Pharisees, so trained, should suppose themselves to be obeying the law, while in truth they entirely overlooked all that is really valuable. Their spiritual consciousness was not awake.

At this point let us make a distinction which is somewhat important in reference to this subject. There is *a natural consciousness*; *a moral consciousness*, and also *a spiritual consciousness*. The *natural consciousness* is exercised upon things merely natural and worldly—external and not in regard to their moral relations. The *moral consciousness* relates to things of a moral nature, and when distinguished from spiritual consciousness should refer to our relations to our fellow human beings. The term *spiritual consciousness* may be applied to our relations to God. An active *spiritual consciousness* keeps our mind awake to the presence of God, just as naturally as we are conscious of the presence of each other. It keeps us alive to all that is embraced in our relationship to God. *Moral consciousness* respects moral questions; yet, in the strict sense, only as they lie between ourselves and our fellow human beings. The difficulty with Paul was that his moral and spiritual eyes were closed; therefore, he entirely overlooked his own subjective state of mind, which is the very thing that God's law primarily regards.

The consequences of being "alive without the law."

Prior to his conversion to Jesus Christ, Paul was in a state of both moral and spiritual delusion. He supposed himself to be performing his duty to others, when really he was doing no such thing. He had only the idea of *objective justice*; that is, *justice viewed in its outward relations*. If he did not cheat a man, it mattered in his view little or nothing how much he coveted his goods, or how utterly void his heart might be of true love to his neighbor. Consequently, Paul never performed the duty which the law required of him toward others; that he love his neighbor from his heart.

The same was true of his spiritual relations to God. He regarded simply what the law required *externally*; therefore, he went round and round with the routine of his *outside duties*, while his heart all this time was dead and cold. This state of mind showed itself subsequently bitter as hell itself toward the lovely and innocent Son of God.

Another consequence was a false hope. Supposing himself to be complying with the law of God, Paul expected to be saved as much as he expected anything whatever. Yet this expectation was altogether unfounded because, although he was very zealous, he was also very bitter in his spirit, showing that his zeal sprang from another source than real benevolence. Indeed, he showed that his spirit was bitter as the bitterness of the pit. How then can it be supposed that his hope of heaven was anything better than a delusion?

Another result was a self-righteous performance of all Paul called his religion. But here I must explain; for I am afraid many are not well aware of what the Bible means by "self-righteousness." Certainly it is the case that many who profess to be Christians do not well understand this matter. For an explanation of the point that is most important for discrimination take the case of Paul. When Paul performed what he called his duties and thanked God, Pharisee-like; when he prayed and fasted and paid his tithes, did he feel himself so utterly lost that he ascribed all his acceptable work to Christ working in him? Far from it! He had done all these things himself.

When Paul came ultimately to know himself and then to know Christ, he could speak on this subject with intelligent discrimination and ever wakeful interest. Then he dwelt much on the fact that the Jews depended on their own works and on themselves alone to do their own works; while on the other hand, he insisted that *while left to themselves they never did anything but sin.* He always maintained that the energetic power of the divine Spirit wrought in them all that was ever acceptable to God. Often does he illustrate this by his own experience. Before he was a Christian, he performed his religious duties as regularly as now; saying, "I profited in the Jews' religion above many of my equals" (Galatians 1:14). But all along, he regarded his obedience as in such a sense rendered in his own strength that he made no hearty acknowledgments of dependence on sovereign grace. Of that grace which comes through divine mercy, and first moves the heart to good, he seemed to know nothing. His own righteousness was self-originating, self-performed. There was nothing but what came of himself. It had no spiritual life or power in it, for the reason that there was *no power of God* in its origin, *no influence from God* molding its character. Paul did not truly recognize God's grace in his obedience, and God did not impart his grace to subdue selfishness and beget true love in his soul.

Now, here is a curious distinction which spiritually-minded people make, but which others, if they use it, never understand. The spiritually-minded say with Paul. "By the grace of God I am what I am" (1 Corinthians 15:10). With many, this language degenerates into trite sentiment; but really there is a world of meaning in it, and a meaning which is inexpressibly dear to the real Christian's heart. The person who truly enters into the spirit of Christian faith never regards himself as having done it; he knows it is all of grace; nothing can offend him more than to have it assumed that it is he himself and not God's grace that has wrought in him all good. He knows deep in his consciousness that if left to himself there never was and never will be any good thing in him. Hence, he honors and praises divine grace with a fullness of meaning and an outpouring of heart which self-righteousness never knew. In the truly converted person, this deep recognition of God's grace comes to be wrought into the very life and intertwined through all the fibers and incorporated into the substance of the soul. Through all his being he feels that all is of rich grace and nothing of praise is due himself.

Not that his exercises are not right, for to deny this would be to impugn the efficiency of God's grace. Not that they are not his own acts, for to deny this would be to set aside human agency and responsibility, and bring the Bible doctrine of God "working to will and to do" in us in entire confusion (Philippians 2:13). The simple idea is that *the Spirit of God, acting upon our minds in harmony with the laws of mind, instructs, stimulates, draws, and thus substantially causes right voluntary action on our part.*

In what sense "the commandment came" to Paul.

The "commandment came" to Paul when the law was set home to both his moral and spiritual consciousness and perception. He was led to see what the law meant in its moral relations to himself and to his neighbor; that *without love all was nothing* (see 1 Corinthians 13). He saw the same also in regard to prayer, to alms, to worship, that all is nothing, only a grievous abomination in the sight of God when the subjective state of the heart is wrong. He became fully aware of this, suddenly, as if a flash of lightning had broken upon him. He saw the reality of this spiritual meaning, and with it a purity and blessedness in the law itself which commanded his most intense regard. And what was the result of this new view of God's law? This is the point we must consider.

When the commandment came, *it quickened his selfishness*. This was the first result of bringing the spirituality of the law home to his selfish heart. This new light as it flashed upon his mind found him in a most self-complacent state, altogether satisfied with himself. However, no sooner did he see the spirituality of the law than one of two results must inevitably take place. He must either break down at once, acknowledge his guilt and empty himself of all his self-righteousness, or if he resists this, his selfishness must be quickened into fresh activity. *In Paul's case, the latter resulted: his selfishness was aroused and stirred up.* The long unnoticed enmity of his heart was developed. We are not to suppose that during all the time he was persecuting the church that he enjoyed an easy, self-complacent state of mind, and that all was quiet until the moment when the great light from heaven broke upon him. By no means. It must not be assumed that he had no serious thought about his moral relations to God prior to the scenes on the road to Damascus (see Acts 9). Doubtless his mind had been stirred up long before. He had heard of Jesus' *Sermon on the Mount* (Matthew 5-7). He had heard about Christ's pungent and terrible denunciations against the Pharisees. He had known that Christ had publicly rebuked and exposed their favorite interpretations of the law, and had torn up their system from its very foundations. He knew that the masses of the common people heard Christ gladly. This had greatly quickened his selfishness and stirred up the enmity of his heart against Jesus so that his very soul was maddened. You recollect he says of himself: "I verily thought with myself that I ought to do many things contrary to the name of Jesus of Nazareth" (Acts 26:9). It was obviously under color of being very zealous for the truth; but really his selfishness was all on fire and all the malign passions of his soul were astir. It is exceedingly plain from the history that Paul was all this time warring against his own consciousness. This great fact was perfectly known to Jesus; hence, when He came down in that flood of overwhelming light and arrested the burning persecutor, what did Jesus ask? He called him by name asking, "Saul, Saul, why persecutest thou me? It is hard for thee to kick against the pricks" (Acts 26:14).

Here we have the secret of Saul's state of mind: he is "kicking against the pricks." *The sharp points of his moral sense are against him*, and he is resisting and is wounding himself upon those piercing points continually. He is like a hampered animal trying to run away, while every step drives the goads into his quivering flesh. He tries to kick. He winces and

Revival of Sin and the Law

shrieks, yet has too much obstinacy to yield. Sometimes, perhaps, he half persuaded himself that he ought to oppose Jesus of Nazareth; but the whole case shows that he was ill at ease in that impression, and that on the whole he knew better and was truly fighting against his prevailing convictions of duty.

When the law came home to his soul, it compelled reflection. This almost always supervenes when the law comes home more and more to the soul. There will be hours of deep and earnest reflection, producing first consternation, then a deep sense of shame, the mind waking up to see things in their true light. This leads to great consternation, remorse, self-condemnation, and then, often to despair. The man is stripped of all his excuses, and then, not having yet seen the great love of God, and having therefore no faith and trust, he settles down in the conviction, "I ought to be damned and I certainly must be! There can be no help for me!" More than one such case have I seen where people, a long time settled down in infidelity, are wakened to see themselves as they are before God and His holy law, and they cry out, "I deserve eternal damnation!" One such I have in my mind's eye. I shall never forget how he looked. Every feature of his countenance depicted horror. Every muscle was in a tremor. A little reflection had brought him into an attitude in which he could not stand before God. There was also the case of a deacon whom I well knew in his years of infidelity. He is now in heaven, but when an infidel, he professed to be entirely satisfied that the Bible was all priest-craft, and verily thought that soon "this delusion" (Christianity), would be swept from the earth. Returning one time from the sale of infidel books, full of self-complacency, all elated with his success, he conversed freely with his wife upon his labors for the day; then, all suddenly, a new view of the truth and meaning of God's word broke in upon his mind; intuitively, he saw himself a sinner and undone. He could no longer shut his eyes to the fact that Jesus, whom he had been opposing, was truly the Savior of the world; that the Bible he had been gainsaying was really God's own revelation to a lost humanity. Seeing all this he was in agony. His wife, alarmed, cried out, "What's the matter with you?" Still he groaned as a man in agony of body. And still she pressed her question, "What's the matter?" At last he broke out saying, "The stubborn oak must bow! Jesus Christ is the Savior of the world!" She was thunderstruck! It could not have surprised her more if a bolt from heaven had broken through the roof and smote him to the floor. There he was; but how changed! He learned what Paul meant by saying, "When the commandment came, sin revived, and I died." If he were alive, he could doubtless tell you.

Paul had long thought on this subject and was troubled. But at last the matter came to a head. Jesus met him in the way and broke him down. He let in light upon his already troubled conscience. He made him see the purity and the spiritual meaning of His law. Now, mark what follows! Notice the self-condemnation, the shame, the dreadful remorse! See him writing his own death-warrant in spite of himself! Nothing is more common than for despair to supervene for a season in such cases as this. In the case of Paul, this was momentary. Yet we must suppose that he utterly gave up his old hope, and this to him was like giving up the ghost and dying. It was as death. No wonder, therefore, that he should say, "Sin revived, and I died." When he saw how strangely the rebellion of his heart burst forth, and sin in this sense "revived," his hope perished, his heart sank within him. Such revelations were made of himself as suddenly blighted all his hopes of being in the divine favor, and he died in the darkness of despair. This seems to be the obvious explanation of his language, and corresponds entirely with what we must infer from the laws of mind and the uniform course of similar experiences.

REMARKS

The Pharisees generally in those days, and all Pharisees in heart in every age, are under the same delusion. Yet they were then and are often supposed to be the most pious people. It was a common saying then that if only two men were to be saved out of all mankind, one of them must be a Pharisee. But they were entirely deceived. Their moral perceptions were blunted. *The subjective state which alone constitutes true faith was not even apprehended in their minds.* When you hear them speak, you hear nothing of spiritual experience, experiences similar to those of David for example. They do not cry out, "O how love I thy law!" (Psalm 119:97). Or, "Cleanse me from secret faults" (Psalm 19:12). Or, "My soul thirsteth for

Revival of Sin and the Law

God, yea, for the living God" (Psalm 52:2). Indeed, you seldom hear any of them go further than to pray for those states of mind which they know God requires. They do not profess to have them already, nor do they use language in the honest simplicity of their hearts which implies that they have a right subjective state of heart now. Many do nothing more than hold on to a hope. With no small difficulty they manage to do so much, and often they call into exercise the utmost pertinacity of purpose to effect even this.

The teachings of Christ roused the Pharisees. He deeply disturbed their peace. They were as a hive of bees when somebody breaks up their house or they are led into battle. So thoroughly had He torn up their entire system, root and branch, and so fully had the Pharisees great defects been laid open to the eye of the world, that they could rest no longer. This general result was produced by the lingering yet almost departing rays of the Spirit's light upon the nation. God was giving a corrupt people their last call. A deep and damning delusion fastened strongly on the hearts of thousands, and if any were to be saved, this terrible delusion must be broken up by outspoken and crushing truth. It was but natural and necessary that in such an effort, many hearts should become excited, maddened, and thrown into a state of most bitter opposition.

Likewise, in our own day, many who profess Christianity, who are living along in a legal and pharisaic state, get now and then some scattering rays of new light. Glimpses of truth break in upon their minds as they hear the true gospel faithfully preached, or as the Spirit sets home upon their souls some portions of God's word. Something within says, "That is true Christianity, and I do not have it. I have no such faith or spiritual experience as described." Sometimes in seasons of searching power, the Spirit of God hurls His arrows broadcast, and many are pricked in their heart and constrained to say, "My hope is vain and I am yet in my selfishness, and know nothing yet of true Christianity as I must know it. I must give up this old rotten hope, or be lost!" But they resist at the moment; they cannot quite bring their minds to give up and throw their bare souls on divine mercy as lost sinners. Thus resisting, they relapse into ten fold greater hardness and spiritual delusion. If under such appeals from God they would not resist, light would increase. They would doubtless be soon brought forth into day.

I knew the case of an elder who took an honest course, unlike most people in similar circumstances. I was preaching in the place of his residence; the Spirit was pressing truth on some minds, as I endeavored to aid His searching scrutiny into the heart by preaching on the case of Achan and the accursed thing (see Joshua 7). I was progressing in my sermon, in search after that accursed thing, when suddenly he rose in the midst of the congregation and cried out: "Mr. Finney, Mr. Finney, you need not say another word, it's found. I am the man, I am the very man!" There he stood pale as ashes. "If there were no other Achan here," said he, "I am enough to curse the whole church. I did not want to disturb the congregation," he added, "but I saw that I must speak. I have been brought almost to this point before, but I drew back and my soul relapsed into darkness. I knew that I must meet the demands of my conscience now, or my soul would be lost."

So with many, there are times when God lifts the veil and lets them see their bare hearts. Constrained by truth they cry out, "I am deceived; I know I am," but instead of making thorough work and acting with decision, they hesitate. They lose the light God gave them. They grieve the Spirit away and fall back to their old position. They go on as before and perish utterly in their own corruptions. I should not be surprised if in fact there has been hundreds in this place who have passed through this very process, doomed, unless they earnestly repent, to reach the same awful end. Influenced by pride of character, and by the force of an old hope, they delay, and put off the thorough examination they ought to make, and thus slide on to ruin. O! That everlasting spirit of DELAY! How many souls it has lured along to ruin!

There are many sinners, who are not Christians, who are laboring under this same difficulty. They have the objective but not the subjective of true faith. *Externally they appear upright*; but alas, *internally there is no true love to God or others*. Some of you are in just this position. I have had business dealings with you and know you to be honest and upright; but what shall I say of your treatment of your God and Savior! Nobody denies you the credit of being prompt in your business with others and of doing your job as you ought to do it. You would scorn to do objective wrong; but

Revival of Sin and the Law

you seem not to think that this in itself is nothing toward real obedience. Suppose you were as upright in externals as Saul of Tarsus himself. You might nevertheless be as guilty a sinner as lives out of hell! What did Paul say of himself when his eyes came to be opened? Speaking of sinners he says, "Of whom I am chief" (1 Timothy 1:15). He looked upon himself as a heart-hypocrite! He did not attempt to say one good thing of his former Pharisee life, but condemned it all. You mean to do right you say, but you think only of objective right—right as to the externals only. You know that all your rightness is only this, no more. You know that all you think of when you speak of doing right is of the external and objective. You do not even inquire whether your heart, your motive, is pure before God. You know that real love to God and others is not the life and spring of your activities. Precisely here is your deep and ruinous delusion!

Suppose my wife should claim to do right in her relations as my wife, and think, like you, only of the objective, the outside appearance. She says she means to do all right, but what does she mean by that? Suppose she trims her ways to answer the demands of external propriety. But suppose also that everybody has reason enough to know that she loves somebody else with all her heart! What would you say to that? Suppose you know that any wife is absolutely devoted to some other man than her husband. Would you not abominate all her professions of doing right toward her husband?

Let every mere moralist know: you never have done one thing in all your life of which God did not say, "Who hath required this at your hand?" You need not come and tell Him it is all right, that you mean to do right; for all is utterly wrong! Your heart is after your idols and is not yielded up trustfully to God. How can all your "right-doing" be anything but an abomination as long as you do not give God your heart!

This text does not profess to give the whole of Paul's conversion. It only gives us his conviction. "I was alive without the law once (in my self-righteous hopes) but when the commandment came (revealing God's holy law) then sin revived, and I died—my hopes perished then." There he was till he gave himself up to the Lord Jesus Christ. Substantially, this experience of being slain by the law must always precede the acceptance of Jesus Christ as our own Savior. The reason is this: people will not accept Christ's robe while their own apparel suits them better. They will not rely on another for salvation while they are strong in their self-dependence.

We can see in the light of our subject what the work of the Spirit is in both conversion and sanctification. Some forever inquire, "What is the work of the Spirit?" Others think there is no need of the divine Spirit in order to produce conviction of wrong, for they assume that natural conscience is all-sufficient for this result. But, the light of nature and all the force of mere conscience will never slay the enmity of the sinner's heart and break him down in real penitence and humiliation. The Spirit of God must wake and rouse the moral and spiritual consciousness. The Spirit must take God's holy law and hold it up as a molten looking-glass. The sinner must see the meaning of God's law and his own awful sin in having so long trampled it beneath his feet. The Spirit also reveals the spiritual nature of the gospel. Having with one hand held up the spiritual nature of the law, with the other He reveals the love of the gospel, unfolding the heart of Jesus till the sinner says, "How can I abuse such love! How can I refuse to trust such a Savior!" Those who are not conscious of such things are not converted. You who have not had before your mind's eye this looking-glass of the law and gospel, what do you know about the gospel? If Christ has not been revealed to your soul, what do you know about faith in Christ?

Do not some of you see that you are certainly deluded? You who are merely moralists, impenitent sinners still, have you utterly failed to see the utter abomination of all your offerings and sacrifices? What awful danger there is lest some of you should put out the light of the Holy Spirit as He shines in upon your souls! What result can be more fatal and more awful than this? How can we account for the moral state of many people except on the supposition that they have grieved away the Spirit of God? They come and go with God's people, but they never seem to see their own self-deception and impending damnation!!

I have seen some writhe under the truth as if an arrow had struck. And did they at once give up all and say, "I am a deceived wretch! I must repent!"? No. Instead, some said, "I will look this subject over after I get home!" Several times during the last season, I thought I saw most clearly that some of you were on the very pivot of life; and I said, "Come now! Come right forward and settle this matter at once for all time!" But you

Revival of Sin and the Law

did not come, and what was the result? Go and see. All gone back. You did not come up to the light and therefore of course fell back into deeper darkness than ever. And are you still waiting for more light? I beseech you, be not so absurd as to wait in such resistance to God as surely grieves away the Spirit and sinks the soul into yet more fatal darkness. Have not some of you young people waited for more light until you have lost all you had? The Bible doctrine is: *Use, and you gain more; neglect and you lose*—"From him that hath not shall be taken away even that which he hath" (Matthew 25:29). Why? Because the fact that he *has not* proves that he has not improved what he had.

Let me say to you who profess to be Christians: It is becoming most alarmingly true that there is a great lack of discrimination in distinguishing what is essential from what is merely incidental to a good Christian life. Often in attending examinations of candidates for admission to the church have I been pained to hear questions put which did not at all touch the real merits of the case. They might have been answered in the most favorable way and yet the answers should have afforded no decisive testimony of real conversion. The questions altogether failed to show whether the candidates had ever really felt themselves to be lost sinners, and as such had thrown themselves upon God's mercy. Did this conviction of being lost and self-ruined fasten on them, and then under its impression, did they search for the remedy and find it in casting themselves wholly on infinite grace? Where this is lacking, there can be no Christian experience.

Often, and perhaps I may say always, where under gospel light true conversion does not take place, something binds the mind. Truth adapted to wake up the consciousness, *first to fear and then to love*, fails to produce its effects. Selfishness has bound up the mind and it has no enlargement, no freedom to go forth in confidence or in penitence. When they attempt to pray, it is as if something bound up their mind; there is no earnest going out of their soul after God. When they say, "I will go and seek God," they go not. It is not with them as with those whom the Spirit of God is drawing, who feel as if their very soul would go out after Christ—even almost out of their body. This going out of the soul I often compare to what you may have noticed often when you put a burning candle in a strong draft of air. The wind bears the blaze away and almost forces it entirely from the wick, yet it flickers and hangs. You can see it borne quite a perceptible distance from the wick, but the connection is still maintained. When you stop the draft, the candle burns again as before. So with Christians. They almost go off from their bodies. Their souls being drawn away by the power of their ravishing views of Jesus.

Opposite to this is the state which I have been emphasizing: there is no spontaneous going out of the heart after God either in prayer or in attempted consecration. Ask such a person, "Do you feel your whole soul going, going, as if nothing were held back?" They may answer, "No; I know nothing about that." Yet when one really yields himself to the drawing of the Spirit, he is as conscious of giving himself up as he ever is of giving anything to another. A lady whom I saw last winter said, "I went to my room to give myself to God there and as soon as I knelt down there was a spontaneous going forth of my heart to God and it seemed hardly necessary for me to say a word for my heart had already gone out to Christ. Words seemed too poor to express my mind to God, for it seemed as if my very soul had gone itself, and no words were needed." She came down from her room so wonderfully filled with the Holy Spirit that her soul was all on fire and some suggested that such a woman must be crazy. But many are utterly hard and unmoved—no going out of heart toward God and no melting of soul before Him.

You who think you are Christians; do you know what it is to be slain by the law and truly made alive by the Holy Spirit? Or is it your case that you are living along with a hope that does not assimilate you to Jesus Christ? Are you aware whether or not you have so long resisted God and His truth that it will not do for you to try it again? Now is your time! You need not pause to make terms with God; for all the terms are fixed already. Let your inward heart go! Say, "Lord, I come to Thee! It is long enough that I have lived on in my sins. I am ashamed to ask another hour's life in which to fight and war against You! Let it be enough that I have lived in sin so long; now and forevermore I will be the Lord's!"*

---

* Charles G. Finney, *The Oberlin Evangelist*, July 6, 1853, *Principles of Liberty*, 65–75. For Review: Answer the Study Questions on page 220, Cowles page 241.

4

Thanks for the Gospel Victory
1856

I thank God through Jesus Christ our Lord. So then with the mind I myself serve the law of God; but with the flesh the law of sin. —Romans 7:25—KJV

Thanks be to God — through Jesus Christ our Lord! So then, I myself in my mind am a slave to God's law, but in the sinful nature a slave to the law of sin. —Romans 7:25—NIV

But thanks be to God, which giveth us the victory through our Lord Jesus Christ. —1 Corinthians 15:57—KJV

But thanks be to God! He gives us the victory through our Lord Jesus Christ. —1 Corinthians 15:57—NIV

Principles of Peace — Finney's Lessons on Romans

In both of these passages, the Apostle Paul gives thanks for deliverance from a sinning and sinful state. The Bible everywhere teaches and the facts prove that the unconverted are morally and spiritually dead. They live as if there were no God. They appreciate neither His rights nor His feelings. To all intents and purposes, they are, toward God, as dead men. Considerations concerning God have no influence on them. This is one of the most obvious facts in human life. So true is this that in fact we often find people pleading as their excuse that they have no inclinations toward God. In this manner, they reveal their moral death, not in their lives only, but in their very excuses. They show that they are conscious of their moral apostasy and death. They are too well aware that they have no tendencies in themselves toward God.

Christians, on the other hand, are often represented as being alive but not in good and perfect health, as not mature in their growth. At first they are newborn babes, needing the pure milk of the word; then youth, needing counsel; then fathers and mothers in Israel, of "full age" and having their senses exercised to discern both good and evil. Often the scriptures represent Christians as being very weak, and having great liability to stumble and fall. This stumbling and falling becomes a sad stumbling-block in the way of the wicked—those who are prone to look for and seek stumbling-blocks for their excuses. They do not realize the condition of those Christians who are only in part reclaimed from their death in sin. They do not consider that though born, they are still newborn babes, or at best, but children. The wicked are not disposed to make allowances for these circumstances—a fact which only serves to show how unreasonable sin is.

Returning to the fact that Christians are usually weak, please note that this weakness is *moral*, not natural. Natural weakness pertains to one's created faculties; *moral weakness* pertains to one's voluntary purposes. Weakness of nature is a misfortune; weakness of moral purpose is a fault. Death in sin is simply a fault—always and altogether a fault. This weakness in Christians is also a fault, because it results from a lack of faith in Christ and love to His name.

This weakness and moral death of sinners is a fact of experience. I have myself had but too much reason to know what it is. I found a total

Thanks for the Gospel Victory

discrepancy between my convictions and my actions. I could say, "So I ought to do, but so I do not." When I questioned myself, asking, "Why is this so?" I could only say, "It is wholly unaccountable." Wide awake on all other subjects, and to all other interests, yet perfectly dead to this. I found myself in a strange state; and if not a wonder to many, I was at least to myself. In a wretched state, I knew I had no disposition to get out of it. And every sinner who reflects knows that this is just his state.

The spiritual weakness of Christians manifests itself in a conscious lack of promptness to act upon, and fully up to, their convictions of duty and sense of obligation. They are more deeply conscious of these defects than sinners are, or can be, of their defects. Sinners have little anxiety or trouble about their own moral death; but not so with Christians. Christians recognize their obligations and are unusually conscious of being ready, prompt, and anxious to meet them; while painfully aware that while "the spirit is willing the flesh is weak" (Matthew 26:41). Sometimes they are strong in the Lord and their sense of weakness has passed away; after awhile, perhaps, they trust to their own strength and find out their weakness to their cost. They fall sadly short and come into darkness and trouble.

This state of spiritual weakness in both true Christians and sinners is among the most patent and obvious facts in the world. Who can doubt that there is moral life in real Christians and moral death in sinners? The Bible everywhere teaches or implies these facts. It is a fact that no one can doubt who has eyes to see and a mind candid enough to apprehend and admit a plain fact.

I often think it strange that the unconverted allow themselves to be so stumbled by the weakness of those who profess Christian faith. I have met some impenitent people who had thought candidly on this subject, and who seemed to appreciate fully the state and difficulties of Christians, and consequently were not stumbled at all by any mistakes or errors into which they might fall. They did not at all marvel that Christians are no better. If I had not considered this matter, and had not ceased to stumble myself on the imperfections of professed Christians, I never could have become a Christian. If I had not seen that all this is according to the Bible and reason, I could not have come into a state of mind toward God and

Christianity in which my conversion from sin would be possible. Usually, in a place where there are many Christians, there will be some who stumble constantly upon them, as if utterly unable or unwilling to apologize for their failures on the score of infant piety, superinduced upon long-standing habits of sin.

The remedy for sin.

If there is not some efficacious remedy for sin in the soul, then sinners must be either annihilated at death or damned. So of Christians, if there be not some efficacious remedy giving them victory over sin, then they too must be lost. In my early life I was much more ready to doubt whether any could be saved than to believe that all would be saved. There seemed to me more reason to suppose all would be damned, than all saved. The great question for me was, "How can any be saved?" I never wondered, "How can God damn any?" Let any sensible person get a clear and full idea of what salvation is and he will see it can be no easy thing. He will assume that the law must go into full execution against all; and that being so, then none can be saved. Before my conversion I mostly thought on this text: "If the righteous scarcely be saved, where shall the ungodly and the sinner appear?" (1 Peter 4:18). I could see that even Christians must have mighty help from some place, since they were only babes in Christ and their salvation a work of many difficulties.

It has always seemed passing strange to me that anyone could be a universalist. Even before my conversion it was a profound mystery. "Why," I asked then, "does not everybody see that a person must become holy or be lost?" If the Holy Spirit does not go down into hell to convert sinners, surely they cannot be saved there. Unless there be some efficacious remedy for sin, taking effect to the full extent of actually giving the victory over sin, salvation in heaven is impossible.

In Romans, chapter seven, Paul describes a state in which there is the greatest effort to get rid of this state of sinfulness. There he cries out, "O wretched man that I am! Who shall deliver me from this body of sin and death?" (Romans 7:24). Then, the gospel opening on his anxious eye, he thanks God for deliverance through Jesus Christ. He saw the remedy!

Thanks for the Gospel Victory

This remedy is never in ourselves. Nowhere in the wide range of the material system all round us can a remedy be found; nowhere outside of God. It might be demonstrated that in our own nature there is no efficacious remedy. Yet by this I do not mean to say that if anyone would use his powers right, he could gain no relief; I do mean to say that apart from God he never will use his own powers right for this purpose. His own will is committed in an opposite direction. He has fallen into the slough of his corrupt propensities (i.e. intense natural inclinations). These propensities are fearful adversaries to his being holy, and must be, until they are subdued. Hence we are constantly pressed with the question, "Where is the power that can subdue them and give us the victory?"

Paul answers by thanking God who gives us the victory through our Lord Jesus Christ. In Christ we have the answer and the victory. Yet, until people come to know the gospel by an inward apprehension, it is to them dark and almost without meaning. They feel but little if any interest in the answer. But, when the Holy Spirit reveals Jesus to the mind, these dark things become precious realities. Light breaks in and illumines the chambers of the mind, so recently in thick darkness. Under the Spirit's influence gospel truth becomes intensely interesting and even exciting. Those who have been swept away by the influence of worldly objects, who would not look at spiritual things, and were almost mad in their pursuit of objects which appeal only to the senses, are now wonderfully changed. Christ reveals himself so clearly that He overbalances and overcomes these earthly excitements. Especially is this the case when the Spirit reveals God as being truly love. God as love at once takes prodigious hold on us. Said one who had long professed faith in Christ, and had known something of the gospel in her own experience, "All at once, after so long walking in comparative darkness, the Lord showed me that I had hitherto known Him but very imperfectly. Before, I did not know God was love. I did not see this in its own true sunlight. I had opinions; I had notions; but it could not be said I had knowledge of the love of God. I had heard of Him by the hearing of the ear; but now mine eye has seen Him, and my heart has been ravished with His love." From this time onward her whole soul seemed all glowing with love to God, and radiant with the love of God revealed to her. So it will always be when the Spirit reveals Jesus to the soul and we see why Christ died for us and why He has in so many ways done so much for us. When these things come up from the realms of theory into the position of fact and of experience, apathy ceases; the sensibilities and emotions are no longer stagnant; all is wakeful; slavish fear is gone; the soul approaches God freely and in the spirit of a child; he is no longer religious because he must be, nor reads the Bible because he must, nor does he pray or give in benevolence for such reasons. All these forms of dead experience have passed away and the mind looks back on it as a loathsome abomination. While these views of Christ are before his mind, he will make no more legal efforts; will no more strive to gain the favor of God by mere works of law. Christ, thus revealed, breaks the power of sin.

Turning now to unrepentant sinners, do you not know and admit that I have given a fair account of your case? You know that you have no proper regard, practically, for God, no more than if your heart and intellect were separated, and all mutual influence of one over the other were broken off. Your convictions of truth are often clear and strong; but the response of your heart to this truth is utterly withheld. The state of your affections and will seems to have no correspondence to your own convictions of what they should be. Yet this strange discrepancy is altogether within your power, and you ought to put an end to it at once. You have no right to live on so, God asserting His claims, but your soul utterly disowning them. This is precisely the state of the sinner. His conscience is separated from his heart. When his attention is turned to this, he is conscious of this utter disagreement and discordance. In my days of sin, I was just as sensible of this as of my own existence.

Do you ask, "What is the reason for this? Am I ever to become self-consistent?" One of the most important lawyers in New York once said, "There is no use in trying to vindicate myself. I can make no defense; can offer no explanation. It avails nothing for me to argue my case, for I have nothing to plead." So you know you have no reason to offer for your course of sin. If I were to put it to you to say by a public expression if this be not your case, you would at once, if honest, rise to give assent. You are in a lost state. Sometimes you feel a deep sense of being spiritually lost. Is there a remedy for you?

Thanks for the Gospel Victory

Some of you who profess to be religious are in great doubt about whether you have any spiritual life. Let me ask you if you have not been greatly tried with the fact of your own spiritual impotence and of your having so little rallying power in yourself? Are you not surprised and troubled at your lack of energy, your inefficiency in duty? Have these things pressed you? Have you been led to inquire anxiously whether or not there is a remedy? Do you want to get hold of one, if it be yet possible?

Our scripture text gives us the true and only remedy. God in Christ is the only efficient and all-sufficient power to reach and remedy this direst of all things, *sin*. Everywhere in the Bible, the condition of this victory over sin is declared to be faith in Jesus Christ. "This is the victory that overcometh the world, even our faith" (1 John 5:4). Without faith the gospel never takes effect in us.

What the Bible thus declares is true also in philosophy and in fact. Goodness revealed has attractions even over sinners. It is its very nature to attract all human hearts. Some of you felt this attraction even when you were in your sins. Perhaps you feel it somewhat even now. In my own case I recollect the circumstance of weeping profusely at an instance of goodness. I thought then it came near to winning me over to sympathy with goodness. I could not help crying out, "This is not in me; I know my heart is not in sympathy with God;" so strangely did this manifestation of goodness affect me.

If you have read *Uncle Tom's Cabin* you will remember the story of Topsy and little Eva.** Topsy seems never to have seen any manifestations of kindness and goodness toward herself. Always beaten about, every influence only driving her further from goodness, no wonder she became surly and morose. Little Eva approached her on one occasion as she sat, and looking her mildly and sweetly in the eye, asked her if she could not be good. Now, for the first time, she saw an interest manifested in her happiness, and saw also, in contrast with Eva's spirit, what her own was. This is represented as the first step before the great moral change.

No doubt this is true in philosophy. There is something in goodness which strongly tends to draw a moral being into sympathy with itself. Christians are made strong by the revelations which Christ makes of himself to their minds. "Beholding as in a glass the glory of the Lord, (Jesus) they are changed from glory to glory" (2 Corinthians 3:18). The view of His own glory, which the Lord gave to Moses when he prayed, "I beseech thee show me thy glory," and the Lord answered, "I will make all my goodness pass before thee," thus strengthened Moses greatly (Exodus 33:18-19). It seemed to cast the mantle of Jehovah upon him and make him a new and wonderful man.

When the Lord gains the confidence of a sinner so that He can reveal himself, the first step is to reveal His goodness. So we should expect, and so it is. But this goodness must be believed. Confidence must be reposed in Christ, else He cannot reveal His goodness in any saving manner. A conscious victory over ourselves and sin is the only evidence of a saving change. An apparent victory is the only evidence to others of our being savingly changed. This victory consists in being saved from sin, and in becoming like God, who does all things from the motive of love.*** Nothing less than this is real salvation.

The power of love.

Love revealed to faith is the power of God unto salvation. Suppose one of you comes into a state in which you have not a particle of confidence in anyone who tries to do you good; all that any friend should attempt to do for you, you ascribe to some sinister motive. So long as you withhold confidence, his love is not revealed to your faith, for you have no faith to which it can be revealed. In this case, by a natural law of mind, all the goodness he reveals to you only makes you more wicked and only works out a deeper ruin.

The love of God revealed to faith is the power of God to bring the soul out of its bondage to sin. But love manifested, yet through unbelief rejected, works ruin to the soul by a natural law. By the same law, the clearer the revelations of God's love, the more rapid and fearful the ruin wrought. The case of the Jews taught by Christ in person is in point a most striking and affecting example. The way they rejected their Messiah served fearfully to deprave their hearts and to hasten the ruin of the nation. Christ himself said, "If I had not come and spoken unto them, they had not had sin, (that is, comparatively none) but now they have no cloak

Thanks for the Gospel Victory

for their sin" (John 15:22). When Christ went through all Judea and Galilee manifesting everywhere the evidences of His being the Messiah, and bearing himself with so much kindness, dignity, love, and humility, it seems amazing that the people in mass and their priests and scribes especially did not open their hearts to bid Him welcome. But when instead of this, they withheld their confidence and rejected Him in stern and wicked unbelief, they became fearfully hardened. Every step in the process of this rejection worked only mischief and ruin. Suppose you have in your family a son whom you are trying to save; but the more you labor for this result so much the more does he withhold his confidence, traduce your motives, and pervert to evil all your intended good. Such a course as this on his part throws him fearfully into the power of Satan, and he is led captive by that arch-deceiver at his will.

Thanks for the victory.

People cannot appreciate our texts, and other passages of this class, unless they have had experience. "Thanks be to God," cries Paul, "who giveth us the victory." Here we have a song in which no one can truly join in singing except those who have gained this victory and know its power and blessedness. What can an impenitent person know of such emotions? What can he say? Can he thank God for victory of which he knows and experiences nothing? No; he has been only vanquished, and Satan sings the song of victory over the ruin of his soul.

To the Christian, really victorious, there is the utmost occasion for gratitude and thanksgiving. He so esteems this far above all his other mercies that he finds himself lifted above the power of temptation, his old chains broken, his religious exercises and purposes become spontaneous, and Christianity the life and joy of his soul. How earnestly does he bless the Lord who hath given him the victory!

It is sad to see how little there is, in our day, of this thanksgiving for victory over sin. How rarely do you hear such thanks for grace received and victory obtained! We have been in the habit here of having a thanksgiving meeting for the purpose of expressing our individual grounds of thanksgiving. When the next thanksgiving day occurs shall we hear any offerings of praise to God for giving the victory over sin? We used to hear thanks for grace received; shall we have such thanks again? It was once more common with us than thanks for temporal mercies; shall it be so again? If the numbers who return to give thanks for this blessing are small, what shall we infer? Is it not fearfully sad and perilous that the gospel should lose its power in any community?

Many seem not to be aware of their real state. It is hard to convince them that they are not altogether right, yet they have no thanks for this victory. Surely, if they had gained this victory, they would acknowledge it and express their gratitude to God for it. No other victors are more grateful than Christian victors. If they find themselves victors, they will not conceal the blessed truth, but will naturally wish to shout the praises of victorious grace!

Many who profess to be Christians spend their time and breath in brooding over their great weakness, talking it over, praying about it, and discouraging themselves and others as if the Lord were a hard master, who imposed heavy tasks and allowed only the least possible amount of grace to help His children perform them. Yet they do not usually quite despair of help in themselves. They do not cease from legal efforts and are not dead to this class of efforts as are those who have utterly renounced them and trust in Christ alone. They still think they shall gain the victory by some work which they shall do in themselves. By efforts made without faith, they hope to get faith, and so work out their own righteousness. But it is only when self is really despaired of that deliverance comes. When you see a sinner on the verge of despair in himself, then you may know he is near the kingdom of grace and mercy. When he has done everything he can do in himself to save himself, and is compelled to despair of doing anything more, then he is ready to trust in Jesus. Who of us has not seen this experience in others and felt it in ourselves? At first we thought we could attain to Christian faith and salvation with a little effort; we started off self-righteously and made some ineffectual struggles to pray, and we soon learned that our case was far worse then we had supposed. Before my conversion I had never prayed much. For a short time previously, I used to lock my office door, stop the keyhole, and whisper out a short prayer in the greatest perturbation lest somebody should hear my

Thanks for the Gospel Victory

voice or in some way learn that I was praying. But this served no purpose. I felt I must pray better than this. I seemed to be bound up and hemmed in on every side and could not pray. But it occurred to me that if I could get entirely away from everybody, and could meet God alone, that then I could pray. So I went off into the woods, far beyond any danger of being overheard or seen. But even then I could not pray. My heart refused to pray. There seemed to be no prayer in it. I felt fearfully faint and said, "All is over with me; I never can pray." Despair came down on my heart for a moment and the last prop was knocked out from under me. There was nothing more I could do but to fall helpless at Jesus' feet and find mercy there!****

People often talk and complain much of their weakness, but do not despair of yet further efforts in their own strength. They are not so shut up to God that they know they cannot take another step to purpose in any other direction. They seem little aware of the fact that Jesus Christ is knocking at the door of their heart every moment. As He said, "Behold, I stand at the door and knock" (Revelation 3:20). Still, they do not bid Him enter with welcome. In fact, they even bolt the door against Him.

A lady of my acquaintance, hopefully a Christian, felt her need of sanctifying grace and really exhausted her strength in efforts after her own ideas of the matter to get the command of her temper. At length she fell into despair. She said she was not a Christian and could do no more and would profess piety no longer. At this crisis Jesus revealed himself to her, and in a moment she found deliverance. She was completely saved from the power of her giant temptation. Years after this she said to me, "I have no more expectation of committing those sins of temper than I have of committing murder." Real despair of help in one's *self* does not make people careless and lead them to drop all efforts. On the contrary, the more they despair, the more their soul reaches out on every side for help and hope.

Until the church is sanctified, the world cannot be converted. Until Christians can testify with their lips and lives, it cannot be expected that the truth will take effect. A man of much prominence in New York had a pious wife. When the subject of sanctification came to be agitated here, some eighteen years ago, she was enough of a Christian to understand it, and to feel her need. She studied it and embraced it. When her unconverted husband saw the astonishing change it wrought in her, he said, "The church must have this. When they do, the world will understand the gospel. They will have something intelligible to aim at." How true! Until the church gets the victory, and, rejoicing in this victory, can show it to the world, she need not think she is greatly recommending Christianity, or is likely to secure many converts.

Converts are likely to be converted only to the current standard of piety in the church where they are. Often you see this illustrated in a very striking manner. Although they have the Bible in their hand, and although they have excellent preaching, yet their practical ideas of Christianity are usually drawn from the observed life and spirit of their Christian friends. The living patterns have the practical power. Hence, if young converts have before them high example, it puts them upon high aims and efforts. They aspire to the standard of those whom they most esteem. O how precious to them to have high and holy examples for their imitation!

Church members are in their own light when they reproach converts, for they only reproach themselves. They often do not consider that these converts are only themselves reproduced; a mirror in which they can see the reflection of their own faces. So, also, for the church to complain of each other is only to complain of themselves. We are every one of us responsible in our measure for the state of the church, and to blame for its state being no better than it is. It is therefore of no use for us to recriminate.

Some who claim to be Christians say, "All this does not apply to me, for I don't profess sanctification." A great mistake; for you have professed sanctification. Scarcely could you make a more solemn profession than you made when you joined the church. Then, you publicly avouched God to be your Father, Jesus to be your Savior, and the Holy Spirit to be your Sanctifier. You solemnly promised to abstain from all ungodliness and every worldly lust, and if this is not a profession of entire sanctification, what is? Certainly, your promise and profession went the whole length of pledging yourself to full and whole-hearted obedience; an obedience not so complete as you may perhaps render in later years, with more and better knowledge; for holy obedience may progress with knowledge, onward through all time and all eternity. But after such a covenant, it avails nothing to say that you have not committed yourself to a life and a state of entire consecration to God.

Is it not the fact that some of you, instead of coming up to the gospel standard, keep shy of it, more than willing to waive the question about entire consecration, and really anxious to build up a new highway to heaven, which shall not be the "highway of holiness"? Brethren, such building of other highways for the Christian life must be a fearful failure. There is perdition at the end of such a pathway, and there ought to be. If God's redeemed people rebel against being constrained by redeeming love, and insist that some little sin must be indulged and admitted into the standard Christian life, ought not God to give them up to their own lusts? Nay more, will He not do this as sure as He is holy, and as surely as He hates sin with utter hatred?

---

* Charles G. Finney, *The Oberlin Evangelist,* January, 30 1856, *Principles of Liberty*, 77–85. For Review: Answer the Study Questions on page 221, Cowles page 242.

** Harriet Beecher Stowe, *Uncle Tom's Cabin*, Boston: John P. Jewett and Company, 1852. You can read Uncle Tom's Cabin for free online at: etext.lib.virginia.edu/toc/modeng/public/StoCabi.html.

***See especially, Charles G. Finney, *Principles of Love*, Minneapolis: Bethany House Publishers, 1986, for a more complete explanation of why and how love motivates God and ought to motivate us as Christians.

****Read about Finney's conversion in Charles G. Finney, *Memoirs of Rev. Charles G. Finney*, New York: A. S. Barnes & Company, 1876, (numerously reprinted by various publishers and still in print) or for free online at: www.gospeltruth.net/1868Memoirs/memoirsindex.htm.

The Psalms on Peace

I will lie down and sleep in peace, for you alone, O Lord, make me dwell in safety. —Psalm 4:8

The Lord gives strength to his people; the Lord blesses his people with peace. —Psalm 29:11

Turn from evil and do good; seek peace and pursue it. —Psalm 34:14

But the meek will inherit the land and enjoy great peace. —Psalm 37:11

Consider the blameless, observe the upright; there is a future for the man of peace. But all sinners will be destroyed; the future of the wicked will be cut off. —Psalm 37:37-38

I will listen to what God the Lord will say; he promises peace to his people, his saints — but let them not return to folly. Surely his salvation is near those who fear him, that his glory may dwell in our land. —Psalm 85:8-9

Love and faithfulness meet together; righteousness and peace kiss each other. Faithfulness springs forth from the earth, and righteousness looks down from heaven. —Psalm 85:10-11

Great peace have they who love your law, and nothing can make them stumble. I wait for your salvation, O Lord, and I follow your commands. —Psalm 119:165-166

Too long have I lived among those who hate peace. I am a man of peace; but when I speak, they are for war. —Psalm 120:6-7

5

Justification
1843

There is therefore now no condemnation to them which are in Christ Jesus, who walk not after the flesh, but after the Spirit.—Romans 8:1—KJV

Therefore, there is now no condemnation for those who are in Christ Jesus, who do not live according to the sinful nature but according to the Spirit.—Romans 8:1—NIV

In this lesson, I shall notice what it means to be "in Christ Jesus;" what is intended by "no condemnation;" why there is "no condemnation" to those "who are in Christ Jesus;" what is intended by not walking "after the flesh, but after the Spirit;" and that only those who walk "after the Spirit" are in a justified state.

What does it mean to be "in Christ Jesus"?

Basically, four different definitions or interpretations have been given to this question, which I will briefly consider. I will give a brief summary of what I suppose to be the true answer in the fourth interpretation, and then explain it more fully in this lesson.

First. Some interpret what it means to be "in Christ Jesus" according to the doctrine of eternal justification by imputed righteousness. This doctrine holds that a certain number of people were unconditionally chosen from all eternity to whom Christ sustained the relation of Covenant Head, and in this sense they are eternally justified. This gross and absurd notion is now exploded and generally rejected.

Second. Others answer the question of what it means to be "in Christ Jesus" according to the doctrine of perpetual justification by one act of faith. This doctrine holds that the first act of faith brings the person into such a relationship to God as never afterwards to be condemned or exposed to the penalty of the law, no matter what sins the person may commit. The simple idea is that with respect to Christians the penalty of the law is wholly set aside.

As we look more closely at the doctrine of perpetual justification, I would like to make several objections to this doctrine. First, notice this: justification is of two kinds, legal and gospel. Legal justification consists in pronouncing a moral agent innocent of all violation of the claims of the law, so that the law has no charge against him. Gospel justification consists in pardoning a sinner for whatever transgressions he may have committed; that is, in arresting or setting aside the execution of the penalty which he has incurred.

Legal justification must be out of the question, because all the world has become guilty before God. To maintain that a person is perpetually justified by once believing is *antinomianism* (the belief that under the gospel dispensation of grace the moral law is of no use or obligation because faith alone is necessary to salvation). *Antinomianism* is one of the worst forms of error, and antinomians maintain that with respect to Christians the law of God is abrogated. The law is made up of precept and penalty, and if either is detached then it ceases to be law. It matters not whether it is maintained that the precept is set aside or the penalty is set aside, for to set aside either is an abrogation of the law and is a ruinous error. It is the nature of a pardon to set aside the execution of the penalty due to past violations of the law, and to restore the person to governmental favor during good behavior. More than this, a pardon cannot do without giving an indulgence to sin. If no future sins can incur the penalty of the law, it follows that the Christian could not be in danger of hell, however many or gross sins he might commit, or even should he die in a state of the foulest apostasy. What an abomination is such a doctrine!

Third, the doctrine of perpetual justification cannot be true for no being can prevent condemnation where there is sin. The law is not founded in the arbitrary will of God, but in the nature and relations of moral beings. Whatever penalty is due to any act of sin, is due therefore, from the nature of the case, so that every act of sin subjects the sinner to the penalty. Pardon for sin cannot be prospective. Sin cannot be forgiven in advance, and to maintain that it is, is to make Christ the minister of sin.

Fourth, if a person holds the doctrine of perpetual justification, then he must agree that if Christians are not condemned when they sin, they cannot be forgiven, since forgiveness is nothing else than setting aside the penalty. Therefore, if they are not condemned, they cannot properly pray for forgiveness. In fact, it would be a sign of unbelief in them if they prayed for forgiveness. What else could it be, if the sin, whatever it may be in enormity, has not exposed its perpetrator at all to the penalty of God's law?

Fifth, this notion of perpetual justification cannot be true, because the Bible uniformly makes perseverance in holiness; that is, in obedience, just as much a condition of final acceptance with God as repentance or one act of faith. For my part, I must say, I don't know where the Bible makes salvation depend on one act of faith. Those who hold this dogma ought to tell us where it is taught in the Bible. The Bible, in fact, expressly declares that "when a righteous man turneth away from his righteousness, and committeth iniquities, and dieth in them, for his iniquity that he hath done, shall he die" (Ezekiel 18:26). What can be more distinct or explicit than this declaration? I know not how it has been overlooked, or can be evaded.

Sixth, if the doctrine of perpetual justification is true, it follows that if Christians are not condemned for one sin, they would not be for ten thousand, and that the greatest apostates could be saved without repentance. But what kind of a gospel is that? It would overthrow the entire government of God. A pretty gospel this is! Strange kind of good news!

Seventh, as I said before, if the penalty is abolished with respect to believers, then the law must be abolished. To them, its precept ceases to be anything else than simple advice, which they may do as they please about adopting as their guide.

Finally, every Christian's experience condemns the doctrine of perpetual justification. Among Christians, who does not feel condemned when he sins? Now, either he is condemned when his conscience affirms that he is condemned; or his conscience is at opposition to the government of God by affirming what is not true. And when, under its rebukes, Christians go and ask for pardon, in yielding to their conscience, they are guilty of unbelief, and thus add one sin to another. The truth is, every Christian's conscience condemns the doctrine of perpetual justification. The doctrine of perpetual justification is obviously evil, and only evil, and that continually, in its whole tendency.

Third. Another answer that is given to the question of what it means to be "in Christ Jesus" is that there will be no *final* condemnation. I will only remark that the Bible teaches no such thing. The Bible says, "there is *now* no condemnation" (Romans 8:1). This agrees with Romans 5:1, "Therefore, being justified by faith, we have peace with God, through our Lord Jesus Christ." Indeed, this is the general representation of the Bible.

Fourth. The fourth answer for what it means to be "in Christ Jesus" is this: to be "in Christ Jesus" is to have a personal, living faith in Him. To be "in Christ Jesus" is to *abide in Him by a living faith*. Consider what Christ himself taught: "Abide (or continue) in me, and I in you. As the branch cannot bear fruit of itself, except it abide in the vine, no more can ye, except ye abide in me. I am the vine, ye are the branches: he that abideth in me, and I in him, the same bringeth forth much fruit; for without me, ye can do nothing. If a man abide not in me, he is cast forth as a branch that is withered; and men gather them and cast them into the fire, and they are burned. If ye abide in me, and my words abide in you, ye shall ask what ye will, and it shall be done unto you" (John 15:4-7). The Apostle John wrote: "And ye know that He was manifested to take away our sins: and in Him is no sin. Whosoever abideth in Him, sinneth not: whoso-

Justification

ever sinneth, hath not seen Him, neither known Him" (1 John 3:5-6). The Apostle Paul wrote to the Corinthians, "Therefore, if any man be *in Christ*, he is a new creature: old things are passed away; behold, all things are become new" (2 Corinthians 5:17). I might quote many other passages, all setting forth that there is no condemnation to those whose faith secures in them an actual conformity to the divine will.

To be "in Christ" is to be so under His influence that you do not walk after the flesh, but after the Spirit; that is, *you receive constant divine influence from Him*, as the branches derive nourishment from the vine. This intimate connection with Christ and spiritual subjection to His control are fully taught in many passages in the Bible. Paul wrote, "I am crucified with Christ: nevertheless I live: yet not I, but Christ liveth in me: and the life which I now live in the flesh, I live by the faith of the Son of God, who loved me, and gave Himself for me" (Galatians 2:20.). And, "This I say then, walk in the Spirit, and ye shall not fulfill the lust of the flesh. For the flesh lusteth against the Spirit, and the Spirit against the flesh, and these are contrary the one to the other: so that ye cannot do the things that ye would. But if ye be led by the Spirit, ye are not under the law. Now, the works of the flesh are manifest, which are these; adultery, fornication, uncleanness, lasciviousness, idolatry, witchcraft, hatred, variance, emulations, wrath, strife, seditions, heresies, envyings, murders, drunkenness, revellings, and such like; of the which I tell you before, as I have also told you in times past, that they which do such things shall not inherit the kingdom of God. But the fruit of the Spirit, is love, joy, peace, long suffering, gentleness, goodness, faith, meekness, temperance: against such there is no law. And they that are Christ's have crucified the flesh with the affections and lusts. If we live in the Spirit, let us also walk in the Spirit" (Galatians 5:16-25).

What is intended by "no condemnation"?

To be condemned is to be under the sentence of law. Those who *are* condemned are not only not pardoned for the past, but also *their present state of mind is blameworthy and condemned.* They are not justified on the ground of either law or gospel. The whole penalty due to all their iniquity is against them.

When it is said there is no condemnation, it is not intended that they never were condemned; rather, their past sin is all pardoned. They are wholly delivered from exposure to the penalty due to their sins. In addition to this, it is intended that in their present state of mind, they obey the law so that the law does not condemn their present state. It does not mean that they will not be again condemned if they sin, but that *while they are in Christ Jesus, they are free from all present condemnation.*

Why there is no condemnation to those who are in Christ Jesus.

There is no condemnation, not because they are of the elect and eternally justified. There is no condemnation, not because Christ's righteousness is so imputed that they can sin without incurring exposure to the penalty of the law. There is no condemnation, not because they are perpetually justified by one act of faith. This, as we have attempted to show, is an antinomian and pernicious error. There is no condemnation, not because God accepts an imperfect obedience. There is a general opinion now current that somehow or other God accepts an imperfect obedience as genuine. Now, it seems to me, that this is a very erroneous view of the subject. The truth is, God has no option about this matter any more than any other being, for the law exists and makes its demands wholly independent of His will. *Whatever the law demands*, that is, *whatever the nature and relations of moral beings demand*, that, *as moral Governor, God is obligated to enforce*, and nothing else. Now what is there in reason or the Bible to sanction the idea that God will or can accept an imperfect obedience? *The Bible insists on our serving God with our whole heart*; on our being perfectly benevolent, and it proposes no lower standard. Nor could we believe it, if it did. What kind of obedience is half or imperfect obedience? No one can tell, and consequently, no one can intentionally render it. The very idea of it is absurd.

To the one in Christ Jesus, there is *now* no condemnation, because he is in Christ Jesus in the sense I have already explained. Not that Christ shields him from the penalty while he continues to violate the precept, but because *Christ saves him from sin*, and thus, from desert of the penalty.

Justification

Our text indicates, "to those who walk not after the flesh, but after the Spirit." Notice the result: read right along. In the seventh chapter of Romans, Paul spoke of a law in his members, which brought him into captivity to sin and death; that is, under condemnation. Now Paul says, "For the law of the Spirit of life in Christ Jesus, hath made me free from the law of sin and death. For what the law could not do, in that it was weak through the flesh, God sending his own Son in the likeness of sinful flesh, and for sin, condemned sin in the flesh, that the righteousness of the law might be fulfilled in us, who walk not after the flesh but after the Spirit" (Romans 8:2-4). Here he asserts that the reason why God sent His own Son in the likeness of sinful flesh and for sin, and condemned sin in the flesh, was, "that the righteousness of the law might be fulfilled in us, who walk not after the flesh, but after the Spirit." Now, public justice has been satisfied by the Atonement, and when a person's heart is thus brought into conformity to the law of God, that is a good reason why they should be pardoned. The same thing is meant, by "writing the law in the heart" (see Psalm 37:31; Psalm 40:8; 2 Corinthians 3:3).

I repeat, *there is no condemnation to the one who is in Christ Jesus*, because he "walks not after the flesh, but after the Spirit." Study carefully once again these verses from Paul's *Letter to the Galatians*: "This I say then, walk in the Spirit and ye shall not fulfill the lusts of the flesh. For the flesh lusteth against the Spirit, and the Spirit against the flesh; and these are contrary the one to the other; so that ye cannot do the things that ye would. But if ye be led by the Spirit ye are not under the law. Now the works of the flesh are manifest, which are these; adultery, fornication, uncleanness, lasciviousness, idolatry, witchcraft, hatred, variance, emulations, wrath, strife, seditions, heresies, evnyings, murders, drunkenness, revellings, and such like; of the which, I tell you before, as I have also told you in times past, that they which do such things, shall not inherit the kingdom of God. But the fruit of the Spirit, is love, joy, peace, long suffering, gentleness, goodness, faith, meekness, temperance; against such there is no law. And they that are Christ's have crucified the flesh with the affections and lusts" (Galatians 5:16-24). The fruit of the Spirit is just what the law requires; therefore, there can be no condemnation.

This assertion must either mean that when we are in Christ we do not sin, or that in Him we can sin without condemnation. Now, what does it mean? It cannot mean that we can sin without condemnation, for that would make Christ the minister of sin. No individual can sin without breaking the law, for sin is the transgression of the law. The meaning must be that *when we are in Christ we do not sin*, and this agrees with what the Scriptures teach: "Without holiness no man shall see the Lord" (see Hebrews 12:14) Here is the reason why there is no condemnation to those who are in Christ Jesus: in Christ, their former sins are pardoned on the ground of His Atonement; while in Him they do not sin, for He saves them from their sins, and therefore from condemnation.

What is intended by not walking after the flesh, but after the Spirit.

By "the flesh," the Bible means "the appetites, desires, and propensities of the sensibility." To walk after the flesh is to indulge these; to give up the will to self-gratification. It is to be in bondage to the propensities so that they are our masters and govern us. It is to be selfish. But to walk after the Spirit is to obey the Spirit of Christ; it is to obey the law of God.

Only those who walk after the Spirit are in a justified state.

By this statement, I do not intend to say that they never were justified. For it is true that individuals who once obeyed, and were of course justified, have fallen. This is the case with the angels who kept not their first estate, and Adam and Eve. These were justified in the legal sense before they sinned. But many have also fallen into grievous iniquity, who have once been justified in the gospel sense.

Furthermore, I do not mean that they are in no sense Christians. In the common acceptation of the term, "Christian" is not limited to those who are in a state of actual conformity to the will of God, but applies to all who give credible evidence of having been converted. Moreover, it is true of Christians that they sustain a peculiar relation to God and the term does not indicate that they never sin or fall into condemnation, but that they sustain a certain relation to God which others do not.

I do mean that no one can commit sin without condemnation. When a Christian sins, he is as really condemned as anyone else, and he is no longer justified any more than he is obedient.

I mean that no one is justified or pardoned until he obeys the law or repents, which is the same thing. By the by, it is important that all should understand that repentance is not sorrow for sin, but a real turning away from all sin and a turning to God. Now, when any individual sins, he must be condemned till he repents or forsakes his sin. A great many people talk about always repenting and say that the best acts we ever perform need to be repented of, &c. Now, this is all nonsense, and nothing but nonsense. I say again, the Christian faith is no such thing as this, and to represent it so is to talk loosely. "The soul that sinneth it shall die" (Ezekiel 18: 4, 20). Repentance is a hearty and entire forsaking of sin; and an entrance upon obedience to God.

When one has truly repented, he is justified, and remains so just as long as he remains obedient, and no longer. When he falls into sin, he is as much condemned as any other sinner, because he is a sinner. Justification follows and does not precede sanctification as some have vainly imagined. I here use the term "sanctification," not in the high sense of *permanent sanctification*, but of *entire consecration* to God. It is not true that people are justified before they forsake sin. They certainly could not be thus legally justified, and the gospel proffers no pardon until after repentance or hearty submission of the will to God. I add: Christians are justified no longer than they are sanctified or obedient; complete permanent justification depends upon complete and permanent sanctification.

REMARKS

I have often thought, and could not help drawing the conclusion, that great numbers of those who profess Christianity are mere antinomians: *they live in the habitual commission of known sin and still expect to be saved.* And when they are pressed up to holiness of heart, they say, "I am not expected to be perfect in this life. I expect Christ to make up for my deficiencies." Now, such belief is no better than universalism or infidelity. See that one who says he is a Christian. What is he doing? Why indulging his appetites and propensities in various ways which he knows to be contrary to the divine will. Ask him about it, and he will confess it. He will confess that this is his daily practice; and yet he thinks he is justified. But the Bible is true, and he is not a true believer. Consider what the Bible teaches: "Know ye not that to whom ye yield yourselves servants to obey, his servants ye are to whom ye obey; whether of sin unto death, or of obedience unto righteousness?" (Romans 6:16). This one who professes to be a Christian can tell you of an experience. Perhaps he wrote it all down lest he should forget it. He tells it over and over again to the hundredth time how he felt when God pardoned his sins, while he is now living in sin every day. Maybe he never tells an experience at all, but rests back upon something which he felt when he imagined he was converted. Now this is nothing but antinomianism, and how astonishing it is that so many should cry out so vehemently about antinomianism who are nothing but antinomians themselves. What a terrible delusion is this!

Believers are justified by faith in Christ, because they are sanctified by faith in Him. They do not have righteousness imputed to them, and thus stand justified by an arbitrary fiction while they are personally unholy, but *they are made righteous by faith*, and that is the reason they are justified.

To talk about depending on Christ to be justified by Him, while indulging in any form of known sin is to insult Him. It is to charge Him with being the minister of sin. A lady, not long ago, was talking with her minister about certain females who were given up to dress in the utmost style of extravagant fashion. He said he thought the most dressy people in his church were the best Christians. They were the most humble, and dependent on Christ. That's his idea about Christian faith and behavior. What did he mean? Why that such people did not pretend to be holy, and professed to depend wholly on Christ. They acknowledged themselves sinners. And well they might! But what kind of Christianity is that? And how did he get such a notion? How else but by supposing that people are not expected to be holy in this life, and that they can be justified while living in sin! Now, I would as soon expect a pirate, whose hands are red with blood, to be saved, as those who profess to be Christians while they indulge in any form of sin, lust, pride, worldliness, or any other iniquity. Contrary to this obvious antinomianism, the Bible clearly teaches: "Do we make void the law through faith? God forbid: Yea, we establish the

Justification

law" (Romans 3:31).

The antinomian idea of justification is open to the infidel objection that the gospel is a system of impunity in sin. The Unitarians have stereotyped this objection against faith. Ask them why they say so. They answer, because the doctrine of justification by faith is injurious to good morals. A circuit judge, some years ago, said, "I cannot admit the Bible to be true. It teaches that men are saved by faith, and I therefore regard the gospel as injurious to good morals, and as involving a principle that would ruin any government on earth." Now, did he get this idea from the Bible? No, but from the false representations made of the teachings of the Bible. It teaches no such thing, but plainly asserts that a *faith that does not sanctify is a dead faith*.

Many hope they are Christians who still live in such a way that their conscience condemns them. The Bible warns those who think this way: "For if our heart condemns us, God is greater than our heart, and knoweth all things" (1 John 3:20). Now, if someone teaches that people may be justified while their conscience condemns them, they contradict the Bible. If our own conscience condemns us, God does. Shall He be less just than our own nature?

A great multitude of those who claim to be Christians are merely careless sinners. Now do let me ask you, if from the way many people live in the Church, compared with the way many careless sinners live, is it not perfectly obvious that they are no different? And is it censorious to say that they are mere hardened sinners? What will become of them?

Many who are accounted the most pious are only convicted sinners. It is a most remarkable thing, and one which I have taken great pains to observe, that many, thought to be converted in the late revivals, are only convicted sinners, that is, mere legalists. The preaching makes them so. The claims of the law are held up, and obligation enforced to comply with God's law. They are told to trust Christ for pardon, and they attempt it. Many really do, while others stop short with mere resolutions to do better. All will fall back or stay in the Church almost constantly distressed by the lashings of conscience. If you hold up the law they are distressed, and if you hold up Christ they are distressed by the consciousness that they do not exercise faith in Him. Hold up either, and they have no rest.

They are really convicted sinners, and yet they think this is Christianity. In time of coldness, they always sink back. In times of revival, they are aroused and driven to the performance of a heartless service which continually fails to appease the demands of conscience. They know of no other experience than this, and they refer you to the seventh chapter of Romans to prove that this is Christian experience, and thus bolster up their hope. I recollect some time ago, after I had preached against this as Christian experience, a minister said to me, "Well, Brother Finney, I can't believe that." Why? "Because that's my experience, and I believe I am a Christian." A strange reason! I suppose it was his experience! Great multitudes have this experience, and they suppose it is genuine Christian experience. I fear that in some instances whole churches are made up of such people, and their ministers teach them that this is genuine Christian faith. What would the minister just referred to say? "That is Paul's experience, and mine too." People often derive much comfort from what the minister says is his experience. Oh, what teaching is this! It is high time there was an overturning in the church on this subject. Whoever has no experience but that of the seventh chapter of Romans is not justified at all, and were it not for the fact that great numbers of people are deluded, it could not be that so many could sit down contented under this view of the subject.

One who walks after the Spirit has this inward testimony that he pleases God. An individual may think he does, when he does not, just as people in a dream may think themselves awake and find it all a dream. So individuals may think they please God when they do not, but it is nevertheless true that those who please God know it. The Bible plainly teaches, "He that believeth on the Son of God hath the witness in himself" (1 John 5:10).

Please notice that *I am not* discussing the final perseverance of the saints. What I am attempting to show is that *true believers are justified or pardoned and treated as righteous on account of the Atonement of Christ*; and furthermore, *those who truly believe are justified because they are actually righteous*. The question is not whether a Christian who has fallen into sin will die in that state, but whether if he does will he be damned. Whether, while in sin, he is justified.

Justification

Those who sin do not abide in Christ. "And ye know that He was manifested to take away our sins; and in Him is no sin. Whosoever abideth in Him sinneth not: whosoever sinneth hath not seen Him neither known Him. Little children, let no man deceive you: he that doeth righteousness is righteous even as he is righteous. He that committeth sin is of the devil; for the devil sinneth from the beginning. For this purpose the Son of God was manifested, that He might destroy the works of the devil. Whosoever is born of God doth not commit sin; for his seed remaineth in him: and he cannot sin because he is born of God" (1 John 3:5-9). While they abide in Christ, they are not condemned, but if they overlook what abiding in Christ is, they are sure to fall into sin, and then, they are condemned as a matter of course. The secret of holy living and freedom from condemnation is to *abide in Christ*. Says Paul, "I am crucified with Christ, nevertheless I live; yet not I, but Christ liveth in me; and the life that I now live in the flesh, I live by the faith of the Son of God" (Galatians 2:20). We must have such confidence in Him as to *let Him have the entire control in all things*.

Sinners can see how to be saved. They must believe in the Lord Jesus Christ with all their heart. They must become holy and walk after the Spirit. Those who profess to be Christians can also see what to do. Have you felt misgivings and a load on your conscience? Are you never able to declare, "I am justified. I am accepted in the Beloved"? If you now experience condemnation by your conscience, you must come to Christ now.

You will have neither peace nor safety unless you are *in Christ*. In Him is all fullness, and all we need. In Him you may come to God, as children, with the utmost confidence. If you are in Christ, you have peace of mind. How sweetly the experience of a Christian answers to this. Many of you perhaps can testify to this. You had been borne down with a burden too heavy, crying out, "O, wretched man that I am; who shall deliver me from the body of this death?" (Romans 7:24). But your faith took hold on Christ, and suddenly all your burden was gone. You could no longer feel condemned. The stains of sin are all wiped out by the hand of grace. You can now look calmly at your sins, and not feel them grind like an iron yoke. Are you in this state? Can you testify from your own experience that there is now no condemnation to those who are in Christ Jesus? If so, you can reflect upon your past sins without being ground down into the dust under the guilty burden which rolls upon you. The instant you experience a freedom from condemnation, your whole soul yearns with benevolence for others. You know what their state is. Ah, yes, you know what it is to drink the wormwood and the gall, to have the arrows of the Almighty drink up your spirit. When you find deliverance you must of course want to teach others what is the great salvation and to strengthen those who are weak. And an individual who can sit down at ease, and not find his benevolence like fire shut up in his bones, who does not even feel agonized, not for himself, but for others, cannot have yet found that there is now no condemnation. He may dream that he has, but if he ever awakes, he will find it but a dream. Oh, how many need to be aroused from this sleep of death!

---

* Charles G. Finney, *The Oberlin Evangelist*, July, 19 1843, *Principles of Liberty*, 87-96. For Review: Answer the Study Questions on page 222, Cowles page 246.

6

Total Depravity
1836

But I know you, that ye have not the love of God in you.—John 5:42—KJV

But I know you. I know that you do not have the love of God in your hearts.—John 5:42—NIV

Because the carnal mind is enmity against God: for it is not subject to the law of God, neither indeed can be.—Romans 8:7—KJV

The sinful mind is hostile to God. It does not submit to God's law, nor can it do so.—Romans 8:7—NIV

The words quoted in *The Gospel of John* above were addressed by the Lord Jesus Christ, on a certain occasion, to those who professed that they loved God. Along with these words of the Apostle Paul in *Romans*, I will establish the doctrine of total depravity.

In doing this, I plan to show what the doctrine of total depravity is not; what it is; and prove the doctrine *according to the definition which I shall give*.

What the doctrine of total depravity is not.

Total depravity does not consist in any lack of faculties to obey God. We have all the powers of moral agency that are needed to render perfect obedience to God. If there were any lack of faculties in our nature; then, our responsibility would cease and we could not be justly blamed for not doing that for the performance of which we do not possess the appropriate moral powers.

Total depravity does not consist in a mutilated state of our moral powers. Neither our powers of body or mind are in a maimed or mutilated state. If they were, our obligation to obey would be diminished precisely in proportion to the imperfection of the faculties of moral agency which we possess.

Total depravity does not consist in any physical pollution transmitted from Adam or from our ancestors to us. It is impossible that moral depravity should consist in physical pollution. Some people have spoken of depravity and of the pollutions of our nature as if there were some moral depravity cleaving to or incorporated with the very substance of our being. Now this is to talk utter nonsense. If such a depravity were possible, it would not be moral, but *physical depravity*. It could not be a depravity for which we were blameworthy. It could not be a sinful depravity. It would be a disease, but not a crime.

Total depravity does not consist in any principle of sin that is incorporated with our being. The word *principle* is used in two senses. It sometimes means a *property* or an *attribute of a substance* which has an inherent tendency to produce results agreeable to its nature. In this sense, depravity is not a principle; it is not a root, or sprout, or essence, or property, or attribute of any substance. Total depravity makes no part of either body or mind. It does not belong to the constitution, but belongs purely and exclusively to character. *Moral depravity is a quality of voluntary action*, and not of substance. If by *principle* is meant *purpose, preference, disposition*,

Total Depravity

voluntary inclination to sin; then, in this sense depravity is a principle, but in no other sense.

Total depravity does not mean that any being is or can be sinful before he has exercised the powers of moral agency.

Total depravity does not mean that there is any sin in human beings or in any other beings separate from actual transgression.

Total depravity is not some constitutional depravity which lies back of and is the cause of actual transgression.

Total depravity is not the same disposition to sin belonging to the substance of body or mind that there is in a serpent to bite or in a wolf to devour sheep. In other words, there is no constitutional appetite or craving for sin implanted in the substance of the body or mind.

Total depravity does not mean that people are as bad as they can be, or as they might be under other circumstances. If they were placed under circumstances of less restraint, or of greater temptation and opportunity, they would doubtless be worse than they are. When we say that people are totally depraved, we are sometimes understood to affirm that people are as bad as they can be. They seem to understand the word *total* as signifying "the highest possible degree of depravity." But certainly this is not the meaning of the word *total*. The sum total of 3 and 2 and 5 is 10. This is not the highest possible number, but is the total of 3 and 2 and 5. The same word when qualifying depravity does not mean the highest possible degree of depravity, but simply that the whole character is depraved; that there is no mixture of good in the person's character. Not that he does and says as wickedly as he could say and do; but that whatever he *does* and *says* and *is*, is sinful. *The Bible describes total depravity* by saying, "Every imagination of the thoughts of his heart was only evil continually" (Genesis 6:5—KJV) and "every inclination of the thoughts of his heart was only evil all the time" (Genesis 6:5—NIV).

What the doctrine of total depravity is.

Total depravity means that unrepentant sinners are universally destitute of love to God. My main business is to establish this position, and conclude with several remarks; then, state further what is meant by total depravity and adduce the proofs of the several positions as I go along.

Jesus said, "But I know you, that ye have not the love of God in you" (John 5:42). He expressly asserts that sinners "have not the love of God" in them. It would be easy to show that this same doctrine is everywhere recognized in the Bible. But, since I am to deal with those of you whom I affirm to be totally depraved, I do not expect that a "thus saith the Lord" will settle the question with you and put it beyond debate. You are unbelievers, and however you assent to the truth of the Bible in general; yet, I know you have no hearty confidence in its doctrines in their detail. To prove to you the doctrine of total depravity by using only the Bible may gain your unfeeling assent. But I am well aware that this kind of evidence will not so bring the subject home to your experience as to make you feel its truth. I might quote these words of Jesus and other passages of Scripture in proof of this doctrine, and then throw the responsibility upon you to receive or reject it. But as there is an exhaustless variety of other proofs within my reach, I will gather up a few of them and lay them before you for your consideration.

Facts are stubborn things, and however people may evade the Bible; however they may turn away from and misunderstand metaphysical reasonings; they find it difficult to resist plain matters of fact; especially when the facts exist in their own experience. I design to gather my proofs of this doctrine from your experience. I plan to point out certain facts in your own history and in the history of those you know that will place this doctrine upon a foundation not to be controverted.

The laws of mind in their detail are but imperfectly understood. Yet there are certain laws of mind that are understood even by children. They are facts of such universal and frequent experience that we know with absolute certainty that such are the laws of mind. For instance, by experience we know it to be a law of mind that we take delight in pleasing the object of our affection. To love an individual is to desire their happiness. To promote their happiness is to gratify that desire. To please the object of our affection will please us. To do that which is pleasing to one whom we love, to add to their honor or to their happiness in any way, is to gratify our desire for their happiness and will naturally and necessarily add to our own happiness. It is not essential that we should aim at gratifying ourselves or at promoting our own happiness in our efforts to please the object of our affections.

When we act virtuously, *to please ourselves* is no part of our design. But, although not entering into our design, it is the natural result of pleasing an object of our affection. It is the gratifying of our love or desire to promote their happiness or honor. This gratifying of our desire is of itself happiness. We find this principle showing itself in all the relations of life. When is the affectionate husband or wife in a state of higher enjoyment than when they are engaged in those employments and in the performance of those offices that contribute to each other's happiness. When is the affectionate wife more cheerful than when busied in those things that she knows will please her husband. How assiduous and unwearied are lovers and other dear friends in their efforts to please the object of their affection. How eager to anticipate each other's desires. How readily and joyfully they engage in those things that they know will give pleasure to one whom they greatly love. It is absurd and a contradiction for you to say that you love an individual if you have no delight in pleasing them. It is impossible that you should love an individual and not be gratified in promoting their happiness. To say that you love a person is the same as to say that you desire their happiness. To say that you can desire their happiness without delighting in promoting it is the same as to say that to gratify virtuous desire is not happiness. In other words, that the gratification of virtuous desire is not a gratification.

This law of mind holds true in all its fullness and extent upon the subject of religion. I appeal to every Christian, whether to do the will of God is not more than your necessary food; whether it is not your meat and drink to do the will of your Heavenly Father. When are you so happy as when you are engaged in those things that you know will promote the honor and glory of God. I do not mean or suppose that it is your design to gratify yourself when you obey and serve God; but, I ask, do you not find it to be a matter of fact that you are never so happy as when you are engaged in doing those things that please God? You search His word to know what will please God; and when you know His will and engage heartily in the performance of it, the happiness you will experience in the performance of these duties may not enter into your design or thoughts; and yet, you know that as a matter of fact the performance of duty promotes your own happiness. To please God, pleases you. And now, let me appeal to the experience of every impenitent sinner in this house: do you not know, from the very constitution of your mind, that you love to please your friends? And do you not know that it makes no part of your happiness to please God? How you delight to gratify your children; to please the objects of your most endeared affection; but I ask your conscience, do you take delight in pleasing God? Do you study to know what will please Him? And when you have learned His will, do you find yourselves inclined, readily and joyfully, to perform it? How much pains you will take. How much expense you will be. How watchful, assiduous, and persevering (not only in conforming the general outline of your conduct to the wishes of one whom you greatly love, but in following out the minutia into the detail) in fulfilling the slightest desires and gratifying even the passing wishes of one upon whom your heart is set. Thus, you give yourself up to promoting the happiness of the object of your affection. This makes up, at once, the history and the substance of your own happiness.

Now, sinner, is this your experience on the subject of Christianity? Do you love to please God? Is it your business? Is it your happiness? In other things in regard to the affairs of this world, everything you say or do is viewed as having a relation to the object of your supreme affection. If you love money supremely, everything is judged of, is hated or loved, is desired or rejected, according to the relation it sustains to your own pecuniary interest. If you can make money by it, you have pleasure in it. If it would prevent the acquisition of wealth, you are displeased with it. So, if you have an earthly friend whom you greatly love, it is natural for you to inquire in everything you say and do how it will be received or looked upon by this object of your affection. You think of what relation it sustains to them, and all your conduct is modified, and all your pursuits are regulated, by this controlling and absorbing affection for this idol. Now, sinner, I ask you again; is it true in your own experience that everything pleases or displeases you, that you love or hate it, that you desire or reject it, according to its relation to the will of God? If you see it will please God, does it please you? If it is agreeable to God's will, is it agreeable to your will? If it will promote God's glory, do you desire it? If it will dishonor God, do you reject and abhor it? If not, why do you pretend to love God? You could not believe that your children or your wife loved you unless you saw that they delighted to please you. And why should you deceive yourself by supposing that you love God when you know it is not your happiness to please Him?

From the constitution of our minds, we delight in the society and conversation of those we greatly love. To commune with them is sweet. To be alone with them, to enjoy their confidence, to pour into each other's lives the overflowing of our affections, constitutes some of the sweetest and most sacred of our joys. This law of mind shows itself in all its strength on the subject of religion. True Christians in all ages have delighted to commune with God. They have sought His society and loved the retirement of the prayer closet where they can be alone with God. Never are they more supremely and sacredly happy than when alone in secret and holy communion with the blessed God. Now, sinner, is this your experience? Do you love to be alone with God? Do you delight to pray? Is it your most sacred and endearing employment to get alone upon your knees and pour out your heart in communion with your God? I do not ask you whether you pray, for this you may do from a variety of motives, but is it because you love to pray? Because you love to be alone and commune with God? If you are an impenitent sinner, you know that you do not love the society of God.

We naturally prize the approbation or approval of one whom we love. We account it the greatest importance, and it is indispensable to our own happiness, that we should have the approval of the object of our supreme affection. We are so constituted that it gives us great pain to know that our conduct is disapproved of by our dearest friends. This is so in regard to our worldly friends, and it is so in regard to God. Nothing will wring a Christian's heart with more intolerable anguish than the conviction that his conduct merits the disapprobation or disapproval of God. And this is not principally, and in many cases not at all, through fear of punishment. The Christian may have, and often does have, the most thrilling and painful emotions in view of his having merited the disapproval of God; while, at the same time, he is not distressed with fear of punishment. But he has offended God! He is ashamed and cannot look up! He feels as an affectionate child or wife would feel under the consciousness of having done what the parent or the husband highly disapproved.

The question naturally arises, and has a controlling influence over our lives, will this or that please or displease the one I love? To gain the approval of this object of affection is our ambition and our highest joy. Now, sinner, I appeal to you, is not this true in your experience respecting the one who is the object of your greatest affection? And is it true that you above all things prize the approval of God? Is it your study? Is it your delight to gain His approbation? Does the consciousness of having done what He disapproves wring your heart with anguish, irrespective of its consequences to yourself and separate from all fear that you shall be punished? Do you feel the same emotions of sadness, of shame, of distress, of sorrow, when you have merited the disapprobation of God that you do when you have incurred the disapprobation of your most beloved earthly friend? I appeal to your own conscience in the sight of God. Sinner, do you not know that you do not supremely desire the approval and commendation of God?

We naturally have reference to the feelings of the object of our supreme affections in all our conduct. The affectionate husband or wife, parent or child, is careful not to wound the feelings of those they love. If they find that they have wounded their feelings, they have no rest until they have confessed, healed the wound, and are forgiven. This is true in religion. If you love God, you cannot reflect that you have wounded His feelings without personal pain. You would not complain that you could not repent. The truth is, if you were in the exercise of love to God, you could not help repenting any more than an affectionate wife could refrain from grief if she had wounded and grieved her husband.

We naturally love to think of the object of our affection. Everyone knows how sweet it is to be alone, to meditate, to call up before the mind and dwell upon some absent object of our love. Thus lovers are apt to seek solitude, and there is a kind of sacredness thrown around those hours, when, in the stillness of our bed-chamber, or in the retirement of the lonely walk, we dwell in silent, but delightful contemplation upon the character and person of the one we fondly love. The deep hour of midnight will often witness the wakeful musing of a heart which in the sweetness of its own fond imagination is dwelling upon that beloved friend, who, though absent, is at once the circumference and the all-absorbing center of its affections. These meditations enkindle our affections into a flame. See that husband away from home? He is a husband and a father. When the bustle of the day is over; when the distractions and cares of business have passed away; see his busy thoughts going out and dwelling upon his absent wife and upon his little prattling babes until his heart is all in a glow and tears of unutterable affection fill his eyes. This is nature. These laws of mind act with equal uniformity when God is the object of supreme affection. The lone walk, the quiet bed-chamber, the hour of sacred retirement, are sweet to the Christian. He loves to send out his thoughts after God, to dwell upon His glories, to look into the mysteries of His love, to think, and think, and meditate, and turn the subject of His glorious character over and over before his mind until his heart dissolves in love. Thus, the Psalmist says, "while I was musing, the fire burned" (Psalm 39:3). Now, sinner, do you love to think of God? Do you delight to have God in all your thoughts? Do you seek solitude and retirement so you may, without being disturbed, dwell upon God in your fondest, holiest meditations? And when you think, meditate, and pray, do you find in it a sweet and tender and all-satisfying happiness? Are you sensible of emotions of love to God, as strong, nay, vastly stronger than those you exercise when thinking of your dearest earthly friend? I appeal to your own experience and to your own conscience in the sight of God.

We naturally delight in conversing about an object of our affections. It gives us pleasure to speak of one we love. It is gratifying to let our lips speak out of the fullness of our hearts. Sometimes an affection is cherished where there is some particular reason for concealing it. But even in those cases, a great affection is seldom cherished without being divulged to someone. Where there is no reason for concealing it, we see how natural it is to make the object of our affection the subject of conversation. This law of mind manifests itself as uniformly on the subject of religion as upon any other subject. It is a maxim in philosophy as well as in morality that "out of the abundance of the heart, the mouth speaketh" (Matthew 12:34). You see a person whose heart is warm with the love of God. If

God is in all their thoughts, God and the interests of God's kingdom will be in all their words. If their heart is set upon God, their lips will speak of God. Unless they are under circumstances to require reserve, they will naturally remain silent rather than converse about a subject upon which their heart is not set. If they are under circumstances where they cannot consistently speak of God, they will be inclined not to speak at all. Now, sinner, look at your own experience; do you love to converse about God? Is it delightful to you to speak of God's character, person, and glory? I leave it with your conscience to decide.

We feel pain when separated from those we love. Everyone knows this is true respecting worldly friends; it is true in a still higher sense respecting God. Every Christian knows, just what the true Christians of old knew, that they cannot live and have the least enjoyment if they are far from God. If God hides His face, if the manifestations of His presence are withdrawn, alas, how mournful and lonely and sad is the Christian in the midst of all the gaiety and enjoyment of the world around him. Sinner, do you know what it is to feel as much pain at the withdrawal of God's presence from you as you do when separated from your dearest earthly friend? Do you feel lonely in the midst of company; sad in the midst of gaiety; away from home in the midst of all your worldly friends, if God's presence is withdrawn from you?

We naturally love the friends of the object of our affection. We feel attached to them for their sake. We love to converse with them and seek their society, because their views and feelings upon the subject that engrosses their attention correspond with our own. Upon this principle, politicians who are in favour of the same candidate are fond of each other's society. Individuals who differ widely in other respects enjoy each other's company if they have one common and absorbing object of affection and conversation. Thus, Christians love to associate with each other. They love other Christians, because they love God. They delight in their society and conversation, because their views, sentiments, and conversation accord with their own. But do sinners love the friends of God? Do you love Christians because they are Christians? Do you delight in their conversation and in their character because they love God? You may love some of them for other reasons and in spite of their religion, but it is not for their Christian faith that you love them.

We naturally avoid the enemies of our friends. See that woman—do you find her every day running in and spending time with a family that is an enemy of her husband? Does she select as her friends and intimates those who speak against her husband or her children? No, she naturally and instinctively avoids them. See that little child—he goes in to play with a neighbor's children; but while there, he hears them speaking against his father; he listens, and looks grieved and offended. He is a little one, and they do not notice him, but continue to vilify and abuse his father. He steals silently and sadly away, and goes weeping home. Hereafter, you will perceive that he will avoid those neighbors as he would a serpent. Just so with Christians. They naturally avoid the society of those that abuse God, unless they mingle with them to warn and save them. Sinners very often imagine that Christians avoid them because they feel above them, but this is not the fact. It is true that some who profess to be religious do not delight in the society and fellowship of true Christians but manifest a preference for the company of the gay and ungodly. But this is a demonstration that they are hypocrites, and is not an exception to the uniform action of this law of mind. "Don't you know that friendship with the world is hatred toward God? Anyone who chooses to be a friend of the world becomes an enemy of God" (James 4:4).

We are grieved when our beloved friend is abused in our presence. It is amazing to see the blindness and stupidity of sinners upon this subject. When Christians manifest grief at the wicked conduct of sinners, they ascribe it all to superstition. If the pious father or mother manifests grief when an impenitent son or daughter is engaged in sin and rebellion against God, they imagine that it is all superstition. Observers say they have forgotten that they were ever young. See that husband—when he breaks the Sabbath, swears, and abuses God; his wife weeps and leaves the room. He says his wife is very superstitious, a great bigot, and under the influence of priest-craft. He wonders that she should concern herself about him. He believes that he will do well enough, that he can take care of himself. He does not seem at all to understand the principle upon which his wickedness affects her. See here, you husbands; suppose you are sitting in your house with your wife and an enemy comes in and begins to abuse you in her presence. When he has heaped numberless vile epithets upon you, he looks, and your wife is in tears. Now, he says, "What ails you, woman? You must be very superstitious. What affects you so?" What would you think of such questions? Could you see no reasons why his abuse of you distressed your wife? Would you not think it strange if he did not understand the reason for her tears? Now, your wife is a Christian; you disobey and abuse God in her presence, and she expostulates and weeps, and you wonder at it and call it superstition. Turn over the leaf. Suppose when this man of whom I have been speaking abuses you to your face that your wife manifests no emotions of grief nor of indignation; but on the contrary, upon casting a glance at her, you perceive her conniving at it and appearing evidently pleased with it. What! A wife pleased to see her husband abused! From that moment, you would set her down as a hypocrite. You would not, you could not, believe that she loved you. The same holds true where God is the object of affection. When God is abused in the presence of His friends, they feel emotions of grief and indignation as a thing of course. This is the reason why the society of impenitent sinners is so disagreeable to a spiritual Christian. It is not because he feels above you, sinner, but because your conduct is a grief to him. When Christians mingle with sinners, it is upon business, or for the purpose of doing them good; not because they have any delight in their impenitent characters or conversation while they are the enemies of God.

I ask you, sinner, whether you are grieved with those who disobey God? Do you feel mingled emotions of grief and indignation; as if your wife or dearest friends were abused in your presence? Does it pain you even to agony to hear people swear in the streets or see them break the Sabbath and trample on God's holy commandments? If you went through the streets and heard execrations and abuses poured upon your dearest earthly friend from every quarter, would it fill you with grief and indignation unutterable? Can you walk the streets and hear God's holy name profaned; see His Sabbath desecrated; see hosts of impenitent sinners trampling with unholy feet upon His high and holy authority, and not be grieved? If so, you are a hardened and shameless hypocrite, if you pretend to love your Maker.

Total Depravity

We are naturally credulous and pleased if we hear any good about one we love. It is a well known fact that it is comparatively easy to believe what we desire to believe. We can believe in accordance with our feelings upon slight testimony. A person will believe what he wants to believe almost against testimony. If the thing accords with our desires, we are not inclined to question the validity of the testimony by which the desired fact is established. We witness the developments of this law of mind in transactions every day. So on the subject of religion; when Christians hear of the conversion of anyone, or of a remarkable revival of religion, or of anything else that glorifies God, they manifest a readiness to believe it because it accords with their desires. But do impenitent sinners show that they love God, that their hearts are set upon His glory and the interests of His kingdom by manifesting a readiness to believe what they hear in favor of the Christian faith? Let your conscience speak.

We love to see means used to promote the interest and happiness of those we love. If we greatly love an individual, we delight in those who honor him and try to promote his interest. If they are successful, we are not apt to be very particular and sticklish about the means that are used to promote this object. We most naturally embrace and most cordially use those means that promise the highest success. Witness the conduct of politicians; see how wise, industrious, and energetic they are in devising and executing means to elect their favorite candidate. You do not hear them stop and cavil and criticise and find fault with any measure merely because it is new. If it is not wicked, and if it promises success, its being new or old will not be a sufficient objection to its being used if it bids fair to accomplish their favorite object. So with Christians whose hearts are set upon promoting the glory and honor of God. They are on the alert and looking for and devising new means of effecting their favorite object. They are industrious and energetic in finding out new ways and adopting new expedients to bring about the salvation of the world. But do sinners apply their minds to this subject and show that they are interested in the glory of God? Are they planning and devising liberal things for Zion? Are they finding out new and more successful methods of promoting the glory of God and the salvation of others? Do you, sinner, rejoice when some new measure is introduced which has a tendency to promote this

Principles of Peace — Finney's Lessons on Romans

great work? Do you hail it as one of the means by which the great object is to be accomplished upon which your heart is supremely set?

It is difficult for us to believe an evil report of one whom we love. Go and tell that affectionate wife of some disgraceful conduct of her husband. Go tell that mother of the dissolute and abandoned conduct of her only son. Do you find them ready and willing to believe these reports? Do they believe them without question? No, but they will sift the testimony, criticise, scrutinize, and perhaps no weight of evidence that you can bring to bear upon them will thoroughly convince them of the facts. What lawyer is there who has not seen the difficulty of convincing a juror against his will? If the juror strongly desires that the testimony of a witness should not be true, what a slight appearance of inconsistency will cause him to give his testimony all to the winds. This law of mind develops itself with equal uniformity upon the subject of Christianity. Go and report among warm-hearted Christians a story, whether true or false, which, if true, is dishonorable to God and injurious to the interests of His kingdom. See how instantly they will ask for your authority, scrutinize, and sift the testimony. You need not expect them to believe, unless it comes upon them with the force of demonstration. But do sinners manifest this unwillingness to believe evil reports of Christians and the Church? If you heard an evil report concerning the family of some near friend of yours, if you heard that one of their sons had greatly disgraced his father, who was your intimate and most beloved friend, would vague report satisfy you? Would the mere say-so of some irresponsible individual be considered by you as sufficient proof to command your belief of the report? No. You would ask for high and unquestionable authority, and even then, you would say, I can hardly believe it. Now, sinner, when you hear any scandalous report of any deacon or minister or any other professed child of God, do you find yourself instantly resisting the report? Do you find yourself inclined to call for further proof; to sift and criticise the testimony, to weigh and scrutinize and give the report to the winds, as false and slanderous, if you find discrepancy or absurdity in it? Do you feel the inward risings of indignation, and your thoughts and feelings taking the attitude of strong repellency, when such a God-dishonoring report is in circulation? Do you feel when such stories are reported about

Christians as you would about slander that was uttered against your wife or dearest earthly friend.

When we are compelled to believe an evil report of the object of our affection, we are careful not to give it unnecessary publicity. Does the mother go and publish all abroad the disgrace of her children? Does the affectionate wife trumpet abroad upon the winds of heaven the disgrace of her beloved husband? No. She locks it up in her faithful and affectionate bosom. The mother and the wife seal up their lips in silence and breathe not aloud the errors of those they love. So with Christians; when they are convinced beyond all contradiction that something has occurred which has dishonored God and the Christian faith, do they go and blaze it all abroad? No. Unless compelled by conscience to give it utterance, it remains a secret in their own breast. And here let me ask, sinner, are you thus careful not to circulate what you know to be true to the discredit of Christianity, the Church, and to the friends of God? Suppose you had seen a minister, or some other professed child of God, off his guard, and had witnessed in him the commission of some disgraceful sin; would you, from love to the cause, lock it up faithfully in your breast and never breathe it forth upon the slightest breath of air lest it should take wings and God should be dishonored? If you hear an individual repeating something that is dishonorable to God and the Christian faith, does it distress you? Do you reprove him for it? Do you endeavour to hush the matter up, and beg him not to repeat it? I leave this question with your conscience.

We naturally try to put the most favorable construction upon any event that might be injurious to the interest or reputation of a friend whom we love. If an event has occurred that admits of different constructions, if possible we naturally put that construction upon it that is most consistent with the honor and reputation of our friend. If a circumstance should occur in the family of a beloved friend of ours which admitted of two opposite constructions; one of which would disgrace our friend and the other not at all, we would, from the very constitution of our being, naturally incline to the construction that was in his favor. It is a law of mind that charity or love hopes all things, believes all things, endures all things, and is ever ready to put the most favorable construction upon any event that the nature of the case will admit. We see the operation of this principle and the developments of this law of mind in the occurrences of every day. You will see Christians inclining to put that construction upon any event that is most consistent with the honor of religion and of God. But do you witness this same disposition in sinners? Do you, sinner, find in yourself a desire to construe every ambiguous occurrence in that way which is most favorable to Christianity? If something is said by someone who professes to be a Christian that turns out not to be true, do you naturally ascribe it to a mistake or to a misunderstanding and find yourself very unwilling to believe that he meant to lie?

When any of the friends of one whom we greatly love falls into any conduct that is greatly dishonorable to the object of our affection, it distresses us, and we are disposed, as far as possible, to prevent a repetition of the event. If the son of our dearest friend fell into a disgraceful crime and in our presence became guilty of things that were calculated greatly to dishonor his father, or if he ran away from his father and was wandering a vagabond up and down the earth, we would naturally desire to reclaim him. We would love and pity him for his father's sake. We would feel grieved and distressed at the dishonor that his son was bringing upon his father. We would feel inclined to warn and expostulate and to pray for him, and instead of going and trumpeting his failings all abroad, we would naturally be tender of his reputation for his father's sake. We would do all that we honestly and consistently could to cover up his faults. Now, sinner, how do you behave when you see Christians err and step out of line? Do you feel distressed that they dishonor God? Do you pity and love them for their heavenly Father's sake? Do you pray for them and warn them and try your utmost to reclaim them? Let your conscience speak. I will not bring a railing accusation against you. Let conscience rebuke you in the name of the Lord.

REMARKS

With all these facts staring sinners in the face and standing out in bold relief upon the very head and front of their own experience, how is it that they can suppose themselves to love God? Nothing is more common than for impenitent sinners to affirm that they love God; and yet nothing is more certain than that they do not love Him. Whence is this mistake? I answer:

They do not distinguish between an admiration of God's natural attributes, which they sometimes feel, and a love of His moral character. The omnipotence, omniscience, omnipresence, eternity, and wisdom of God are attributes, which, when considered, are calculated to inspire awe and admiration in the breast of intelligent beings, whether they are sinful or holy. These attributes have no moral character. The devil himself may be filled with awe and admiration when contemplating the displays of God's natural attributes, which are manifested throughout all creation.

Sinners mistake a selfish gratitude for love of God. A supremely selfish being may be grateful for favors bestowed upon him without any true regard to the character of the one who bestowed the blessings. Sometimes, when sinners escape from death and some marked providence is interposed in their behalf, they feel a kind of gratitude. They might feel the same kind of gratitude to Satan as they do to God, if Satan bestowed the same favor upon them.

Sinners make their own god and fall in love with an idol of their own creation. They think God is the being they desire Him to be. They strip the true God of His essential moral attributes, and then ascribe to God a moral character that suits them. Then, they fall in love with their imaginary god and walk by the light of their own fire. They compass themselves with sparks of their own kindling. The Universalist creates a god for himself. He conceives his god as a being just suited to his tastes. If you keep out of his view the essential attributes of justice and truth, he will talk and feel very piously; but, bring before his mind the true moral character of God, and his heart becomes at once like the troubled ocean when it cannot rest, whose waters cast up mire and dirt.

Do you see why impenitent sinners think Christianity is something very gloomy? They have no love for God. What would you think of a wife who thought it a very gloomy business to be with her husband? What if she complained of it as an irksome and disagreeable task to engage in those offices that she knew would please him? What if she accounted it a grief, a burden, and a vexation to engage in the duties of a wife? You would say it was an absolute demonstration that she did not love her husband. So it is with sinners. When they conceive of Christianity as something gloomy, and calculated to rob them of all their joys, it is a demonstration that they do not love God; that they have no delight in pleasing Him.

Now you see from this subject why sinners grow weary and complain of having too many and too long meetings. What would you think if you heard an individual who professed to love you complain of weariness on account of the length of your conversations? Suppose he said, "Oh! The time seems so long. I do wish our time together was ended." You would understand it. You would not, and could not, believe that his heart was greatly set upon you. So, when you hear sinners complain that there are too many meetings, and when you hear them express a wish that they were not more than an hour in length, this is an index to their feelings. They do not love God. They have no delight in His service. It is a burden and vexation to them to spend a short time in God's presence or worship with those who love to sing God's praises.

Do you now see why some who profess to be Christians prefer parties of pleasure to prayer meetings? Prayer meetings are the most delightful parties to those that love God. To those who do not love God, they are not a source of happiness. When they are attended by such people, it is from other motives than from love to God. Whenever you see those who claim to be Christians manifesting more interest in worldly parties than in prayer meetings or Bible studies, you know they are hypocrites.

You see from this subject that some are deceived if they say they always loved God. There may be some instances where people may have been converted so young that they cannot remember the time when they did not love God. If there are such people, I am persuaded that such instances have been very rare; with these exceptions, it is certain that they are deceived who suppose they have always loved God. Why, by their own showing they have never had a change of heart. They feel toward God as they always did. If they ever truly loved God, when they first exercised this true love, they would know that it was something new to them, and could not possibly suppose that they had always loved him.

You see from this discussion that impenitent sinners are often great hypocrites. They profess to be very much opposed to hypocrisy, and they

Total Depravity

say they like true Christian faith. They say they desire to see people who are sincere in what they profess; they think true Christianity is a good thing and are very much in favor of it. They pretend to be very friendly to God, and they say they love Him. Now, in these professions of favor, they are arrant hypocrites. Christ might say to them, "I know that you do not have the love of God in your hearts" (John 5:42). "Do people pick grapes from thornbushes, or figs from thistles?" (Matthew 7:16). "You are the ones who justify yourselves in the eyes of men, but God knows your hearts. What is highly valued among men is detestable in God's sight" (Luke 16:15). "You snakes! You brood of vipers! How will you escape being condemned to hell?" (Matthew 23:33).

Now you see the obvious and barefaced hypocrisy of those professing to be Christians who unnecessarily publish the faults of other Christians. We sometimes see professed Christians as forward in speaking in all companies and on all occasions of the faults real or supposed of the professed children of God as infidels are. They will load down the winds with their complaining of the imprudences and errors of those whose characters are nearly associated with all the endeared interests of Christianity. And this they often do when no such thing is called for, and where there can be no just pretence that God or the interests of Christian faith requires this service at their hands. They will even sometimes give these things the greater publicity, publish them in the newspapers, and all this under the sheer pretence of doing God a service and benefitting the cause of Christ. But, this is the precise method and pretended motive of the Universalists in their slanderous publications against God and His servants; and there is no more reason to believe that such professors of religion have the true interests of Christ's kingdom at heart than there is to believe that Universalists are actuated by a regard to the glory of God. Cases have occurred in which those who profess to be Christians have entertained passengers in steamboats and in other public places by retailing slanderous reports of revival men and measures. Vast prejudice has been created and immense evil has resulted from this infidel conduct of those who profess to love the blessed God. Oh shame! Where is thy blush!

From the very laws of mind, it is impossible for people to engage in this work of death and mischief of hell, if they truly loved the cause of

Christ. They would not wantonly hang up the cause of Christ to reproach by blazing abroad the failings, real or supposed, of those whose name, character, and influence are identified with the dearest interests of Christ. This is an absolute proof that they are hypocrites; just as if they themselves had taken an oath of it.

In conclusion, while sinners imagine they love God already, it is not likely that they ever will love Him. Sinner, if you think that you love God already, you will never realize that you need a change of heart. If you really do love God, you certainly do not need a new heart, unless you would have a heart that does not love Him. Sinner, in pretending that you love God, you deny the very foundation of the doctrine of the new birth. But let me tell you, sinner, your delusion will soon be torn away. You cannot always deceive yourself with the imagination that you love God. You are going rapidly to eternity. There is, even now, perhaps, but a step between you and death. The moment that you appear in the presence of your Maker, and behold the infinite contrariety there is between your character and His, your delusion will vanish forever. You pretend to love God, while you know that you have no delight in His word, or worship, or service. Oh! What would heaven be to you! If you cannot enjoy a prayer meeting for one hour, and what would you do in heaven, employed in God's service forever and ever. Would heaven be heaven to you? Would you feel at home? Would you be happy there? What! Without the love of God in your heart? Away with this delusion! "I tell you the truth, no one can see the kingdom of God unless he is born again" (John 3:3).

In part two of this lecture, we will now look more closely at the meaning of *Total Depravity*, and I would remind you of what the Apostle Paul wrote to the Romans: "The mind of sinful man is death, but the mind controlled by the Spirit is life and peace; the sinful mind is hostile to God. It does not submit to God's law, nor can it do so. Those controlled by the sinful nature cannot please God" (Romans 8:6-8).

The *law* that Paul writes about here is *the moral law*; or that law which requires people to love God with all their heart and their neighbor as themselves. The facts affirmed by the apostle are that the carnal mind is "enmity against God" or "hostile to God." For that reason, the sinful mind is not subject to the law of God; that is, *it does not obey the law of God*, neither, of course, can it obey this law while it continues to be enmity against God or hostile to God. The apostle does not affirm that a sinner cannot love God, but that *a carnal mind cannot love God*; for, to affirm that a carnal mind can love God would be the same as to affirm that enmity itself can be love. To understand this truth better, we need to know what is not meant by the *carnal mind*; what the *carnal mind*, as used in the text, does mean; that those who have not been born by the Spirit of God have a *carnal mind*; that this *carnal mind* is enmity against God or hostile to God.

What we mean by the carnal mind.

First, by the *carnal mind* as used in the text, it is not meant that any part of the substance of the soul or body is enmity against God. It is not meant that there is anything in the constitution or substance of body or mind that is opposed to God. The mind is not saturated or soaked with hostility toward God. Nor is it meant that the mind or body is so constructed that from the constitution of our nature we are opposed to God. It is not meant that there are appetites or propensities that are constitutional which are enmity against God. Nor is it meant that all unconverted people feel sensible emotions of enmity or hatred toward God. Enmity may exist in the mind either as a volition or an emotion. When existing in the form of a volition, it is a settled aversion to God's character and government; hostility of such a nature that while it may have an abiding influence over our conduct, it may not have a felt existence in the mind.

When existing in the form of an emotion, hostility toward God constitutes what we call feeling; and its existence is a matter of consciousness. I said that enmity may exist in the form of a volition or a settled aversion to God. As a settled aversion, hostility toward God has an abiding influence over our conduct and leads us to treat God as an enemy, without rising into the form of an emotion that may be sensibly felt and be the object of consciousness. Emotions exist in the mind only when those objects are before it that are calculated to produce them; and a principle reason why sinners do not more frequently exercise such emotions of hatred toward God as to be sensible of their enmity against Him is they seldom think of God. God is not in all their thoughts. And when they do think of God, they do not think justly of Him, or think of God as He really is. They deceive themselves with vain imaginations and hide from their own view God's real character; and thus cover up their enmity.

Second, the *carnal mind* means *the minding of the flesh* is enmity against God. The *minding of the flesh* is a voluntary state of mind. It is *the state of supreme selfishness* in which all people exist previous to their conversion to God. The *minding of the flesh* is a state of mind in which, probably, people are not born with, but into which they appear to fall very early after their birth. The gratification of their appetites is made by them the supreme object of desire and pursuit. Selfish gratification becomes the law of their lives or that law in their members that wars against the law of their minds of which the apostle speaks. They conform their lives and all their actions to this rule of action which they have established for themselves, which is nothing more nor less than voluntary selfishness; or a controlling and abiding preference of self-gratification above the commandments, authority, and glory of God.

Understand well and remember: the carnal mind, as used by the apostle, is not the mind itself but a voluntary action of the mind. In other words, it is not any part of the mind or body, but a choice or preference of the mind. It is a minding of the flesh. *The carnal mind prefers self-gratification more than obedience to God.*

The constitutional appetites, both of body and mind, are in themselves innocent. However, making their gratification the supreme object of pursuit is enmity or hostility against God. Minding the flesh is the direct opposite of the character and the requirements of God. God requires us to subordinate all our appetites of body and mind to His glory, and to aim supremely at honoring and glorifying Him. God requires us to love Him with all our hearts, to bring all our powers of body and mind under obedience to the law of love: and, whatever we do, whether we eat or drink, we should do all to the glory of God. Now the carnal mind, or the minding of the flesh, is the direct opposite of this. The carnal mind pursues as a supreme end or goal that which is the direct opposite of God's requirements, the direct opposite of the character of God. Minding the flesh is a choice, a preference, an abiding temper or disposition of the mind which consists in a determination to gratify self, and to make self-gratification the high and supreme object of pursuit.

Third, previous to conversion, all people are in the state of enmity or hostility against God. The Bible speaks of people as possessing by nature one common heart or disposition. This text does not say that the carnal minds of *some* people are hostile toward God; rather, the carnal mind is enmity against God. In another place, God says, "every imagination of the thoughts of his heart was only evil continually" (Genesis 6:5). Another passage says, "the heart of the sons of men is full of evil, and madness is in their heart while they live" (Ecclesiastes 9:3). Indeed, the unconverted, throughout the Bible, are spoken of as having a common heart; and what the Bible asserts is seen to be a matter of fact. Go throughout all the ranks of the human family from the sensitive female that faints at the sight of blood to the horrid pirate whose eyes flash fire and whose lips burn with blasphemy. Present to them all the claims of God and the gospel of His Son; require them to repent and give their hearts to God; and with one consent they will plead their inability. Go to the refined and unrefined; the learned and unlearned; the high and low; rich and poor; old and young; male and female; bond and free of every country and of every clime; and not one of them can be persuaded to embrace the Gospel without the interposition of the Holy Spirit. Now, how is it possible to account for this notorious fact but upon the principle that however the external deportment of different individuals may be modified by circumstances, however much the natural temper may be made to differ as respects people, by education, by animal temperament, by the state of the nervous system, and a variety of other considerations; still, as it respects God, they possess the same disposition and will, all, with one consent begin to make excuses for not loving and obeying Him.

Fourth, let us look closely at what it means to affirm that the carnal mind or minding of the flesh is enmity against God. In part one of this lecture on the subject of total depravity, I endeavoured to demonstrate by an appeal to facts that *the unconverted do not love God*. Now, the first point to be established under this fourth heading is that *impenitent sinners hate God.*

In what follows, I shall use the same method, appeal to the same sources for proof, and go into the same field to gather facts, to establish the truth that *impenitent sinner hate God* that I did in proof of the position that *the unconverted do not love God.* My appeal will be to the well known laws of mind as we see them develop in everyday transactions.

We are naturally pleased with those things that are displeasing to our enemies. Hatred is ill-will; therefore, whatever displeases or disobliges our enemy gratifies our ill-will. It is a contradiction to say that we hate an individual with a malevolent hatred, and yet have no satisfaction in what displeases him. It is the same as to say that the gratification of our desires is not pleasing to us. We witness the developments of this law of mind not only in our own case but in the manifested feelings of those around us. Imagine this person—if something happened greatly to disoblige his enemy, he cannot conceal the pleasure he takes in this event. If the same event has in some measure injured himself, and he is in some degree partaker in the common calamity, yet, if it has much more deeply injured or completely ruined his bitter enemy, he feels upon the whole gratified with the event. He considers the ruin of his enemy as more than a compensation for his own loss, and he does not mind bearing the portion that has fallen to him, inasmuch as it has overwhelmed the one that he so deeply hates. Now, whatever he may say, under whatever hypocritical pretence he may conceal the satisfaction that he feels in this event, it remains certain that his hatred is gratified, that he really at heart takes pleasure in an event which has gratified his malignant opposition to his enemy.

We see this same law of mind developing itself toward God. Sinners manifest the greatest pleasure in sin. Pleasure in sin is the element in which they live and move. They roll sin as a sweet morsel or piece of candy under their tongue. They drink in iniquity like water. They even weary themselves to commit iniquity. They not only do these things themselves, but take pleasure in those who do likewise. The very things that are the most displeasing to God are the most pleasing to them. The things that are the most pleasing to God are the most displeasing to them. They love what God hates. They hate what God loves. This demonstrates that they are in a state of mind which is the direct opposite of the character and will of God. The whole bent and current and inclination of their minds are the direct opposite of God's requirements and are enmity against Him. This is matter of fact.

In addition, people are naturally gratified to see the friends of their enemy forsake and dishonor him. If a man hates another, and if the children or friend of this enemy of his does anything to grieve or dishonor or injure him in any way, he may speak of it as if he regretted it; but, if he pretends to regret it, he is a hypocrite. It is just as certain that, upon the whole, he rejoices in it as it is that he hates him. He rejoices in it, because it gratifies his hatred. You see this law of mind manifesting itself with equal uniformity and strength toward the blessed God. When the professed friends of God forsake His cause and do anything to dishonor Him, you may perceive that impenitent sinners are gratified. They will speak of it with exultation. While Christians converse about it with sorrow, weep over it, and betake themselves to prayer that God will wipe away the reproach, it will become the song of the drunkard and the wicked in barrooms and in the corners of the streets. Sinners will laugh at it and rejoice over it.

We are apt to see and magnify the faults of the friends of our enemies. With what scrutiny will politicians search after the faults of the friends and supporters of an opposing candidate! How eagle-eyed is the person in searching out all the failings of those who favor his enemy. How politicians and others will not only see their real faults, but will greatly magnify them, and dwell upon them, until they fill their whole field of vision! They give their attention so exclusively to their faults as to forget that they have any virtues. So enormous do their faults appear that where they have the appearance of virtue it is ascribed to duplicity and hypocrisy. Now, you see this same spirit often manifesting itself toward God. With what a searching and malignant gaze are the eyes of the unconverted fastened upon the professed friends of God! How eagerly they note their faults. How enormously they magnify them! How apt they are to ascribe every appearance of virtue in them to bigotry and hypocrisy.

Very naturally, we are apt to misinterpret the motives and put the worst construction upon the conduct of the enemies of our friends. If they are favoring the interests and endeavouring to promote the happiness of one whom we greatly hate, we behold all their conduct through a jaundiced eye. The best things in them are often ascribed by us to the worst of motives; and those things in them which deserve the most praise are often by us the most severely reprobated. Your acquaintance with your own heart, and with the developments of the human character around you, will instantly supply abundant proofs of this remark. Often, this feature of the human character most odiously develops itself toward God. How frequently do we hear impenitent sinners ascribing the most praiseworthy deeds of God's professed friends to the most unworthy motives. How often are their acts of greatest self-denial, those things in which they most humbly serve and most nearly resemble God, misrepresented; ascribed to the basest of motives and made the very reasons upon which they ground their pertinacious opposition to them. It is impossible to account for this upon any other principle than that of their enmity against God; for the persons against whom this enmity is vented are often entire strangers to them; individuals against whom they can have no personal hostility. Obviously, it is enmity against Christians when they resemble Jesus Christ, against the cause in which they are engaged, and against the Master they serve.

We naturally shun the friends of our enemies. We naturally avoid the society of a person we know to be particularly friendly to our enemy; his company and conversation is irksome to us. We see this same spirit manifested by impenitent sinners toward the friends of God. They avoid them; they feel uneasy in their company. Their presence seems to impose restraints upon sinners; they cannot abuse God with quite as much freedom when Christians are present. They are therefore glad to dispense with their company. How often do you observe impenitent sinners, in making up a party for a stage-coach or rail-road car, so arrange matters as to exclude a minister or any engaged Christian from their company. They feel uneasy at his presence and manifest the same temper that we should witness if some distinguished friend of their greatest enemy were present with them. How can this be accounted for on any other principle than that of enmity against God. With these ministers or Christians, they have perhaps had very little personal acquaintance. They never have had any misunderstanding with them; nor has any personal controversy existed between them. It must be on account of the cause in which they are engaged and the Master they serve that they wish to avoid them.

We naturally admire and magnify the virtues and overlook the vices of the enemies of those we hate. How enthusiastic are politicians in their admiration of the talents, wisdom and virtues of those who take sides with them and are opposed to the election of their political enemy. If anyone has an enemy, he regards it as an evidence of wisdom in anyone else to be opposed to the same person. He is inclined greatly to overrate the number, the talents, and the influence of those who are opposed to his enemy. If he hears of a few that are opposed to him, and among them anyone of more than ordinary talents, he is apt to imagine that almost everybody is opposed to him, especially all the talented and virtuous part of the community. He comes to think that nobody favors his enemy but the weak, the servile, and the selfish.

The situation is similar regarding religion. How often do you hear impenitent sinners boasting of the talents, the numbers, and the virtues of infidels and of those that make no pretension to religion. Boasting of the excellent characters, high standing, and great influence of the leaders among the irreligious: while, at the same time, they depreciate both the numbers and the talents of those that are the friends of God. They often consider them as a sickly, bigoted, and priest-ridden people: and they promote this prejudice without any definite knowledge of their numbers, their characters, or their influence. What is this but the out-breaking of enmity against God and the cause which they love?

We naturally hate to think of our enemies. The human mind is so constituted that malevolent emotions distress it and are the source of misery. Whenever our thoughts are intensely occupied in thinking of an individual whom we hate, those malevolent emotions will naturally arise which are condemned by the conscience, and which of themselves constitute misery. For this reason, unless it be for the purpose of studying revenge, or in some way to gratify our hatred, we naturally turn our thoughts away from an object which we hate. And while, as I have shown in a former discourse, we naturally dwell upon a beloved object, we just as naturally abstract our thoughts from a hated one. Behold the developments of this law of mind in its action toward God. Sinners banish God from their thoughts. They are "unwilling to retain God in their knowledge." If at any time the thought of God is intruded upon them, they manifest uneasiness and immediately divert their attention. If they are really convinced that they are sinners, and are in danger of His wrath, their selfish regard to their own happiness may lead them to reflection and induce them to think of God for the purpose of devising some means of escaping His just indignation.

We dislike to converse about those that we hate. Unless we want to calumniate and pour forth our malignant hostility against them, we choose to remain silent and say nothing about them. You often hear someone say of his enemy, "I desire not to talk about him." As I have shown above, we love to converse about our friends, because such conversation at once enkindles and expresses our love for them. Such conversation gratifies us. But we hate to converse about our enemies. For although there is a kind of gratification in giving vent to our enmity, it is at the same time the source and the essence of pain. Who has not witnessed the manifestations of this law of mind on the subject of Christian faith? Who does not know that sinners are averse to talking about God? That they converse about God seldom, reservedly, and in a manner that shows they have no pleasure in it; but, on the contrary, that such conversation gives them pain?

We are naturally pained to hear our enemy praised. Think about a group of ladies and gentlemen; everyone but one of them are particularly friendly to a distinguished and absent individual. The one who is not friendly is his bitter enemy. His enmity, however, is unknown to the group. They, of course, bring up their favorite person as the subject of their conversation. They indulge themselves in enthusiastic commendations of their absent friend. They are delighted with the common bond of sympathy that exists among them upon this subject. Now, think of the embarrassment and distress of the person listening to his enemy being so lavishly praised. While they, without heeding his agony, indulge themselves in the most lavish pouring forth of applause, this enemy is filled with the most irrepressible distress and indignation. He looks at his watch. He takes out his snuff-box. He walks to the window. He tries to read a newspaper. He turns up and down the room. He tries to divert the attention of the company and introduce some other topic of conversation. Now, suppose that one of the ladies turns to him and demands his opinion, remarking that he seems to be absent-minded and does not enjoy the conversation. If he is a gentleman, he may wish to be very civil to the lady and endeavour to waive an answer to her question. But suppose she presses him and wonders at his hesitancy until his conduct attracts the attention of the other members of the group. Suppose they all, with one consent, coincide with the lady and insist upon an expression of his opinion. Now, an hundred to one, if, in spite of his good breeding, he does not manifest the enmity of his heart and clearly exhibit to the entire company the deep malignity of his feelings toward his enemy.

Under similar circumstances you may often witness the breaking out of enmity against God. Let a group of Christians in a steamboat or stagecoach engage in conversation upon their favorite topic. Let them converse of Jesus Christ. After a warm conversation, let them appeal to impenitent sinners in the midst of them for an expression of their opinion. Or if, when in a proper place, they propose to conclude their conversation with prayer; how often are impenitent sinners offended. Go and visit a family where some are Christians and others not. Sit down and converse warmly with the pious wife on the subject of Christian faith in the presence of her husband and unconverted family. What looks you will instantly perceive about the house. Perhaps one will go out at this door and another out that door. If any of the impenitent remain, turn and direct your conversation to one of them. If it be the husband, perhaps he will almost forget that he is a gentleman and abuse you to your face. Perhaps he will say that his religion is a matter between him and God and he does not thank you for your impertinence. That it is none of your business; that he does not thank you for coming there to disturb him and his family upon the subject of Christianity. Now, why does he consider this a disturbance? Why does he look upon it as an impertinence? Why is he so displeased? Certainly he has no reason to fear that you will injure him or his family. If he loved the subject and loved God, it is certain that he would thank you for your visit and be pleased with the interview. Is it not proof to demonstration that he hates God and Christianity when he considers the kind introduction of the subject as an intrusion and a vexation.

We are naturally pained and incredulous on hearing of the prosperity of our enemy. If we hear that our enemy is gaining friends, popularity, property or influence, it distresses us. We are inclined to disbelieve it. If there is any room for doubt, we are sure to hang a doubt on every point that admits debate. See that person with a hypocritical face: he hears of the prosperity of his enemy and professes to rejoice in it. But if he believes it, he only mentions it on occasions where he cannot avoid it. Then, the spirit and manner of his conversation (if he pretends to rejoice in it) will to a discerning mind develop the deep hypocrisy of his heart. But if there is a possibility of calling the truth of it in question, you will find that he disbelieves it altogether. You will find him dwelling upon and greatly magnifying any little circumstance that will render it improbable. He will depreciate and cast into the shade the weighty considerations that demonstrate its truth. Who has not witnessed the exhibitions of this principle on the subject of Christianity? Let a report of the prosperity of the Church and great revivals be circulated through the community. See how Universalists and other impenitent sinners will manifest uneasiness and try to disprove it all. See how they will question the evidence and try to pour contempt upon the report and those who believe it. They do not believe that so many have been converted. "You will see," say they, "the professed converts will all go back again and be worse than ever. The reports are greatly exaggerated. If there are any Christians in these revivals, there are probably ten hypocrites to one Christian." Such facts as these speak for themselves. They manifest a state of mind that cannot be mistaken. It is the boiling over of enmity against God.

We naturally hate efforts to promote the interests of our enemies. We are very apt to cavil at the measures which they use. We call their motives into question. When we are opposed to their goals, we find a great deal of fault with the spirit and manner of their efforts. If someone seeks to promote the interests of our enemy, we are naturally watching for objections and are captious and ill-natured in regard to their movements. We are apt to ridicule and oppose such efforts. By us, anything like zeal in such a case is looked upon as enthusiasm and madness. Witness the conduct of impenitent sinners on the subject of Christianity. If any efforts are made to promote the interests of the kingdom of God, to honor and glorify Him, they are offended. They get up an opposition. They not

Total Depravity

infrequently ridicule their meetings; speak evil of those that are engaged in them; denounce their zeal as enthusiasm and madness, and something for which they deserve the execration of all their neighbors. People may get together and dance all night, and impenitent sinners do not think it objectionable. The theater may be opened every night at great expense, and the actors and multitudes of others may be engaged all day in preparing for the entertainment of the evening. In this way, the devil may get up a protracted meeting and continue it for years; and they see no harm in it: no enthusiasm in all this. Ladies may go and stay till midnight every evening. Poor people may go and spend their time and money and waste their health and lives and ruin their souls; and they see no harm in all this. But let Christians do anything like this and exercise one tenth part of this zeal in promoting the honor of God, and the salvation of souls; why, it would be talked against from Dan to Beersheba. Sinners may go to a ball, or a party, and stay nearly all night; but excessively indecorous it is for ladies to go out to evening church meetings. For Christians to have protracted meetings and pray till 10 o'clock at night. "Abominable!" they say. Why, such things are spoken against in the newspapers. They are the subjects of remark and reprobation in steamboats, stagecoaches, and barrooms; wherever impenitent sinners are assembled. Politicians may manifest the greatest zeal on the subject of politics; may hold their caucuses; post up their handbills; blaze away in the public journals; appoint their ward committees; ransack every nook and corner; parade through the streets with their music; fire their guns; show their flags; transport their frigates through the streets on wheels: send their coaches up and down the streets with handbills posted on their sides to bring men to the polls. Hundreds of thousands of dollars may be expended to carry an election; and all this is well enough to impenitent sinners. But, Oh! Let Christians begin to serve God with such zeal and make such efforts to build up His kingdom and save souls. Ten to one, if the wicked do not absolutely mob them and cry out that such efforts will ruin the nation. They would brand such proceedings as the most arrant enthusiasm and downright madness. But, is it because politics is so much more important than the salvation of souls? Is it because no effort is necessary to arouse a slumbering world and bring sinners to act, think, and feel as they ought on the subject of salvation? No, there is reason enough for the highest possible degree of Christian effort and sinners know it very well, but their enmity against God is so great that such efforts cannot be made without arousing all the hell there is within them.

We easily believe an ill report of one we hate. If a man hears any evil of an enemy, he believes it on the slightest testimony. He does not care to inquire whether the report may be relied upon. He eagerly listens to every breath of slander and yields the most unqualified credence to almost any and every falsehood that serves to blacken the reputation of his enemy. The reason for this is his ill-will is gratified with such reports. He hopes they are true; therefore, he easily believes them. How frequently we see this feature of the human heart developing itself on the subject of Christian faith! With what eagerness do sinners listen to every false and slanderous report that may be circulated about the friends of God. It is surprising to see what absurd and ridiculous things they will believe. They manifest the most unequivocal desire to believe evil of those who profess friendship to God. It is amazing to see the enmity of their hearts manifesting itself to such a degree that often there is nothing too absurd, ridiculous, and contradictory for them to believe if it only has a tendency to cast contempt and ridicule upon the cause of God.

We naturally love to give publicity to any evil report about our enemies. We desire to have others feel toward them as we do. It gratifies our malignant feelings to hear and circulate those reports that are injurious to the enemy we hate. Have you ever heard of this happening? A man meets his neighbor and asks, "Have you heard such and such a report about so-and-so?" His neighbor replies, "No. I have not." So the man replies, "Ah! I supposed that you knew it; else I would have said nothing about it." Now listen to him go into the whole subject and relate and aggravate every circumstance of which he has heard. He will comment upon each report as he goes along. At length he closes by saying I hope you will not mention this, but it is a matter of fact. Then he goes around to the other neighbors and relates the same to them as though it were a great secret. And he says he hopes they will say nothing about it, but he thinks the facts cannot be disputed. Everywhere he goes he takes this same course. He says he hopes the thing will not get around to others for it might do injury to the poor

Total Depravity

man. He relates how this is a mournful event, and he is truly sorry that these things have happened. In all this he is a hypocrite, and he knows it. He is glad the event has happened. He delights to publish it wherever he can. He seems to covet the exclusive privilege of being the bearer of the first intelligence to every door.

How often do we witness the developments of this principle against God! If something takes place that is disgraceful among the professed friends of God, injurious to the interests of the church, harmful to the spread of the Gospel, how ready sinners are to give it universal publicity. They will talk about it. Publish it on all occasions. Blaze it abroad in the public prints and send it in every direction upon the wings of the wind. If anyone becomes deranged in connection with a revival; alas, what an ado is made about it! Thirty thousand citizens of the United States may be murdered every year by strong drink. The liquor industry may fill bedlam with maniacs. Homicide, suicide, and all manner of abominations may be the result of rum selling; yet the indignation of sinners is not aroused. But if some nervous individual becomes deranged in view of his abominable crimes against his Maker in connection with a revival or a protracted meeting; the press groans under the burden of the doleful complaints that are poured out upon the public ear.

Unrepentant sinners hate God with a mortal hatred.

Hating God with a *mortal hatred* means that if an unrepentant sinner had it in his power, he would destroy God's very existence. Probably, very few sinners recognize that they have this degree of enmity against God, and they may feel shocked at the assertion. Nevertheless, it is true. There are several reasons why they may never have known that such was the state of their hearts. It is probable that most of them have never dared to indulge any such feelings. Another reason why they may have never had the desire to destroy God is that they have never thought it possible to destroy Him. There are many things which sinners have never designed or desired to do because they have never thought it possible. Have you ever designed to be a king? Did you ever entertain a thought of being a king? Have you ever felt any ambition to be a king? Probably you never did; for the very reason that you have never thought it possible. Suppose a throne, a crown, and a scepter were put within your reach and the robe of royalty was tendered to your acceptance. Do you not think that you have pride and ambition enough under such circumstances to desire to be a king? And suppose, when you had accepted the crown, and swayed the scepter over one nation, you had the opportunity of extending your empire and making your dominion universal over all nations. Do you not believe that you would instantly desire to do it? And now, suppose that when all the governments of this world were subject to your rule; suppose an opportunity should offer for you to extend your dominion over the entire universe of worlds, and you conceived it possible to subject God himself to your control. Are you too good under such circumstances to aim at exercising dominion over all the universe and over God himself? Sinners, who of you would trust the best among you? You know not your hearts, if you suppose that under such circumstances there would be any limit to your ambition.

Sinners do not realize the greatness of their enmity against God, because God still lets them go unpunished for their sins. They do not believe that God will send them to hell for their sins. If God lets them have their own way, as long as He does not interfere with their desires, as long as He does not seem to be punishing them for their sins or disturbing them in their courses of iniquity, their enmity remains comparatively at rest. But who among them would not rise up and murder God, were it in their power, if God should attempt to punish them for their sins? No, they would sooner wish God in hell than consent that God should deal with them in justice.

It is obvious that the enmity of sinners against God is *mortal* from the fact that they are in rebellion against God and in league with devils to oppose God's government and undermine His throne. Sinners do not obey God. The whole weight of their influence and example is opposed to God's government. They do everything that the nature of the case admits to annihilate God's authority and destroy His government. Rebellion is always aimed at the life of the sovereign, and it is impossible for sinners to be more absolutely in rebellion against God than they are.

Note. The question has been tried. God once put himself as much in the power of men as in the nature of things was possible. The Second Person in the Godhead, Jesus Christ, took human nature on himself. He put His human nature within the power of men. And what was the result? They rested not until they had murdered Him. Do you say that those were the Jews? That you are of a different spirit? This has always been the favorite plea of sinners, but it is an empty plea.

The ancient Jews persecuted and murdered the prophets. The Jews of Christ's day professed to honor the prophets. They built their sepulchres and insisted that if they had lived in the days of the prophets they would not have persecuted them. But they persecuted and murdered Christ. And Christ himself informs them that by persecuting Him, they showed that they approved the deeds of their fathers. Now sinner, suppose you lived under a government that was a monarchy. Suppose your fathers had rebelled against the rightful king and placed an usurper upon the throne; and that you, their children, although you did not participate in the original rebellion, yet now, you maintain the same ground which they took. You support the usurper and refuse obedience to your rightful sovereign. Now, is this not in law and equity, is this not to all intents and purposes, justifying the conduct of your fathers and becoming a partaker in their crimes and incurring the same guilt and deserving the same condemnation? Suppose you did not originally murder Christ. Still, is it not a fact that you now refuse to obey Him as your rightful sovereign? You support the authority of Satan, who has usurped the government of this world by refusing to repent, when you withhold your service and your heart from Jesus Christ. Do you not, to all intents and purposes, become a partaker in the crime of those who murdered him? He claimed their obedience, and they arose and imbrued their hands in His blood. When He claims your obedience and you utterly refuse it, you show that you approve the deeds of the Jews. If Jesus Christ were in your power, you would show that rather than submit to His authority, you would murder Him again. This conduct makes you in the eye of common law a partaker in their crime. In the eye of conscience, of reason, and of common sense; in the eye of God, and in the judgment of heaven, earth and hell, you are guilty of the blood of Christ. You prove to a demonstration that were it in your power, you would dethrone and murder the Almighty.

Sinners hate God *supremely*. They hate God more than they do anything, everything, anybody, and everybody else in the universe. Do not startle at this, as if it were a rash and extravagant assertion. It is a sober and awful truth. Look at this. All other enmity can be overcome by kindness. The greatest enemy you have on earth may subdue your enmity by kindness and win you over to become his friend. But how is it that all the kindness of God, an infinitely greater kindness than any human being has had it in his power to show you, has not overcome your enmity, but you still remain in rebellion against Him.

A mere change of circumstances in any other case of enmity will change the human heart. Consider two political opponents between whom an hereditary enmity exists. Their fathers were enemies. They have always been enemies. They have both believed and spoken all evil of each other. Now let a change of politics bring them both upon the same side of a political question and they will instantly become friends. Let them have an opportunity to play into each other's hands; let both their hearts be set upon the election of the same candidate; notice how cordially they will cooperate. How warmly they will take each other by the hand. They will walk, sit, and dine together. They will attend political meetings, defend each other's reputation, magnify each other's virtues, and throw the kind mantle of charity over each other's vices. And all this they will do heartily. Their real feelings toward each other are changed by circumstances. Their hearts are really changed toward each other, and they can truly say, "Whereas we formerly hated, now we love each other." All this has been effected merely by a change of circumstances without any interference by the Holy Spirit. Let the President of the United States appoint his greatest political opponent to the first office in his gift, and he will make him his friend. Suppose the greatest anti-Jackson man in this city, who has said and done the most of any man in the United States to prevent his election, should be reduced to poverty and had no means of support for himself and family. Now suppose, when the news of his extremity should reach President Jackson, that the President should appoint him to a post of high honor and emolument, would not this change his heart? Would he complain that he could not become the president's friend until the Holy Spirit had changed his heart? No. Such kindness would be like pouring coals of fire upon his head; would melt him down in an instant; would change the whole current of his soul. How then does it happen that all the offers of heaven, and all the threatening of hell, that all the boundless love and compassion manifested in God giving His only-begotten, and well-beloved Son to die for you; when mercy stoops from heaven with bleeding hands and offers to save, and hell roars from beneath and threatens to devour; when God approaches you with a world of moving, melting motives, gathered from earth, heaven, and hell, and rolls their mountain-weight upon you; that these considerations will never change your heart unless made effectual by the Holy Spirit?

If people did not hate God supremely they would instantly repent. Suppose that when you go home tonight, at the deep hour of midnight; when you are all asleep in an upper apartment of your house, you are awaked by the cry of fire. You look up and find your dwelling wrapped in flames around you. You leap from your bed and find the floor under your feet just ready to give way. The roof over your head is beginning to give way and ready to fall in upon you with a crash. Your little ones awake and are shrieking and clinging to your night-clothes. You see no way of escape. At this moment of unutterable anguish and despair, someone comes dashing through the flames with his hair and clothes on fire; he seizes you in your distraction with one hand and gathers his other long and strong arm around your little ones, and he again rushes through the flames at the hazard of his life. You absolutely swoon with terror. In a few moments, you open your eyes in the street and find yourself supported in the arms of your deliverer. He is rubbing your temples with camphor and fanning you to restore your fainting life. You look up and behold in the scorched and smoky features of him who rescued you the man whom you have supremely hated. He smiles in your face and says fear not, your children are all alive; they are all standing around you. Now would you, could you, look coldly at him, and say, "Oh, I wish I could repent for having hated you so much. I wish I could be sorry for my sin against you, for hating you." Could you say this? No. You would instantly roll over upon your face and wash his feet with your tears and wipe them with the hair of your head. This scene would change your heart in a moment, and ever after the name of that man would be music in your ears. If you heard him slandered or saw him abused, it would enkindle your grief and indignation. And now, sinner, how is it that you complain that you cannot repent of your sins against God? Behold God's loving-kindness. Consider His tender mercy. How can you look up? How can you refrain from repentance? How can you help being dissolved in broken-hearted repentance at His blessed feet? Behold Christ's bleeding hands! See His wounded side! Hark! Hear His deep death-groan, when He cries, "It is finished," and gives up His Spirit for your sins. Sinner, are you marble or adamant! Has your heart become so case-hardened in the fires of hell that you will not repent? Surely nothing but your enmity deep as perdition can be proof against the infinitely moving inducements to repentance.

Now perhaps you will say that you do not like to hear about hell and damnation, that you love mercy; and if ministers would present the love and mercy of God, and present God as a God of mercy, sinners would love Him. But this is all a mistake. Sinners are as much opposed to the mercy of God as they are to any of His attributes. This is a matter of fact and everyday experience. Hark! What is that din and outcry? Whence are those cries of "Crucify Him! Crucify Him!" that load down the winds and break upon our ears from the distance of almost 2000 years? God has revealed His mercy, and all the world are up in arms against Him. Jesus Christ has come upon the kind errand of salvation, and the world is filled with uproar to murder Him. Mercy is the very attribute of God against which mankind are arrayed. For thousands of years, the sword of vindictive justice has slept in its scabbard and God has been unfolding and holding out the attribute of mercy. All the opposition in the world against God and the Christian faith is aimed particularly at God's mercy. What is Christianity? What is the Bible? What are revival? What are all those things that have called forth so much of the opposition of earth and hell, except so many exhibitions of the mercy of the blessed God! When justice ascends the throne, the cavilling mouths of sinners will be stopped. Justice will soon hush the tumult and the loud opposition of sinners against their Maker. Then, every mouth shall be stopped. All the world shall be found guilty before God. But now is the dispensation of God's mercy and all the earth is up in arms against it; why are you such a hypocrite as to pretend to love the mercy of God? If you love it, why do

Total Depravity

you not accept it? If you love a God of mercy, why have not all the moving manifestations of it that have passed before you melted you down and subdued your heart? O sinner, sinner, speak no more proudly. Boast not yourself that you love any attribute of God; for if, while you remain impenitent, you say you love God, you are a liar and the truth is not in you.

REMARKS

Do you see why Universalists and other sinners are so disturbed with revivals? It is because God comes so manifestly forth in the exercise of mercy. They cannot bear such an exhibition of God. It disturbs all the sediment and lurking enmity of their hearts. These professed friends of God and men, as soon as God displays himself and people become the recipients of His mercy, they are greatly offended by it.

Do you see the importance of preaching clearly and frequently the enmity of sinners' hearts against God. There is, and has been for ages, in most instances, a striking defect in exhibiting this most important subject. Ministers seem to have been afraid to charge unrepentant sinners with being the enemies of God. I never heard this doctrine declared in my life in such a way that I understood it previous to my own conversion. Many ministers seem to have regarded total depravity as consisting in nothing more than the absence of love to God.

The church does not seem to have realized or believed that the carnal mind is absolutely enmity against God. Although there is no other truth more abundantly taught in the word of God, or more unanswerably evident from matter of fact, few sinners have been made to see and believe it. I have, in hundreds of instances, conversed with people who have sat under the preaching of the Gospel all their days who never had been made to see this fundamental truth of the Gospel.

The truth of total depravity and the carnal mind is a truth upon which is founded the necessity of the new birth and the Holy Spirit's influences. Without understanding and believing it, how are we to expect the world to be converted to God?

From this subject, it is obvious that if sinners should take their oath that they hate God, it would not make it at all more evident. If everyone on earth took an oath that the sun shines at noonday, it would not add a particle to the evidence that the sun shines or render it any more certain or evident to others. It is a simple matter of fact, of which we can have no higher testimony than our own senses. So it is matter of fact that sinners are the enemies of God. They act it out before everyone. It is as evident as their existence. How it ever came to be questioned, or forgotten, or overlooked is most mysterious to me.

As I remarked earlier, there are many who profess to be Christians who could not make it more evident that they are the enemies of God if they should take their oath on it. They speak against revivals and those engaged in promoting them. They give publicity to the faults, real or supposed, of those who are the friends of God. They retail slander and manifest their opposition to God in so many ways that their hypocrisy and enmity against God are perfectly obvious.

Those who have not known by their own experience that they have been enemies of God have not been converted, nor so much as truly convicted of sin. What have they repented of? Have they repented merely of their outward sins? This is impossible, unless they have understood and condemned the fountain of iniquity from which these abominations have proceeded. The head and front of their offending is that they have been the enemies of God. Their *minding of the flesh* has been of itself enmity against God. And now, do they talk of having repented, when they have never so much as known that in which their chief guilt consists? Impossible!

Those sinners who deny that they are the enemies of God are never likely to be converted until they confess their enmity. "He who conceals his sins does not prosper, but whoever confesses and renounces them finds mercy" (Proverbs 28:13). There are many who will confess themselves sinners, but will deny that they are the enemies of God. Thus they cover up the great amount of their sins. They acknowledge their outward acts of wickedness, but deny the enmity from which they flow. While they do this, God will never forgive them.

This discourse exhibits a very different view of total depravity from that which regards depravity as physical or constitutional or as belonging to the substance of the body or mind. *Total depravity is voluntary*, consisting

Total Depravity

in *voluntary transgression,* the sinner's own act, something of his own creation. As voluntary transgression, depravity is that over which the sinner has a perfect control and for which he is entirely responsible. O, the darkness, confusion, and utter nonsense of that view of depravity which exhibits it as something lying back and the cause of all actual transgression. Something created in the sinner; something born with him. Some physical pollution transmitted from Adam through the agency of God or the devil which is in itself sinful and deserving the wrath of God previous to the exercise of voluntary agency on the part of the sinner. This is absurd and impossible.

It is not only absurd and impossible, but is virtually charging all the sin in the world upon God; and if it is firmly believed, it renders repentance in every such case a natural impossibility. While the sinner supposes himself to be condemned not only for his conduct but for his nature; and while he believes that his conduct is the natural and necessary result of a depraved constitution; and that his nature must be changed before he can obey his Maker, it is obviously impossible for him to blame himself for his sins. He must cease not only to be a reasonable being, but cease to have commonsense, before he can justify God and condemn himself upon these principles. No wonder that people who maintain such a view of depravity as this should also maintain that sinners are *unable* to repent. It is true, based on the definition of total depravity and the carnal mind as I have defined it, that sinners cannot repent of themselves, nor can God make them repent. It is manifest that *the only way in which God can bring a sinner to repentance is by correcting his views; by showing him what sin is; and causing him to see that it is for his conduct, and not for his nature, that he is to repent; and that his conduct and not his nature needs to be changed.* To teach physical or constitutional depravity is not only to teach heresy and nonsense; but it leads the sinner inevitably to justify himself and condemn God; and it renders repentance, while the sinner believes it, impossible.

Do you see why sinners find it so hard to be Christian in their behavior and obey God? The total difficulty consists in their unwillingness to yield up their selfishness.

No one can pretend with any show of reason that my discourses amount to any denial of moral depravity. *I have purposely denied physical depravity; but certainly this discourse maintains moral depravity*; that for which the sinner is to blame, that of which he must repent in all its length and breadth. It would seem that in the estimation of some, a denial that human nature is in itself depraved is a virtual denial of all depravity. In other words, they seem to think it a virtual denial of the guilty source of all actual transgression. I have endeavoured to show that the cause of out-breaking sin is not to be found in a sinful constitution or nature. *The cause of sinful actions is a wrong original choice; in which the sinner prefers self-gratification to the will of his Maker, and which choice has become the settled preference of his soul that constitutes the deep fountain from which flow the putrid waters of spiritual and eternal death.* I am unable to see by what figure of speech that is called *moral depravity* which either consists in a depraved constitution or is the natural result of it. Why should it be called *moral* depravity? Certainly it can have no such relation to moral law as to deserve punishment. It is indeed amazing that in this century it should be thought heresy to call *sin a transgression of the law* and insist that sin must be the act of a voluntary agent. For, the Bible clearly teaches, "Whosoever committeth sin transgresseth also the law: for sin is the transgression of the law" (1 John 3:4—KJV) and "Everyone who sins breaks the law; in fact, sin is lawlessness" (1 John 3:4—NIV). Unhappily, it has it come to this: those who virtually deny all moral depravity and virtually charge all the sins of the world upon God gravely complain of heresy in those who maintain moral depravity in all its length and breadth and deny physical or constitutional depravity. What next? If it be heresy to say that sin is a transgression of the law, certainly the Apostle John was not orthodox, nor the other apostles.

From this subject it is plain, sinners must be annihilated, converted, or forever lost. With a mind that is enmity against God, it is impossible for them to be happy. Infidels have no cause to sneer at the doctrine of the new birth. If there were no Bible in the world, the doctrine of total depravity as exhibited in these lessons on Romans would be abundantly obvious as a matter of fact. It cannot be denied that unless a person passes through just that change of mind which is in the Bible called the new birth or a change of heart, they must, self-evidently, be annihilated or

Total Depravity

damned to all eternity.

Sinners are not *almost* Christians. We sometimes hear people say of some unrepentant sinner that he is *almost* a Christian. The truth is, the most moral impenitent sinner in the world is much nearer a devil than a Christian. Look at that sensitive young lady. Is she an impenitent sinner; then she only needs to die to be as very a devil as there is in hell. Any slight occurrence that should destroy her life would make her a devil. Nay, she needs no positive influence to be exerted upon her to make a fiend of her; only remove all restraints and the very enmity of hell boils over in her heart at once. Let God take from under her His supporting hand. Let Him cease, but for a moment, to fan her heaving lungs, and she would open her eyes in eternity; and if she dared, would curse Him to His face.

How impossible it would be for sinners to enjoy heaven, if permitted to go there in their present state of mind. Only break down the body; let the mind burst forth into the presence of God; let it look abroad, and behold His glories, and see "Holiness to the Lord" inscribed on everything around them. Let them listen to the songs of praise. Let them perch upon the loftiest battlement of heaven. Let them hear the song of "Holy, Holy, Holy, Lord God Almighty," and so great would be their enmity, if unconverted, that, if permitted, they would dive into the darkest cavern of hell to escape from the presence of the infinitely holy Lord God.

While sinners remain unrepentant, they yield to God no sort of obedience any more than the devil does. Their carnal mind is not subject to the law of God, neither indeed can it be. In this state of mind, until the supreme preference of their mind is changed, until they have given up minding the flesh and obey God, it is in vain to talk of obedience. *The first act of obedience that you ever will or can perform is to cease minding the flesh and give your heart to God.*

Do you see the wickedness and folly of those parents who think their unconverted children friendly to Christianity? You cannot teach them a greater heresy than that they are friendly to the Christian faith or to God. I have often heard professing parents say that their children were not enemies of Christianity. No wonder that such children were not converted under such teaching as this. It is just the doctrine that the devil desires you to teach them. You only give your children the impression that they are friendly to God and Christianity already and they will never know why they need a new heart. While in this state of mind and laboring under this delusion they cannot so much as be convicted of sin, much less be converted to Jesus Christ.

Do you see from this subject the folly and the falsehood of saying of an impenitent sinner that he is a good-hearted man when the fact is that his heart is enmity against God? Do you see how necessary it is that there should be a hell? What shall be done with these enemies of God, if they die in their sins? Heaven is no place for you, if you are an enemy of God and hate Him. Heaven would doubtlessly be worse to you than hell, if you were allowed to go there. Hell is deserved by sinners, and is obviously needed for those who die in enmity against God. And now, sinner, do you see your state? You must be convinced of the truth of what I have said: your enmity is voluntary. Your hatred of God is of your own creation; that which you have long cherished and exercised. Will you give it up? What has God done that you should continue to hate him? What is there in sin that you should prefer your disobedience to God? Why, O why, will you indulge for a moment longer this spirit of horrible rebellion and enmity against the blessed God? Go but a little further; cleave to your enmity but a little longer; and the knell of eternal death shall toll over your damned soul, and all the corners of despair will echo with your groans.

---

*This lesson combines two of Finney's sermons [he preached this long lesson in two parts] on Romans 8:7. Both came from his *Sermons on Important Subjects* (sermons 4 and 5). The first sermon, "Total Depravity," was broken into small "bite-sized" principles and published in my edition of Finney's *Principles of Revival*, pages 115-156. The second sermon, "Total Depravity" appeared in my first book of Finney's sermons in the *Finney's Principles Series*, titled *Principles of Victory*, pages 109-127. At that time, I was unaware of Finney's other sermons on Romans that came to be published in the later books in the *Finney's Principles Series*. The Lesson that follows this one is also on Romans 8:7, "Moral Depravity." For Review: Answer the Study Questions on page 224, Cowles page 249.

7

Moral Depravity
1862

Because the carnal mind is enmity against God: for it is not subject to the law of God, neither indeed can be.—Romans 8:7—KJV

The sinful mind is hostile to God. It does not submit to God's law, nor can it do so.—Romans 8:7—NIV

The words "moral depravity" mean, literally, *crooked manners*, from *mos*, "manners," and *pravus*, "crooked." The *de* is intensive. Hence, "moral depravity" means "manners wholly crooked." By *manners*, I do not intend to mean merely the outward life or way of living, because the outward life has not in itself any morality or immorality. All that is strictly or properly moral, all that has moral character, belongs to the mind. *Moral manners*, therefore, are the manners of the inner will, the moral agent, the mind itself. The outward or bodily manners are only expressions of the inward or real manners of the subject. When we speak of manners as *crooked*, we of necessity refer to something straight with which the manners are compared. A thing may have a natural crookedness, a physical crookedness, or a moral crookedness. Moral crookedness is a deviation from the straight rule of action prescribed by the moral law. It is crooked when compared with the moral straightness of the law of God. I repeat, *moral depravity lies entirely back of individual actions and volitions, and is the source from which these actions and volitions spring.*

What are the attributes or qualities of moral depravity?

Unlawfulness is a quality or attribute of moral depravity. Moral depravity must be a thing prohibited by the moral law. If it were not, it would not be *morally* crooked. Whatever has moral character must be either in accordance with moral law or in violation of it.

Sinfulness is a quality or attribute of moral depravity. Dr. Woods defines moral depravity as being "sinfulness."* Sinfulness means moral depravity as a *state of mind* is contrary to God's law and is sinful. This is the term by which we express moral turpitude or the inherent baseness of sin.

Blame-worthiness is another attribute of moral depravity. It means moral depravity is not only contrary to God's law and sinful; but it is worthy of blame and of punishment, and justly brings the subject of it under the penalty of moral law.

Moral depravity is a violation of moral obligation. It is a *state of mind* the opposite of that which we are bound to be in. We ought not to be morally depraved. If it were not a violation of moral obligation, it would be neither unlawful or blame-worthy.

Moral depravity is a state of mind that ought to be instantly abandoned. Of course, if it is sinful, if it is blame-worthy, if it is a violation of moral obligation, it ought to be instantly renounced.

Moral depravity is a state that can be instantly abandoned. It ought to be; therefore, it can be. To say that it *ought* to be abandoned, that we are under moral obligation to abandon it instantly, and yet to deny the possibility of abandoning it instantly, involves a gross contradiction.

Moral depravity must be a state of mind. It cannot be a state of body. Depravity of body is physical depravity, not moral. It is simply disease.

Moral Depravity

Observe closely, moral depravity consists in moral manners; that is, in mental action. Moral depravity is no part or quality of soul or body. Whatever belongs to the essence or substance of either soul or body must of necessity be in its nature physical; and if depraved, therefore, its depravity must be physical and not moral. It is plain that whatever is strictly constitutional in the sense of being an attribute, quality, or part of soul or body, cannot have the distinctive characteristics of moral depravity. For example, if something is physically depraved, it cannot be unlawful or contrary to the law of God, for the law legislates over our mental activities, and not over the essential qualities of either body or mind.

That which is a part or attribute of either soul or body cannot be a violation of moral obligation. Nor can any attribute of body or mind be a violation of conscience, because it cannot be a violation of duty; it cannot be instantly abandoned, and it cannot be blame-worthy.

Moral depravity cannot consist in things created or transmitted; such as, the appetites, passions, or propensities. These have none of the attributes of moral depravity. They are not contrary to moral law. It is only their *unreasonable indulgence* that is contrary to moral law, and not the appetites or propensities themselves. They are not blame-worthy. They cannot be immediately abandoned so as to exist no longer. Their existence is no violation of moral obligation. Consequently, the existence in the constitution of these appetites and propensities is not moral depravity or bad manners.

Moral depravity should not be confused with temptation, excited feelings, or propensities. I have just said that the existence of these sensibilities in the soul is not in itself sinful. Nor is an excited state of the propensities necessarily in itself sinful. If they are indulged unreasonably, this is sin. No merely excited state of feeling that does not secure the consent of the will can be a violation of moral obligation.

Moral depravity must certainly be a voluntary state of mind. For whatever is involuntary has none of the attributes of moral depravity.

In the Scriptures, moral depravity is the state of mind called "the wicked heart." It is that in us to which moral character belongs. I speak of it as *a state of mind* to distinguish it from mere volitions or mere executive acts of mind. It is that *state of mind* from which wicked words and acts naturally proceed. Words and acts are means to an end. They proceed from the choice of an end, goal, or supreme purpose. They have moral character only as they partake of the moral qualities of the choice that gives them existence.

Moral depravity must consist in a settled *ultimate choice*, the choice of an end. *Moral depravity must consist in the voluntary devotion of the mind to self—self-interest and self-gratification.*

Human activity is rational and responsible. People are moral agents; that is, they act under the responsibilities of moral obligation and are subjects of moral law and of moral government. Moral law requires of all moral agents sincere, perfect, universal devotion to God and to the interests of His kingdom. In other words, moral law requires perfect, universal, perpetual, unselfish benevolence. Moral depravity is the opposite of what this law requires; or, more strictly, it is lack of conformity to this law. It is primarily a withholding—a refusal to be devoted to God and to the interests of His kingdom. It sets up "self" above God. A morally depraved being deliberately prefers self-interest and self-will to God's interest and God's will. Practically speaking, moral depravity makes the self of supreme importance. *In one word, moral depravity is selfishness.* A morally depraved person commits their mind to "self" as the great supreme good of life.

Moral depravity is a standing choice as distinct from a volition. A "standing choice" is the choice of the supreme end to which the mind shall devote itself. Moral depravity is the standing choice of self-gratification as an ultimate end. Selfishness or self-gratification is chosen for its own sake. We know from consciousness that when the mind is made up and has decided upon the end to be secured, its whole activities will be directed to the accomplishment of that end. Volition, as distinguished from the choice of an end, is the mind's effort to secure the end. When we speak of individual sins, we speak of volition and consequent action. When we speak of moral depravity as distinct from individual sinful acts, we mean that abiding and wrong selfish choice from which these volitions proceed.

Please carefully observe the distinction I make between sinful acts and moral depravity. Moral depravity is originally a choice, and therefore a

Moral Depravity

mental act. It is the choice of an end, and therefore an abiding, standing choice. Volitions are individual efforts to secure the end chosen. Sinful acts are found in life, in the way we live outwardly. *Moral depravity lies back of the outward life, back of volition, and is a standing preference of self-interest over God's interests and all other interests.*

What is the "carnal mind"?

The *carnal mind* is not the substance of either soul or body. It has been common to speak of the "carnal mind" as being identical with the mind itself. Dr. Griffin, in his Park Street Lectures, confuses the "carnal mind" with the substance of the soul; hence, since the Bible affirms the carnal mind to be enmity against God, he insists that the more clearly God is revealed to the mind, the more the mind will hate God. He believes that there is nothing in the Gospel at all adapted to win the mind; rather, he thinks that the character of God as presented in the Gospel is adapted only to repel the soul. He maintains this on the ground that the soul of the sinner is in its very substance enmity against God.** But this must be a great mistake.

The carnal mind must be *a voluntary state*. If you have Bibles with marginal references and readings, you will observe that in the margin it is written, "the minding of the flesh." The carnal mind is the fleshly mind, or *the mind in a state of committal to the indulgence of the appetites*, passions, and propensities.

The carnal mind is that state of mind into which Adam fell. It appears that, for a time, Adam preferred the will of God to his own, the pleasure of God to his own, and the interests of God to his own. But a temptation of peculiar nature was presented to him through Eve. The wily serpent addressed Eve, "Yea, hath God said, Ye shall not eat of every tree of the garden?" She answered, "We may eat of the fruit of the trees of the garden; but of the fruit of the tree which is in the midst of the garden, God hath said, Ye shall not eat of it, neither shall ye touch it, lest ye die." And the serpent said unto the woman, "Ye shall not surely die: for God doth know, that in the day ye eat thereof, then your eyes shall be opened; and ye shall be as gods, knowing good and evil." And when the woman saw that the tree was good for food, and that it was pleasant to the eyes, and a tree to be desired to make one wise, she took of the fruit thereof, and did eat; and gave also unto her husband with her, and he did eat" (Genesis 3:1-6). In this situation, two constitutional propensities, innocent in themselves, were strongly excited by this appeal of the tempter. The desire of knowledge is constitutional; the appetite for food is constitutional; that is, the way God made us physically and mentally to survive. These appetites are not wrong in themselves, nor is it morally wrong that they should be in an excited state. But the question as put by the tempter amounted to a proposal to Eve and to Adam to gratify their appetites, although their gratification involved disobedience to God. This question was really fundamental to their moral character. They could not yield to this temptation without preferring their own self-gratification to the will of God, and their own pleasure to God's pleasure. To yield to this temptation would be to revolt from the government of God. It would break off their allegiance to God. In the very act, they must decide to seek their own pleasure in their own way as their supreme good. This would really be *a change of the supreme ultimate end of life*. Instead of loving God supremely, they now love themselves supremely. They reject God's authority, God's rights, God's happiness and His glory, as all subordinate to their own gratification. You will observe that the temptation was not merely to put forth a single volition to secure some good, without any reference to the ultimate end in view. It was nothing else than a proposal from the tempter to set aside God as the great end for which they should live, and set up self-gratification as the supreme object of life. *Yielding to this temptation plunged them into a state of choice—a settled state of voluntary preference of self-interest above all other interests, and of self-gratification above all other good.*

A voluntary state as distinguished from a voluntary act is a matter familiar to us all. We all know what is meant by choosing a partner for life, and abiding in that choice. We know that when that choice is settled and abiding, the volitions and the outward life flow from it. The choice, abiding, gives direction to all the subsequent life.

Just so with respect to this choice made by Adam. It became a fixed state of mind. He lapsed into a state of supreme selfishness, which is nothing

Moral Depravity

else than a strong committal of the will, and consequently of the whole being, to self-gratification.

The carnal mind, or the state of minding the flesh, reveals itself in fulfilling the desires of the flesh and of the mind. As the Apostle Paul wrote in Ephesians 2:1-3, "And you hath he quickened who were dead in trespasses and sins; wherein in time past ye walked according to the course of this world, according to the prince of the power of the air, the spirit that now worketh in the children of disobedience; among whom also we all had our conversation in times past in the lusts of our flesh, fulfilling the desires of the flesh and of the mind; and were by nature the children of wrath, even as others." The mind being settled in its great ultimate aim and end, the supreme choice being to gratify the deepest desires and propensities, it will of course reveal itself in all the myriad ways of self-indulgence in which unconverted sinners actually live.

The carnal mind has all the attributes of moral depravity. It is directly contrary to moral law; it is utterly sinful; it deserves punishment; it ought to be instantly abandoned; it can be instantly abandoned; to abandon it would be a change of heart.

The "carnal mind" is a state of enmity against God.

I say "a state of enmity;" that is, the carnal mind as an abiding choice is enmity against God, because it is the exact opposite of what His law requires. His law requires us to love Him supremely and to make His glory, pleasure, will and interests, the supreme object of our lives. However, minding of the flesh is making self-indulgence the supreme object of our lives. This is not only a refusal to obey God's law, but a state of mind the direct opposite of it.

The minding of the flesh is directly opposite to the whole character of God. It is a state of voluntary alienation from God, and of intense committal against Him. It is the wicked heart. It is so treated in the Bible itself. It is spoken of in the chapter of our text as being "in the flesh," and a state of mind in which it is impossible to please God. Furthermore, in this same chapter it is affirmed to be *a state of death in sin*. "To be carnally minded is death" (Romans 8:6). Also in Ephesians 2:1-3, this carnal mind is represented as *a state of spiritual death*, of bondage to the flesh, of enmity against God.

I observe again that this carnal mind is a state of total moral depravity. As is said in Romans 8: 8, "So then they that are in the flesh cannot please God." The carnal mind reveals itself in the neglect of God. This is the reason why sinners neglect worship, prayer, and communion with God; and why they do not love to think of God or speak of Him.

The carnal mind reveals itself also in contempt for God's authority. The Psalmist enquires, "Wherefore doth the wicked contemn [despise] God?"(Psalms 10:13). I answer, "Just because they are wicked. And their wickedness consists in this carnal-mindedness." Perhaps you will say, "I do not contemn [despise] the authority of God." But how much do you care for His authority? Do you, in fact, treat it as if it were of the slightest importance? You will set aside the authority of God for the most trifling indulgence. See that young man smoking that cigar. Do you think, young man, that that is right? Do you think God wants you to smoke that cigar? Do you believe he is pleased with it? You know he is not; and yet you care less for God's authority than you do for smoking that cigar. Everyday you live, you gratify yourself in ways which you know to be unlawful, without the slightest regard to God's authority. What do you mean, then, by saying that you do not contemn the authority of God? Is there anything in the world that you treat as of less importance than the authority of God? Your daily conduct is equivalent to saying, "What do I care for the authority of God? Who is God that I should obey him, or what profit should I have if I should pray unto him?"

The carnal mind reveals itself in opposition to God's people and cause. Who does not know that unconverted sinners are always picking at God's people, and in a multitude of ways manifesting opposition to them. They magnify their faults and publish them as widely as possible. They ridicule their piety, accuse them of hypocrisy, and in every way manifest opposition to them. Now, this is not because they have received any injury from God's people, nor is it really because God's people are worse than other people; but it is because of their own enmity to God that they oppose Him in His people.

The carnal mind also reveals itself in a lack of confidence in God. Sinners very well know that they have every reason to confide in God, but yet they do not. They have not the slightest confidence in all His professions of love for them, nor are they at all inclined to trust God.

The carnal mind reveals itself in a total lack of sympathy with God. In every way, this state of mind shows itself the opposite of God's state of mind. His revealed will and way are an abomination to them, and their will and way are an abomination to Him.

The carnal mind reveals itself in a whole life of rebellion against God. That the unconverted are in a state of rebellion against the authority of God is one of the plainest facts that lie on the face of society.

The carnal mind is a state of mortal enmity against God.

By this I mean that the human mind is so firmly entrenched against God, and so utterly opposed to God that, sooner than be governed by Him, it would take His life if this were possible. Rebellion against any government always implies this.

The crucifixion of Christ demonstrated this fact so far as it is possible for human beings to make such demonstration. Christ was God manifest in the flesh. Unrepentant sinners slew His human nature, and, no doubt, they would have slain His divine, if they could. It does not answer this fact to say that it was only the Jews who were highly prejudiced against Him slew Him. Nor is it any answer to say that if the Jews had known that He was God, they would not have crucified Him; for, we see now on every side that those who acknowledge Jesus to be God, yet reject His authority and give the most unmistakable evidence that they would oppose Him to the death sooner than be governed by Him.

The carnal mind is a state of supreme opposition to God.

The carnal mind is more deeply set in opposition to God than to any other being in the universe. God is infinitely holy, and the carnal mind is in a state of entire sinfulness. These two things are infinitely opposed, the one to the other. There is nothing in the universe to which the sinner is so much opposed as real holiness, and there is nothing in heaven to which he is so much opposed as to infinite holiness. Remember, all other enmities besides this can be subdued by a change of circumstances without the interposition of the Holy Spirit. But so intensified is the enmity of the carnal mind against God that sinners complain that it is utterly impossible for them to love God unless the Holy Spirit induces them to do so. I do not admit that it is impossible, as they pretend; but I do admit that without divine influence they never will love God, whatever the consequences might be of their refusal.

REMARKS

The human mind is obviously in a physically diseased state. By this I mean that sin has deranged its developments, insomuch that there are various tendencies in the constitution that result in selfishness. But remember, this is a physical and not a moral depravity. To illustrate this: Many persons come into being with depraved appetites—a strong natural appetite, say, for strong drink, or some other sensual enjoyment. Now, these appetites, although in a diseased state, yet being constitutional, are not in themselves sinful. It is only their unlawful indulgence that is sinful. In fact, no appetite of human beings can be sinful that is strictly constitutional and normal, nor can it become in itself sinful by being in an unhealthy or depraved condition. The sin must consist in its unlawful indulgence.

Adam and Eve had constitutional appetites for knowledge and for food. These were not sinful, not even when strongly excited by the temptation to indulge. It was only the consent of the mind to indulge them in a prohibited manner that constituted their sin.

It has been very common to confuse temptation and sin. None of the constitutional appetites or propensities can be in themselves sinful, because they are involuntary and are a part of our nature. Nevertheless, these appetites and propensities, when excited, are of course temptations to seek their indulgence. It must be their unlawful indulgence and this only that constitutes sin. But it has been very common to speak of their very existence, and especially of their excited state, as sin.

Now, unless the soul, by an act of will, indulges this excitement, there

Moral Depravity

can be no sin. If the mind resists the excitement, suppresses it so far as possible, and refuses to gratify it, there can be no sin. Indeed, when the appetite is strongly excited, but yet resisted, we cannot possibly deny that the virtue is the higher, as the temptation is the greater and the mind more strongly and perseveringly resists it.

It is a great mistake to confuse physical depravity with moral depravity. It is very curious to see how the Bible has been interpreted on the question of constitutional sinfulness. It seems to me that people often interpret it without the least reference to any sound principles of biblical criticism. For example, one of these principles is: no passage is to be so interpreted as flatly to contradict human reason, unless it is so irresistibly plain that it can bear no other interpretation.

Now I have no time to examine all the passages that have been misinterpreted on this subject. But take one, generally made very prominent in the attempt to prove from Scripture that the human constitution is morally depraved. Consider Psalm 51:5—"Behold, I was shapen in iniquity, and in sin did my mother conceive me." ["Surely I was sinful at birth, sinful from the time my mother conceived me" (Psalm 55:5—NIV).] What is this text quoted to prove? That the human constitution, or in other words, the very nature of all people, is morally depraved. But this dogma is certainly contrary to human reason. If by moral depravity we mean something sinful, it is certainly inconceivable by reason that that should be morally blameworthy over which the person never had any control—a thing that belongs to his very constitution as he came from the hand of his Maker. That any human soul should be blame-worthy for such a constitution—should be guilty of moral wrong for possessing it, is certainly as contrary as possible to human reason.

Now remember, we are never to interpret any passage of Scripture so as to make it teach a doctrine palpably contrary to human reason, if it will bear any other interpretation. I say *contrary to human reason*, and *not merely above its reach*. Now, the doctrine that the human constitution is in itself sinful, blame-worthy, morally wrong, morally depraved—is not so much above reason as opposite to the irresistible decisions of the human reason. It cannot therefore be proved, unless from passages unequivocally clear, explicit, and incapable of any other interpretation.

Let us now apply these remarks to the passage quoted above, Psalm 51:5. What does it say? Some quote the passage in an attempt to prove that sin is universal; in other words, that moral depravity is constitutional and pertains to the entire human race. But this verse does not affirm a *universal* proposition. The verse, "Behold, I was shapen in iniquity, and in sin did my mother conceive me" affirms nothing of human beings in general, and we are not to extend and torture the passage to make it teach so absurd a doctrine. In this verse, the Psalmist does not even affirm his own sin. If he accused any one of sin, it was his mother: "Behold, I was shapen in iniquity, and in sin did my mother conceive me."

Psalm 51:5 uses the language of poetry. The Psalmist was smarting bitterly, and was deeply moved under a sense of his great sin in the matter of Bathsheba and Uriah. As is natural in such cases, he has expressed himself in a highly figurative and poetic manner, and undoubtedly had a strong sense of his great sinfulness, and meant to say that he had been a sinner ever since he was capable of being so. Now, surely, *to make such a passage teach so monstrous a dogma as the universal sinfulness of human nature is a flagrant perversion of God's word*. It cannot be made to teach any such thing without greatly over-straining what is really said in the passage. But most surely no passage should be over-strained to make it teach an unreasonable dogma. You must not force strong poetical expressions to mean more than they really say when this super-addition is contrary to reason.

The usual interpretation of this passage totally perverts the real meaning of the Psalmist. He was greatly agonized in view of his own sinfulness, and was confessing his own sin to God. He was far from being in a state of mind to accuse anybody else or to make any excuses for his own sin. But the usual interpretation would represent him as searching for some excuse for his sin, and really charging the blame upon God, as if he had said, "O Lord, You gave me a sinful nature, so how am I to blame for my sin?" This is a gross misrepresentation of the meaning of the passage and of the spirit of its author.

Ephesians 2:3 is another passage extensively quoted to prove that human nature is itself sinful. "Among whom also we all had our conversation in times past in the lusts of our flesh, fulfilling the desires of the flesh and of the mind; and were by nature the children of wrath, even as oth-

Moral Depravity

ers." ["All of us also lived among them at one time, gratifying the cravings of our sinful nature and following its desires and thoughts. Like the rest, we were by nature objects of wrath" (Ephesians 2:3—NIV).]

Upon this verse I remark: The apostle represents the sinfulness of human beings as consisting in fulfilling the desires of the flesh and of the mind, and not in the desires themselves. This is the same view of moral depravity that I have given in this discourse. Paul does not represent these desires as being in themselves wrong; it is only their sinful indulgence which makes human beings the children of wrath.

Another remark is due here to show why Paul uses the words "by nature." Suppose a child were born with a natural appetite for strong drink. This natural appetite does not make him a drunkard before he indulges it. But suppose he grows up to adulthood, does indulge himself and becomes a drunkard. Now, looking to the occasion of his fall, we should naturally say, he was a drunkard "BY NATURE." The same is true with those who have a natural propensity (as some have) to lie and steal. If they were born with a natural tendency in those directions, and we knew it, we should speak of them as liars or thieves "by nature." By this language we should not mean that they were actually guilty of any of these crimes before they had indulged these physically depraved propensities; much less should we assume that these inherited propensities were sins of their own.

There is no doubt in my mind that this is the real meaning of the Apostle Paul in this passage from Ephesians. The constitutional desires (*Epithumiai*, Greek,) were natural to humans, and in this sense people are "by nature children of wrath." The appetites being constitutional to human beings in their physically depraved state, it is quite natural to speak of him as being by nature a sinner, when really we can mean no more than that he inherits the temptation to sin, and not that the temptation is itself sin. The desires are natural to him; the fulfilling or indulging of them is voluntary, and therefore sinful. Now, this is all that this passage can be made to mean by a fair interpretation.

I say of this passage in Ephesians and all the passages that are quoted to prove the doctrine of constitutional sinfulness as I have said of Psalm 51:5—they have not been soberly interpreted. They have been made to teach a most irrational doctrine by straining them and making them mean more than they say. They naturally mean no more than that people inherit a physically depraved constitution. Certainly no one of them asserts in language that can admit no other interpretation that human nature is itself sinful. I have quoted the two strongest passages on this point that are to be found (as I suppose) in the Bible. Surely it requires no great ingenuity to show that these passages naturally admit a very different interpretation from that which has been generally given them.

You can see from this subject of moral depravity why people need regeneration, and also what regeneration is. Regeneration involves the giving up of the carnal mind, a ceasing to mind the flesh, and giving up the whole mind to obey God. It is a change from being committed to self-gratification, to committing the whole soul to obedience to God.

From what we have learned, it is evident that each one is and must be the author of his own moral depravity. For moral depravity consists, as has been shown, in committing the mind, voluntarily, to self-indulgence. No one can do this for another. Physical depravity, or a diseased state of the constitution or human nature, is no doubt the occasion (*not the cause*) of moral depravity. Remember: the propensities are no doubt depraved; so they act as a temptation, to which, as a matter of fact, people at first universally yield.

Many people who think they are the friends of God are deceived. They have never been converted. It is a great mistake, and they need only die to know it. It would be far better to learn it and correct it here and now.***

---

*Leonard Woods (1774-1854) was a member of the Andover faculty. He wrote *Letters to Unitarians* in 1820 to challenge their view of human nature.

** Edward Dorr Griffin (1770-1837) was pastor of Park Street Church from 1811-1815, and published his *Lectures in the Park Street Church*: Boston, 1813. He also wrote *The Extent of the Atonement*: New York, 1819.

*** Charles G. Finney, *The Oberlin Evangelist,* March 12 and March 26, 1862, *Principles of Liberty,* 97-107. For Review: Answer the Study Questions on page 225, Cowles page 249.

8

License, Bondage and Liberty
1854

For ye have not received the spirit of bondage again to fear; but ye have received the Spirit of adoption, whereby we cry, Abba, Father.—Romans 8:15—KJV

For you did not receive a spirit that makes you a slave again to fear, but you received the Spirit of sonship. And by him we cry, "Abba, Father."—Romans 8:15—NIV

The Lord has three classes of servants; bondmen, mercenaries and those who serve Him in love. I wish to make another three-fold distinction. People may be classified according to their spirit. Some have a spirit of license; others a spirit of bondage; and others a spirit of true Christian liberty. Into one or the other of these classes all moral agents who have any knowledge of God must necessarily fall. My present object is to show the prominent characteristics of each class.

Principles of Peace — Finney's Lessons on Romans

People who have the spirit of license.

License differs essentially from liberty. *License is selfishness unrestrained by moral considerations*—a state in which people do as they want with no fear of God before their eyes; they follow out their own selfish ends without moral restraint. The spirit of license includes the characteristic of an *undeveloped conscience*. Those with the spirit of license have had so little moral training that their views on moral questions are yet immature, or merely negative, and not infrequently erroneous. I once belonged to this class of people. Many things which I have since regarded as gross sins gave me no trouble then. My conscience was undeveloped. Back then, nothing had transpired to develop my conscience. Some of my earliest impressions of moral restraint were produced by seeing my mother weep because my father would let his sons go to the lake fishing on the Sabbath. Her tears reminded me forcibly that there was something wrong in this. I was then old enough to know all about such matters of duty, but not having my attention turned to these subjects, I remained, practically speaking, as if I had no conscience.

Others have only a *seared conscience*. These people go on much as if they had no conscience at all; although at one time they may have had a conscience very considerably developed. They can recollect when they could not lie or swear. When tempted, they were often obliged to refrain by the demands of their conscience. Today, they are inclined perhaps to smile over their former notions.

Those who have a spirit of license are not restrained, even though they are ever so much upbraided. *They have no faith* in the great things revealed of God. Indeed, they act as if there were no God; for although they admit God exists, they do not allow God's existence to have any practical influence on their minds. They have no practical regard for what is morally right. Having *no vivid sense of moral obligation*, their minds are wholly open to the impulses of selfishness. If they forbear to cheat, lie, or steal, it is not through any moral consideration, but under the influence of some form of selfishness. They manifest the spirit of license in this particular: their conscience has no practical control over them. The desire to do good has no influence. They do not care to do any good, although they know they have the power and the opportunity.

Now, how does this apply to you? What testimony does your heart and life bear when tried by such tests as these I have just mentioned? Are you living as you know you ought not to live? Are you doing what your conscience condemns? Are you going on in your own way under a spirit of moral recklessness in spite of all God may require? Inquire into this matter. You may not be reckless with respect to other considerations; but if you are reckless regarding moral considerations, the fact ought to alarm you. If the motives which ought to control you fail to do so, your heart must be fearfully wrong. If your condition is such that in order to influence you others must appeal to something besides your conscience and your sense of duty, you may know that you are far gone in moral recklessness and ruin.

It is curious to see how this downward tendency acts on the moral nature. The perception of moral principles grows dim; moral relations seem to fade away gradually from the mind. The person will tell you he doubts whether such and such things are sinful at all. He does not quite see how there need be any wrong in them. If you try to point out to him their moral qualities and relations, you are amazed to find that his perceptions on such questions are so dull that you cannot make him see a sin. This is naturally the state of all those who have the spirit of license. If people have clear, sharp moral perceptions, they will fall into one of the two later classes. Those with the spirit of license have but few moral principles. As you consider each one individually, you will see that these principles have dropped out of their mind until there is little moral principle left. They can now laugh over the commission of sins which once made them sweat with agony. All moral principles become lax in their minds. Things they once deemed wrong they learn to excuse. They look back on their former scruples as superstitious and foolish. They talk largely of their "progress"—little thing, alas, that their way of progress is toward hell.

Young people with the spirit of license will manifest it in their pleasure loving tendencies and their passion for fancy clothes. Amusement is often their chief delight, and of course their spirit of license develops itself in this direction. "What," they say, "were we not made that we might enjoy ourselves? Does not God like to see us happy?" But if you search carefully into their state of mind, you will see that they are "lovers of pleasure more than lovers of God" (2 Timothy 3:4). They care little about what will please God, but much about what will please themselves. They know how to make excuses for anything that pleases them.

Developments of the same reckless spirit vary according to age and tastes. Young people are pleasure-loving. Middle-aged people are covetous and money-loving; or perhaps they aspire after distinction in their professions. Whenever the heart goes in that direction, you will find the spirit of license in sin developing itself. Under such a state of moral feeling, people will be sure to leave a broad margin for deviations from moral right. They can justify a great many dishonest ways of getting gain or promoting their favorite schemes of ambition.

It is striking and sad to see how their worldly-mindedness can deface and even efface all their notions of right and of wrong; how they will plead for sin; defend various forms of sin and indulgence; roll their sin as a sweet morsel under the tongue without scruples. They will violate the Sabbath and allow themselves almost any amount of latitude in this direction, especially if among strangers. They will take a little strong drink and say, "What's the harm if nobody knows it and it brings no disgrace?" In business, what will they not do if they can escape detection? If there is danger of detection, they will call it a mistake and rectify it, but they will never rectify a mistake in their benefit for the sake of moral principle. In political life, they will manage any way to subserve their ends; their object is never the general good, but always their own personal interests. In whatever form of self-seeking, they care not for the eye of God, nor for the dictates of conscience.

The law of progress with all people of this class is from bad to worse. If you notice where they started and trace along their secret history, you will see this distinctly and fearfully illustrated. You young people who yield yourselves to sin, do you not see that your law of progress is from bad to worse? Have you thought of the moral and spiritual decline of your life if you give yourselves up to license in sin? Some of you have been almost surfeited with religious instruction. You have heard prayers enough and have seen tears enough to melt any heart but yours. Where will you be when once removed forever from these restraints and given up to the full sweep of that fearful law of downward progress?

For those of you whose conscience has been rightly developed, I have great hope. How many have we seen here who, when they first came among us, had hardly conscience enough to make them appear decent in the house of God; but not having been hardened in their conscience, they began to listen, and as they listened began to feel and think. Soon you meet them in the enquiry meeting; and then soon at the feet of Jesus.

On the other hand, some go the other way. With a conscience already fearfully hardened, they wince under the truth. Their hearts rebel against the truth of God's word. They fall into some low form of skepticism, and they cast off God and His truth. With fearful strides they rush downward, downward to the depths of hell!

Where young people are you? Where are you of every age and of all conditions, whether professing or not professing Christian faith and piety? I ask you to apply these tests to your own heart and life. Where are you? Have you the spirit of license? And more than all this, let me ask, "Have you that most fearful of all symptoms of being far gone in the way of death—that you know your state to be as bad as it can be, and yet you do not care?"

People who have the spirit of bondage.

Very commonly but improperly those who have the spirit of bondage are often called conscientious Christians. They get this name especially because they differ so widely from those who have the spirit of license. It is true that this class of people differ very much from those with the spirit of license. Their conscience is not seared, but tender. Their conscience is not undeveloped or inactive, but wakeful and efficient in certain directions. Yet, they are not conscientious for the right reasons, because they do not go deep enough. *Their conscience reaches only to the exterior of life—not to the interior.* Their conscience restrains them from external conduct which they deem to be wrong, but *it does not control their heart.* It is a conscience without faith or love. Hence their life is not spontaneously seeking the will of God to obey Him. They are in bondage in the sense that they are not at liberty to do what they really would like to do. Since their heart does not sympathize with God, all His ways are irksome and all their own ways are pleasant; so of course, all their religious duties must come hard for them. Now, if their hearts were truly given to God, they would be filled with the Holy Spirit, and nothing could please them more than the things that please God. In a state of love for God, they can serve God without bondage, "Tis love that makes our cheerful feet, In swift obedience move."* This obedience is the highest freedom and the purest blessedness. When the heart is right it asks nothing wrong, and people have only to go according to their heart; or more strictly, they have only to follow the Lord, and to this the heart makes no resistance but yields with the utmost delight.

However, those whose hearts are still in sin will sometimes do a bond-service for God, as they suppose; but, their service is really for self. They would prefer to lessen their religious services if they could. They would stay away from Christian gatherings and worship if they could do so. They lust for the fleshpots of Egypt, and would return there if they dared. They are in bondage to their consciences. For the sake of peace with conscience, they conform to its dictates in part, in the way of compromise, pleading to be let off as much as possible, and making the best turns they can, as people are prone to do with a hard master.

This class of people are *in bondage to God*, so far as they render Him any service, *they serve Him in the spirit of slaves and not of sons*. They think they must be religious, or do worse, and they are afraid of the worse alternative. They would do many things which God forbids, but they dare not. Hence they submit, yet their heart yields only the form of service.

They are *in bondage to the church*. They are afraid of censure. To have Christians watch over them is about the equivalent of having spies watching their path. So far from rejoicing to have the kind and watchful care of Christian brothers and sisters on them, they feel this to be an unwelcome restraint.

Now, beloved, how does this test apply to your heart? This group of people are abound in resolutions. Making resolutions constitutes their

License, Bondage and Liberty

principal Christian exercises. To make resolutions and to break them; to endeavor, yet to fail to perform; to resolve and resolve, yet go on as ever before—this is their religious history. The reason for their failure is they never break up the deep foundations of selfishness and let their souls settle down into the great depths of benevolence. They are often greatly pressed with conviction, a deep sense of sin troubles them. Their conscience upbraids them, they say. They refuse to confess and turn from the many things for which they condemn themselves, and hence they feel exceedingly uneasy. If they are students they scarcely get a lesson. In fact they are simply convicted sinners, not converted, true Christians.

The knowledge of those in a spirit of bondage controls the judgment they form of others, and hence they judge others harshly. They cannot conceive how a Christian can smile without sin. They do not understand that buoyancy of spirit which is so congenial to the peaceful Christian. Always dissatisfied with themselves, how can they be satisfied with others? Always conscious of doing wrong, how can they, naturally, judge otherwise of their friends? Their own mind screwed up under a feeling of bondage and a sense of constraint, they give no credit for honest piety to those who walk peacefully and calmly in the light of the Savior's presence. Spontaneously forming harsh judgments, first of themselves and next of others, they have no idea what a change would come over these judgments of others if once they were to come themselves into gospel liberty.

Set these bond-servants to the work of Christian discipline; they almost never reclaim or reform the offender. It is quite beyond their power to love him–for the love of Christ is not in them. Or let another commence discipline in the church; and you will find them almost surely throwing themselves in the way. Their sympathies will be on the side of the wrong-doer. They will treat everything as persecution which is intended to reform and subdue.

Commonly they are strict and punctual in their religious duties, yet not willingly and joyfully, but of constraint. Take the constraint away, and no such duties would be done. In Christian duties, they get no real comfort. The true child of God gets real comfort without seeking it. Those in bondage seek it much and long but in vain. They value it highly.

They want somebody to give them comfort. They applaud the ministers who speak comfortably to them; but, not complying with the conditions of comfort, they must fail to find it. They have but little hope, and the hope they have is unsettled, hard to keep, and of little practical worth. Anxious, unhappy, an annoyance to others, they are prone to be sour, morose and censorious. It is natural that they should misunderstand those who pass into real peace by submission to God. When they see such people enter into a state of gospel light and liberty, they are alarmed, and say, "How can he be so cheerful? What can make him so lighthearted? There must be something wrong."

Now, those under the spirit of bondage have not gone far enough even to see where the peaceful Christian stands. They are also characterized by a religious zeal and a sanctimoniousness which must put on something, and which to a discerning eye will have the air of something put on and not spontaneous. It is not a natural solemnity, but a constrained formality. Their prayers amount to this, that they may be converted. They do not so understand it, for they think they have been converted, perhaps long ago; yet their convictions lead them to pray for just what would, if granted, be conversion. The amount of their prayer is that God would give them repentance, a new heart, gospel faith; in short would make them Christians. They struggle earnestly in their way; but going perpetually about to establish their own righteousness, they come not into gospel rest.

With those in the spirit of bondage, religion seems a hard business— as it always must seem to be while the heart is wrong. "What," they say, "how can a man love God with all his heart? How can one love his neighbor as himself?" The best they can do is to struggle on and find no peace. One perpetual round of tasked duty-doing makes up their religion. In it all, there is no real service done for God from a heart devoted lovingly to His character and service. Such people have only the spirit of bondage again to fear.

People who have the spirit of liberty.

Some understand Christian liberty to be the privilege of doing as they

License, Bondage and Liberty

please, right or wrong: but they greatly mistake; for this is only license.

Liberty, psychologically considered, *is the power to do the contrary—* the free ability to choose and to act otherwise than the actual choice. But, considered in reference to the Christian life, it may be better defined as *the spirit of doing right spontaneously*. The heart is united to God by thoroughly choosing God's goals, purposes, and ends, and hence becoming unified with Him in sympathy and interest, even as the Son with the Father whom He respects and loves.

The Bible speaks of Christians as being "children of God." The Apostle John wrote: "Yet to all who received him, to those who believed in his name, he gave the right to become children of God—children born not of natural descent, nor of human decision or a husband's will, but born of God" (John 1:12-13—NIV). In context here, the Apostle Paul wrote: "For the creation was subjected to frustration, not by its own choice, but by the will of the one who subjected it, in hope that the creation itself will be liberated from its bondage to decay and brought into the glorious freedom of the children of God" (Rom 8:20-21—NIV). The Bible represents Christians as becoming *children of God both by being begotten of His Spirit in regeneration and by adoption*. Indeed the Spirit of God dwells in them, takes up His abode in their hearts; and hence creates a living union between their souls and His. They come to have the same great reason for action; the same radical purpose and aim that God has. They have chosen the same great end or goal, have adopted the same views, and have submitted their heart to the control and guidance of His truth and Spirit; therefore, genuine benevolence issues from their very hearts spontaneously. Hence, they enjoy a harmony with God in their ends, aims and affections, and this becomes an established, settled state of life; therefore, they are no more in bondage than Christ was. You need not appeal to their conscience to prick them on to duty. They have a conscience to be sure; but it is to them *a guide and not a goad*, a very important distinction. Their conscience is not a goad under which they move along, stung, wincing, bleeding. Their conscience is a guide, given by God to lead their way and point out moral relations. When cordially accepted as a guide, the conscience has no sting; the conscience comes not to lacerate any more than if it were wrapped in the softest silk. As soon as the heart settles and sinks sweetly into the will of God, conscience needs no rod, no scorpion sting, not even a word of command. Conscience has only to say, "This is the way, Here you are to go. This is the will of your Father in heaven."

Those who are not in this state of liberty, and who are strangers to it, may suppose that the conscience of true Christian believers has fallen away and dropped out. Someone said of a wife: "She is dutiful, but has no love." But suppose this woman is married to one she tenderly loves, to whom her heart is bound with bonds stronger than death. She might then say: "It seems to me that my conscience has fallen away. It seems as if I had no conscience. Formerly, my conscience compelled me as a goad, and not merely a guide. Now it has no such work to do as before. My heart needs only to know the way and it rejoices with great joy to walk therein." This is a spirit of spontaneous cooperation with God. It is love acting itself out and manifesting itself in a way natural and easy. Everything is done as is supposed will please God. The mind acts on high principles; the law of love and of God is written on the heart; all obedience is natural and free because spontaneous and in harmony with the Christian's supreme choice.

The full idea of Christian liberty is acting as we please when our pleasure is to act only right; *taking the right course because this pleases God, and nothing can please us but what pleases God.* The mind entrusts all its own interests and destinies with God. The Christian commits his future to God, a future unknown and untried. He commends the present to God, with its toils and interests. He also commends his past to God, in the hope of free forgiveness through a Redeemer. Hence the Christian is free and at ease. He is conscientious in the true sense; the state of his conscience and acts are so entirely in harmony with an enlightened conscience that he experiences no collision with its dictates. All is right, says the conscience; and of course there is peace as long as Christian feeling and duty are spontaneous.

REMARKS

It is hardly necessary to say that the first class of people I have described,

License, Bondage and Liberty

those having the spirit of license, are spiritually blind and dead. This is abundantly obvious. The second class of people, those in bondage, are regarded as very exemplary Christians, but they are in fact only convicted sinners. That they are not saved is very evident from the fact that they are constantly praying for salvation; that is, when they are stirred up to any religious exercise. You may try to get them to pray and to labor for others; you cannot; they fall right back to praying for themselves.

After preaching one evening, I went to the library room of the church, and at the door a young lady met me and said she wanted to speak with me. She wanted to ask me what she should do to be saved. Her father, long a leading man in the church, was standing by us; so, after talking awhile with his daughter, I said to him, "Let us pray for this dear child of yours." He seemed as one confused. I observed his strange appearance, yet thought it best to press on our work; therefore I said, "You lead first in prayer for your daughter, and I will follow." He prayed awhile, yet for himself only. He had not the face to say even once, "Lord, have mercy on my daughter." He could only pray, "Lord have mercy on me." Not one word could he say for his daughter, though under such circumstances of heart-thrilling interest.

It is of no use to try to drive a person out of this rut. They will forever slump back into it. But as soon as they come into the liberty of the gospel, it becomes as natural as their breath to pray for sinners. A forcible illustration of this occurred in a meeting for enquiry in which I had no assistance. I spoke to the inquirers for a while, trying to lead them to Christ, and then I proposed to pray. Before I commenced, I said to them. "After I close, if any of you want to pray, just open your mouth and your heart freely." After I stopped, one of them began; prayed a minute for himself; seemed really to come in humble faith to Christ; and then immediately began to pray for the one next to him. When he stopped, this next one began in the same way, first for himself; then coming to Christ, he launched out in most earnest prayer for his next neighbor. And this went on for a long time, each one praying first for himself until his heart committed itself to Jesus; and then he began pouring out his heartfelt prayer for sinners. It was a most affecting season, and especially instructive in showing how naturally the heart that has laid itself over

8 Romans 8:15

upon the arms of the Savior prays for those yet in their sins.

Those who are really in bondage often remain so through pride. They are not humble enough to disclose their real state. When a full pouring out of their souls in confession would do them good and would honor the gospel, they refrain, too proud to take their place before God and others as humbled penitents. Especially is the danger extreme when those who have held a prominent position in the church get into bondage. Very often, such people never get out of bondage. I could tell you of many cases that would surprise you. They are prone to say, "If I confess, I shall stumble others. Who will believe I am converted, or will have any confidence in me if I confess the real truth of myself?" Hence Satan shuts them in all round about, and few of any class are in so great a danger of losing their souls.

People in bondage often seem *to themselves* to have a much deeper sense of sin than those who are in gospel liberty. They think they have a deeper sense of sin, but they are entirely mistaken. Those who are free in the gospel have altogether the keenest sense of sin. Yet the bones broken under the law are set and healed, and God has caused rejoicing where only pains were before. But if people from this state were to fall into sin, you would see their conscience wake to a searching and a fearful retribution.

Young people who have not associated with Christians in gospel liberty and acting under the impulses of love will almost always have false conceptions of Christianity. Their idea of it will lack the amenities and the charities of the true gospel life. They do not see how anybody can be in such a state as not to lust after the flesh-pots of selfishness. They have no conception of that state in which the soul rises to a new level of aspirations and sympathies, a level far above the murky and foul atmosphere of earth—where the soul bathes itself in the love and the light of heaven. They need to come into close communion with Christians who are in this state before they can properly appreciate the idea of true Christian faith and liberty.

Do you lack this glorious gospel light and liberty? How is it with you today? Those of you who are not claiming to be Christians; what attitude will you take? Is it not time that you should set your face toward

License, Bondage and Liberty

your Father's house, saying, "From this day, my whole heart is Yours?" What do you say to this! Is it not time that you should get out of darkness? Think of your bondage. Is it not time that you should awake and accept the offered boon of freedom? Jesus Christ has proclaimed you free, if you will; and is it not time that you should accept it? Will you longer remain of choice a slave?

Currently, in some of the southern states, the emancipation of a slave is so great a matter that it is done only by means of special forms and by a solemn public transaction. The master brings his slave before the court and there in a special form makes out and subscribes his papers, and thus gives the slave his freedom.

A far more wonderful transaction has taken place in another quarter; a far higher court has been in session. The supreme Executive of the universe has come forth to act on this great emancipation. He has made out true papers for giving gospel liberty to a race of lost, enslaved sinners. Have you heard of this? The thing was done many years ago, but the business still lingers unfinished. In fact, there have not been messengers enough to carry the glad news yet to every creature; and what is worse, very many to whom it has come cannot be persuaded to accept the boon. Hence much time has been lost and the work still lingers.

And now, what will you do with this proposal? It comes to you; what will you do with it? Do you say, "I am not a slave!" Ah, but you are, and you know it! Do you say, "If I were only sure that I could get such a faith, one of true gospel liberty, I would have it"? Let me tell you, there is no other true religion than Christianity, a Christianity that holds out the promise of gospel liberty, none. All others are counterfeit. You can have this if you will.

Suppose a young person said, "If you can tell me what to do, I will do it. Anything I can do, I am ready to do." This would be hopeful and right; and nothing less than this can be right. How many of you will pledge yourselves to do your duty, if you were told what it is? If you are willing to do what God requires you to do to be saved even to the cutting off a right hand, then you can be readily directed to Christ and you may surely come and find life and peace.

Unfortunately, many sinners come and ask what they shall do, and then, having heard, they refuse to do it. They come to the door and knock; but when bidden to come in, they say, "O no, I had no thought of coming in;" and then they turn coolly, or it may be, scornfully, away. Alas, "the turning away of the simple shall slay them" (Proverbs 1:32). They cannot many times repel the gospel from their hearts and dash salvation's offered cup from their lips and still be welcomed in when they shall have pressing occasion to call in fearful earnest for admission.**

---

*From *The Puritan Hymn and Tune Book Designed for Congregational Singing, Social Meetings, and the Family*. Third Edition. Boston: Congregational Board of Publication, Chauncy Street, 1859. Number 178, *Love*, Page 42.

1 Happy the heart where graces reign,
  Where love inspires the breast:
  Love is the highest of the train,
  And strengthens all the rest.

2 Knowledge, alas! 'tis all in vain,
  And all in vain our fear;
  Our stubborn sins will fight and win,
  If love be absent there.

3 'Tis love that makes our cheerful feet,
  In swift obedience move;
  The devils know, and tremble too,
  But Satan cannot love.

4 This is the grace that lives, and sings,
  When faith and hope will cease;
  'Tis this shall strike our joyful strings.
  In the sweet realms of bliss.

** Charles G. Finney, *The Oberlin Evangelist*, May 24, 1854, *Principles of Liberty*, 109-118. For Review: Answer the Study Questions on page 226, Cowles page 250.

9

The Spirit of Prayer
1835

Likewise the Spirit also helpeth our infirmities: for we know not what we should pray for as we ought: but the Spirit itself maketh intercession for us with groanings which cannot be uttered. And he that searcheth the hearts knoweth what is the mind of the Spirit, because he maketh intercession for the saints according to the will of God. —Romans 8:26-27—KJV

In the same way, the Spirit helps us in our weakness. We do not know what we ought to pray for, but the Spirit himself intercedes for us with groans that words cannot express. And he who searches our hearts knows the mind of the Spirit, because the Spirit intercedes for the saints in accordance with God's will. —Romans 8:26-27—KJV

One grand design in preaching is to exhibit the truth in such a way as to answer the questions which would naturally arise in the minds of those who read the Bible with attention, and who want to know what it means so they can put it into practice. In explaining this text from Romans 8, I propose to show: What Spirit is spoken of in the words, "The Spirit also helpeth our infirmities." What this Spirit does for us. Why He does what the text declares He does. How He accomplishes it. The degree in which He influences the minds of those who are under His influence. How His influences are to be distinguished from the influences of evil spirits or the suggestions of our own minds. How we are to obtain this agency of the Holy Spirit. Who has a right to expect to enjoy His influences in this matter, or for whom does the Spirit do the things spoken of in our text.

Paul wrote of the Holy Spirit helping us.

Some have supposed that the Spirit spoken of in the text means our own spirit—our own mind. But a little attention to the text will show plainly that this cannot be the meaning. If they were correct, "The Spirit helpeth our infirmities" would be translated, "Our own spirit helpeth the infirmities of our own spirit" and "Our own spirit likewise maketh intercession for our own spirit." It is evident from the manner in which the text is introduced that the Spirit referred to is the Holy Spirit. The scripture text for our lesson plainly speaks of the same Spirit that Paul wrote of earlier: "For if ye live after the flesh, ye shall die: but if ye through the Spirit do mortify the deeds of the body, ye shall live. For as many as are led by the Spirit of God, they are the sons of God. For ye have not received the spirit of bondage again to fear; but ye have received the spirit of adoption, whereby we cry, Abba, Father, The Spirit itself beareth witness with our spirit, that we are the children of God" (Romans 8:13-16).

What the Holy Spirit does for Christians.

The Holy Spirit intercedes for Christians. "He maketh intercession for us" and "helpeth our infirmities" when "we know not what to pray for as we ought." He helps Christians pray according to the will of God, or for those things that God desires Christians to pray for and obtain.

The Spirit of Prayer

Why the Holy Spirit helps Christians.

The Holy Spirit intercedes for us because of our *ignorance*. Because we know not what we should pray for as we ought. We are very ignorant both of the will of God as revealed in the Bible and of His unrevealed will as we ought to learn it from His providence. People are vastly ignorant of the promises and prophecies of the Bible, and they are also blind to the providence of God. They are still more in the dark about those points of which God has said nothing except by the leading of His Spirit. In one of my earlier messages in *Lectures on Revival of Religion*, I named these four sources of evidence on which to ground faith in prayer—promises, prophecies, providences, and the Holy Spirit.* When all other means fail of leading us to the knowledge of what we ought to pray for, the Holy Spirit will give us the knowledge we need.

How the Holy Spirit makes intercession for Christians.

We need to understand the mode of the Holy Spirit's operation to help us in our infirmities. The Holy Spirit does not supersede the use of our faculties. The Holy Spirit does not pray for us while we do nothing. He prays for us by exciting our faculties. Not that the Holy Spirit immediately suggests to us words or guides our language. *He enlightens our minds and makes the truth take hold of our souls.* He leads us to consider the state of the church and the condition of sinners around us. The manner in which He brings the truth before the mind and keeps it there till it produces its effect, we cannot tell. But we can know as much as this—*He leads us to a deep consideration of the state of things; and the result of this (the natural and philosophical result) is deep feeling.* When the Holy Spirit brings the truth before a person's mind, there is only one way in which the person can keep from deep feeling. He must turn away his thoughts and lead his mind to think of other things than that which the Holy Spirit is impressing upon his mind. When the Spirit of God brings the truth before sinners, they must feel. They feel wrong as long as they remain unrepentant. So, if a person is a Christian and the Holy Spirit brings a subject into warm contact with his heart, it is just as impossible for him not to feel as it is that your hand should not feel it if you put it into the fire. If the Spirit of God leads someone to dwell on things calculated to excite warm and overpowering feelings, and he is not excited by them, it proves that he has no love for souls, nothing of the Spirit of Christ, and knows nothing about Christian experience.

The Holy Spirit makes the Christian feel the value of souls and the guilt and danger of sinners in their present condition. It is amazing how dark and stupid Christians often are about this danger. Even Christian parents let their children go right down to hell before their eyes, and scarcely seem to exercise a single feeling or put forth an effort to save them. And why? Because they are so blind to what hell is, so unbelieving about the Bible, so ignorant of the precious promises which God has made to faithful parents. They grieve the Spirit of God away, and it is in vain to try to make them pray for their children while the Spirit of God is away from them.

The Holy Spirit leads Christians to understand and apply the promises of Scripture. Amazingly, in no age have Christians been able *fully* to apply the promises of Scripture to the events of life as they live each day. This is not because the promises themselves are obscure. The promises themselves are plain enough. But there has always been an amazing disposition to overlook the Scriptures as a source of light respecting the passing events of life. How astonished the apostles were at Christ's application of so many prophecies to himself! They seemed to be continually ready to exclaim, "Astonishing! Can it be so? We never understood it before." Think of the manner in which the apostles, influenced and inspired by the Holy Spirit, applied passages of the Old Testament to gospel times. How amazing that they found such a richness of meaning in the Scriptures! So it has been with many Christians; while deeply engaged in prayer, they have seen the passages of Scripture that are appropriate, which they never thought of before as having such an application in prayer.

I once knew an individual who was in great spiritual darkness. He had retired for prayer, resolved that he would not desist till he had found the Lord. He kneeled down and tried to pray. All was dark, and he could not pray. He rose from his knees, and stood for a while, but he could not give it up, for he had promised that he would not let the sun go down before he had given himself to God. He knelt again, but it was all dark, and his heart was as hard as before. He was nearly in despair, and said in agony, "I have grieved the Spirit of God away, and there is no promise for me. I am shut out from the presence of God." But his resolution was formed not to give up, and again he knelt down. He had said but a few words, when this passage came into his mind as fresh as if he had just read it; it seemed as if he had just been reading the words, "Ye shall seek me, and find me, when ye shall search for me with all your heart" (Jeremiah 29:13). Though this promise was in the Old Testament, and was addressed to the Jews, it was still as applicable to him as to them. It broke his heart like the hammer of the Lord in a moment. He prayed and rose up happy in God.**

This often happens when those who profess to be Christians pray for their children. Sometimes they pray and are in darkness and doubt, feeling as if there were no foundation for faith and no special promises for the children of believers. But while they plead, God shows them the full meaning of some promise, and their soul rests on it as on the mighty arm of God. I once heard of a widow who was greatly exercised about her children till this passage was brought powerfully to her mind: "Leave thy fatherless children with me, I will preserve them alive" (Jeremiah 49:11). She saw it had an extended meaning. She was enabled to lay hold on it, as it were, with her hands. Then, she prevailed in prayer and her children were converted. The Holy Spirit was sent into the world by the Savior to guide His people, instruct them, bring things to their remembrance, and convince the world of sin.

The Holy Spirit leads Christians to desire and pray for things of which nothing is specifically said in the Bible. For example, that God is willing to save is a general truth; therefore, it is also a general truth that He is willing to answer prayer. But how shall I know the will of God respecting a specific individual; that is, whether or not I can pray in faith according to the will of God for the conversion and salvation of a specific individual? In this situation, the agency of the Holy Spirit comes in and begins His work. The Holy Spirit will lead the minds of God's people to pray for those individuals, and at those times, when God is prepared to bless them. When we know not what to pray for, the Holy Spirit leads the mind to dwell on some object, to consider its situation, to realize

Principles of Peace — Finney's Lessons on Romans

its value, and to feel for it, and pray, and travail in birth, till the object is attained. This sort of experience I know is less common in cities than it is in some parts of the country, because of the infinite number of things to divert the attention and grieve the Spirit of God in cities. I have had much opportunity to know how it has been in some sections of the country. I was acquainted with an individual who used to keep a list of persons that he was specially concerned for; and I have had the opportunity to know a multitude of persons for whom he became thus interested who were immediately converted. I have seen him pray for persons on his list when he was literally in an agony for them; and have sometimes known him to call on some other person to help him pray for such a person. I have known his mind to fasten on an individual of hardened, abandoned character who could not be reached in any ordinary way. In a town in the northern part of New York, where there was a revival, there was a certain individual who was a most violent and outrageous opposer of the gospel. He kept a tavern and used to delight in swearing at a desperate rate whenever there were Christians within hearing; he did so on purpose to hurt their feelings. He was so bad that one man said he believed he should have to sell his place, or give it away, and move out of town, for he could not live near a man who swore so. A good man of prayer, the one I was speaking of, was passing through the town and heard of the case. He was very much grieved and distressed for the individual. He put him on his praying list. The case weighed on his mind when he was asleep and when he was awake. He kept thinking about him and praying for him for days. And the first we knew of it, this ungodly man came into a meeting and got up and confessed his sins and poured out his soul. His barroom immediately became the place where they held prayer meetings. In this manner the Spirit of God leads individual Christians to pray for things which they would not pray for unless they were led by the Spirit. And thus they pray for things according to the will of God.

Some may say this is a revelation from God. I do not doubt that great evil has been done by saying that this kind of influence amounts to "a new revelation." And many people will be afraid of it if they hear it called "a new revelation;" so much so that they will not stop to inquire what it means or whether the Scriptures teach it or not. They suppose their op-

The Spirit of Prayer

position to "a new revelation" is a complete answer to the idea. But the plain truth of the matter is this: the Holy Spirit leads people to pray. And if God leads a person to pray for an individual, the inference from the Bible is that God designs to save that individual. If we find by comparing our state of mind with the Bible that we are led by the Holy Spirit to pray for a person, we have good evidence to believe that God is prepared to bless him.

The Holy Spirit leads Christians to desire and pray for things of which nothing is specifically said in the Bible by giving to Christians a spiritual discernment respecting the movements and developments of God's providence. Devoted, praying Christians often see these things so clearly, and look so far ahead, as greatly to stumble others. They sometimes almost seem to prophesy. No doubt, some people may be deluded, and sometimes are so, by leaning to their own understanding when they think they are led by the Holy Spirit. But there is no doubt that a Christian may be made to see and to discern clearly the signs of the times so as to understand *by providence* what to expect, and thus to pray for it in faith. Thus they are often led to expect a revival, and to pray for it in faith, when nobody else can see the least signs of it.

For example, in a place where there had been a revival, a woman in New Jersey was very positive there was going to be another revival. She insisted that they had had the former rain, and were now going to have the latter rain. She wanted to have conference meetings appointed. But the minister and elders saw nothing to encourage it and would do nothing. She saw they were spiritually blind. So, she went forward and got a carpenter to make seats for her so she could have the meetings in her own house. There was certainly going to be a revival. She had scarcely opened her doors for meetings before the Spirit of God came down in great power. These sleepy church members found themselves surrounded all at once with sinners under conviction of sin. And they could only say, "Surely the Lord was in this place, and we knew it not." The reason such people as this woman understand the indication of God's will is not because of the superior wisdom that is in them, but because the Spirit of God leads them to see the signs of the times. Understanding the signs of the times is not by "a new revelation;" rather, they are led to see that converging of providences of God to a single point which produces in them a confident expectation of a certain result.

The degree to which the Spirit of God affects the minds of believers.

The text says, "The Spirit maketh intercession with groanings that cannot be uttered." The text means that the Spirit excites *desires too great to be uttered except by groans*. The Holy Spirit gives us desires that language cannot utter. The Spirit makes the soul too full to utter its feelings by words; therefore, the person can only groan them out to God, who understands the language of the heart.

How we know if it is the Spirit of God that influences our minds.

We will not know the influence of the Holy Spirit by feeling some *external* influence or agency being applied to us. Do not expect to feel your mind in direct *physical* contact with God. If such a thing can be, we know of no way in which it can be made sensible. We know that we exercise our minds freely, and we know when our thoughts are exercised on something that excites our feelings. However, we are not to expect a miracle to be wrought as if we were led by the hand, sensibly, or like something whispered in the ear, or any miraculous manifestation of the will of God. People often grieve the Holy Spirit away because they do not harbor Him and cherish His influences. Sinners often do this ignorantly. They *suppose* that if they were under conviction by the Holy Spirit that they would have such and such mysterious feelings, or perhaps a shock would come upon them which they could not mistake. Many Christians are so ignorant of the Spirit's influences, and have thought so little about having His assistance in prayer, that when they receive His influences they do not know it, and so do not cherish them, and yield to them, and preserve them. We are conscious of nothing in the case except the movement of our own minds. There is nothing else that we can feel. *We are merely aware that our thoughts are intensely employed on a certain subject.* Christians are often unnecessarily misled and distressed on this point, because they fear they do not have the Spirit of God. They feel intensely,

The Spirit of Prayer

but they know not what makes them feel this way. They are distressed about sinners; but why should they not be distressed, when they think of their condition? They keep thinking about them all the time, and why shouldn't they be distressed? Now, the truth is: the very fact that you are thinking upon the destiny of sinners is evidence that the Spirit of God is leading you. Do you not know that the greater part of the time these thoughts do not affect you so? Most of the time you do not think much about the case of sinners. You know their salvation is always equally important. But at other times, even when you are quite at leisure, your mind is entirely dark and vacant of any feeling for them. But now, although you may be busy about other things, you think, pray, and feel intensely about them, even while you are about business that at other times would occupy all your thoughts. Under the Spirit's influence, almost every thought you have is: "God have mercy on them." Why is this? Why, their case is placed in a strong light before your mind by the Spirit. Do you ask what it is that leads your mind to exercise benevolence for sinners, and to agonize in prayer for them? What can it be but the Spirit of God? There are no devils that would lead you so. If your feelings are truly benevolent, you are to consider it as the Holy Spirit leading you to pray for things according to the will of God.

You can recognize the influence of the Holy Spirit by testing or trying the spirits by the Bible and what the Bible teaches. People are sometimes led astray by strange fantasies and crazy impulses. If you faithfully compare your impulses with the Bible, you never need to be led astray. You can always know whether your feelings are produced by the Holy Spirit's influences by comparing your desires with the spirit and temper of true belief as described in the Bible. The Bible commands you to try the spirits: "Beloved, believe not every spirit, but try the spirits, whether they be of God" (1 John 4:1). Observe not only your own feelings in regard to others, but also, and more especially, study the teachings of the Spirit within you respecting our Lord Jesus Christ. "Hereby know ye the Spirit of God. Every spirit that confesseth that Jesus Christ is come in the flesh is of God. And every spirit that confesseth not that Jesus Christ is come in the flesh is not of God; and this is that spirit of Antichrist whereof ye have heard that it shall come; and even now already it is in the world" (1 John 4:2-3).

How to receive the influence of the Holy Spirit.

The influence of the Holy Spirit must be sought by fervent, believing prayer. Jesus Christ declared, "If ye then, being evil, know how to give good gifts to your children, how much more shall your heavenly Father give the Holy Spirit to them that ask him!" (Luke 11:13). Do you say, "I have prayed for Him, and He does not come"? It is because you do not pray right: "Ye ask and receive not, because ye ask amiss, that ye may consume it upon your lusts" (James 4:3). You do not pray from right motives. For example, a person who professed to be a Christian, and a principal member in a church, once asked a minister what he thought of his case: he had been praying week after week for the influence of the Holy Spirit and had not received Him. The minister asked him what his motive was in praying. He said he wanted to be happy. He knew those who had the Holy Spirit were happy, and he wanted to enjoy his mind as much as they did. Why, the devil himself might pray so! His motive was mere selfishness. When the minister told him this, the man turned away in anger. The minister saw that the man had never known what it was to pray. He was convinced he was a hypocrite, and that his prayers were all selfish, dictated only by a desire for his own happiness. David prayed with a right motive, that God would uphold him by His Spirit so he could teach transgressors: "Restore unto me the joy of thy salvation; and uphold me with thy free spirit. Then will I teach transgressors thy ways; and sinners shall be converted unto thee" (Psalm 51:12-13). Likewise, a Christian should pray for the Holy Spirit so he can be more useful and glorify God more; not in order to be more happy. Eventually, the man saw clearly where he had been wrong and he was converted. Perhaps you have been this way. You ought to examine and see if all your prayers are not selfish.

To receive the influence of the Holy Spirit, use the means adapted to stir up your mind on the subject and to keep your attention fixed there. If a person prays for the Holy Spirit, and then diverts his mind to other objects; uses no other means, but goes right away to worldly objects; he tempts God. He swings loose from his object, and it would be a miracle if he should get what he prays for. How is a sinner to get conviction of sin? Why, by thinking of his sins. That is the way for a Christian to obtain deep feeling, by thinking on the object. God is not going to pour these things on you without any effort of your own. You must cherish the slightest impressions of the Spirit. Take your Bible and go over the passages that show the condition and prospects of the world. Look at the world, look at your children, consider your neighbors; see their condition while they remain in sin; then, persevere in prayer and effort till you obtain the blessing of the Spirit of God to dwell in you. This was the way, doubtless, that Dr. Isaac Watts came to have the feelings which he has described in the second Hymn of the second Book, which you would do well to read:

My thoughts on awful subjects roll,
Damnation and the dead:
What horrors seize the guilty soul
Upon a dying bed!

Lingering about these mortal shores,
She makes a long delay,
Till, like a flood, with rapid force
Death sweeps the wretch away.

Then, swift and dreadful, she descends
Down to the fiery coast,
Amongst abominable fiends,
Herself a frighted ghost.

There endless crowds of sinners lie,
And darkness makes their chains;
Tortured with keen despair they cry,
Yet wait for fiercer pains.

Not all their anguish and their blood
For their past guilt atones,
Nor the compassion of a God
Shall hearken to their groans.

> Amazing grace, that kept my breath,
> Nor bid my soul remove,
> Till I had learned my Saviour's death,
> And well insured his love!***

Look, as it were, through a telescope that will bring it up near to you; look into hell, and hear them groan; then turn the glass upwards and look at heaven, and see the true Christians there, in their white robes, with their harps in their hands, and hear them sing the song of redeeming love; and ask yourself, "Is it possible, that I should prevail with God to elevate the sinner there?" Do this, and if you are not a wicked man, and a stranger to God, you will soon have as much of the spirit of prayer as your body can sustain.

To receive the influence of the Holy Spirit, you must watch unto prayer. You must keep a look out, and see if God grants the blessing when you ask Him. People sometimes pray and never look to see if the prayer is answered. Be careful also that you do not grieve the Spirit of God. Confess and forsake your sins. God will never lead you as one of His hidden ones, and let you into His secrets, unless you confess and forsake your sins. Not be always confessing and never forsake, but confess and forsake too. Make restitution wherever you have committed an injury. You cannot expect to get the spirit of prayer first and then repent. You cannot fight it through so. Church members and those who profess to be Christians, who are proud and unyielding and justify themselves, will never force God to dwell with them.

To receive the Spirit's influence, aim to obey perfectly the written law. In other words, have no fellowship with sin. Aim at being entirely above the world. Jesus commanded: "Be ye therefore perfect, even as your Father which is in heaven is perfect" (Matthew 5:48). If you sin at all, let it be your daily grief. The person who does not aim at this goal means to live in sin. Such a person need not expect God's blessing, for he is not sincere in desiring to keep all God's commandments.

The Spirit of Prayer

Those for whom the Holy Spirit intercedes.

The Holy Spirit intercedes for the saints, *for all true Christians*, for any who are saints. "Likewise the Spirit also helpeth our infirmities: for we know not what we should pray for as we ought; but the Spirit itself maketh intercession for us with groanings which cannot be uttered. And he that searcheth the hearts knoweth what is the mind of the Spirit, because he maketh intercession for the saints according to the will of God" (Romans 8: 26-27).

REMARKS

Why do you suppose so little stress is laid on the influences of the Holy Spirit in prayer, when so much is said about His influences in conversion? Many people are amazingly afraid the Holy Spirit's influences will be left out. They lay great stress on the Holy Spirit's influences in converting sinners. But how little is said, how little is printed, about His influence in prayer! How little complaining that people do not make enough of the Spirit's influences in leading Christians to pray according to the will of God! Never forget: *unless led by the Spirit, no Christian ever prays right*. He has natural power to pray, and so far as the will of God is revealed, is able to do it; but he never does unless the Spirit of God influences him. Just as sinners are able to repent, but never do unless influenced by the Holy Spirit.

This subject lays open the foundation of the difficulty felt by many on the subject of the "Prayer of Faith." They object to the idea that faith in prayer is a belief that we shall receive the very things for which we ask. They insist that there can be no foundation or evidence upon which to rest such a belief. In a sermon published a few years ago upon this subject, the writer brings forward this difficulty and presents it in its full strength. "I have," says he, "no evidence that the thing prayed for will be granted, until I have prayed in faith; because, praying in faith is the condition upon which it is promised. And of course I cannot claim the promise, until I have fulfilled the condition. Now, if the condition is that I am to believe I shall receive the very blessing for which I ask, it is evident that the promise is given upon the performance of an impossible condition, and is of course a mere nullity. The promise would amount to just this: You shall have whatsoever you ask, upon the condition that you first believe that you shall receive it. Now, I must fulfill the condition before I can claim the promise. But I can have no evidence that I shall receive it until I have believed that I shall receive it. This reduces me to the necessity of believing that I shall receive it before I have any evidence that I shall receive it—which is impossible."

The writer of that sermon misunderstands the influence of the Holy Spirit when leading the believer to pray the Prayer of Faith. The whole force of his objection arises out of the fact that he overlooks entirely the Holy Spirit's influences, which the Spirit exerts in leading an individual to the exercise of faith. It has been supposed that Mark 11:22-24 (and other similar promises on the subject of the Prayer of Faith) relate exclusively to miracles. However, suppose this were true. I would ask, "What were the apostles to believe when they prayed for a miracle? Were they to believe that the precise miracle would be performed for which they prayed?" It is evident that they were praying for the precise miracle. In the verses just alluded to, Christ says, "For verily I say unto you, that whosoever shall say unto this mountain, Be thou removed, and be thou cast into the sea, and shall not doubt in his heart, but SHALL BELIEVE THAT THESE THINGS WHICH HE SAITH SHALL COME TO PASS, he shall have whatsoever he saith. Therefore I say unto you, what things soever ye desire, when ye pray, BELIEVE THAT YE RECEIVE THEM, and ye shall have them." Jesus' teaching makes it evident that the thing to be believed, and which they were not to doubt in their heart, was that they should have the very blessing for which they prayed. Now, the objection of the writer (stated above) lies in all its force against this kind of faith when praying for the performance of a miracle. I argue. "If it be impossible to believe this in praying for any other blessing. it was equally so in praying for a miracle." I might also ask, "Could an apostle believe that the miracle would be wrought before he had fulfilled the condition?" I would answer, "Inasmuch as the condition was that he should believe that he should receive that for which he prayed. Either the promise is a nullity and a deception, or there is a possibility of performing the condition. Of course, Christ's promise was no deception, but a promise with conditions that could be fulfilled."

Now, I repeat, the whole difficulty lies in the fact that the Spirit's influences are entirely overlooked, and that faith which is of the operation of God is left out of the question. If the objection is good against praying for any object, it is as good against praying in faith for the performance of a miracle. The fact is, the Spirit of God could give evidence on which to believe that any particular miracle would be granted; could lead the mind to a firm reliance upon God, and to trust that the blessing sought would be obtained. Even today, the Holy Spirit can give the same assurance in praying for any blessing that we need. Neither in the one case nor the other are the influences of the Spirit miraculous. Praying is the same thing, whether you pray for the conversion of a soul or for a miracle. Faith is the same thing in the one case as in the other; it only terminates on a different object; in the one case on the conversion of a soul, and in the other on the performance of a miracle. Nor is faith exercised in the one more than in the other without reference to a promise; and a general promise may with the same propriety be applied to the conversion of a soul as to the performance of a miracle. And it is equally true in the one case as the other, that *no one ever prays in faith without being influenced by the Spirit of God*. And if the Spirit could lead the mind of an apostle to exercise faith in regard to a miracle, the Spirit can lead the mind of another Christian to exercise faith in regard to receiving any other blessing by a reference to the same general promise.

We are under *obligation* to believe that we shall receive the blessing for which we ask when a divine blessing is particularly named in a *biblical promise*. When the Bible makes a promise of a particular blessing, we have evidence, and are bound to believe, whether we receive any divine influence or not. Similarly, sinners are obligated to repent whether the Holy Spirit strives with them or not. Their obligation does not rest upon the Spirit's influences, but upon the powers of moral agency which they possess; upon their ability to do their duty. And *while it is true that not one sinner will ever repent without the influences of the Holy Spirit, still they have power to do so, and are under obligation to do so*, whether the Spirit strives with them or not. The same with the Christian. Christians are obligated to believe where they have evidence. And although the Christian never does believe, even where he has an express promise, without the Spirit of God, yet his obligation to believe rests upon his ability and not upon the divine influence.

We are under an *obligation* to believe that we shall receive the blessing for which we ask when God makes a revelation by *His providence*. We are bound to believe in proportion to the clearness of the providential indication.

We are under an *obligation* to believe that we shall receive the blessing for which we ask when there is a *biblical prophecy*. But in fact, we will not believe a providential indication or a biblical prophecy without the influence of the Spirit of God.

Where there is no biblical *promise*, divine *providence*, or biblical *prophecy*, on which to repose our faith, we are under no obligation to believe, *unless*, as I have shown in this discourse, *the Holy Spirit gives us evidence* by creating desires and leading us to pray for a particular object. In the case of those promises of a general nature, where we are honestly at a loss to know in what particular cases to apply them, it may be considered rather as our privilege than as our duty, in many instances, to apply them to particular cases; but whenever the Spirit of God leads us to apply them to a particular object, then it becomes our duty so to apply them. In this case, God explains His own promise and shows how He designed His promise to be applied; then, our obligation to make this application and believe in reference to this particular object remains in full force.

Some have supposed that Paul prayed *in faith* for the removal of the thorn in his flesh, and that his prayer was not granted. But they cannot prove that Paul prayed *in faith*. The presumption is all on the other side. Paul had no biblical promise, no biblical prophecy, no divine providence, no influence of the Spirit of God to lead him to believe and pray *in faith*. Some seem to think that the apostle might pray *in faith* without being led by the Holy Spirit, but this is impossible. Obviously, for them to assume that Paul prayed *in faith* is to assume either that he prayed in faith *without being led by the Spirit*, or that *the Spirit of God led him to pray for that which was not according to the will of God*. Impossible! The Holy Spirit will never lead anyone to pray contrary to the will of God or the Bible's

The Spirit of Prayer

teachings, commands, promises, or prophecies.

I have dwelt on this subject, because I want you to be careful not to grieve the Holy Spirit. *I want you to have high ideas of the Holy Spirit and feel that nothing good will be done without His influences.* No praying or preaching will be of any avail without the Holy Spirit. If Jesus Christ were to come down here and preach to sinners, not one would be converted without the Holy Spirit. Be careful then not to grieve Him away by slighting or neglecting His heavenly influences when He invites you to pray.

In praying for an object, you must persevere till you obtain it. Oh, with what eagerness Christians sometimes pursue a sinner in their prayers, when the Spirit of God has fixed their desires on him! No miser pursues his gold with so fixed a determination.

The fear of being led by impulses has done great injury by not being duly considered. A person's mind *may be led* by an *ignis fatuus* (a will-o'-the-wisp, a delusion or an illusion). But we do wrong if we let the fear of impulses lead us to resist the good impulses of the Holy Spirit. No wonder Christians do not have the spirit of prayer, if they are unwilling to take the trouble to distinguish the spirits; and therefore reject or resist all impulses and all leadings of invisible agents. A great deal has been said about fanaticism that is very unguarded and causes many minds to reject the leadings of the Spirit of God. "As many as are the sons of God are led by the Spirit of God" (Romans 8:14). It is our duty to try the spirits whether they be of God or not. We should insist on a close scrutiny and an accurate discrimination. There must be such a thing as being led by the Spirit. And when we are convinced the leading is from the Spirit of God, we should be sure to follow—follow on with full confidence that He will not lead us wrong.

We see from this subject the absurdity of using *forms of prayer*. The very idea of using *a form* rejects, of course, the leading of the Spirit. Nothing is more calculated to destroy the spirit of prayer and entirely to darken and confuse the mind as to what constitutes prayer than to use forms. *Forms of prayer* are not only absurd in themselves, but they are the very device of the devil to destroy the spirit and break the power of prayer. It is of no use to say the form is a good one. Prayer does not consist in words. And it matters not what the words are, if the heart is not led by the Spirit of God. If the desire is not enkindled, the thoughts directed, and the whole current of feeling produced and led by the Spirit of God, it is not prayer. Set forms are, of all things, best calculated to keep an individual from praying as he ought.

The spirit of prayer furnishes a test of character. The Spirit maketh intercession—for whom? For the saints. Those who are true Christians are thus exercised. If you are true Christians, you know by experience what it is to be thus exercised to pray by the Holy Spirit. Or you know when you have grieved the Spirit of God, so that He will not lead you. You live in such a manner that this Holy Comforter will not dwell with you or give you the spirit of prayer. If this is so, you must repent. Whether you are a Christian or not, do not stop to settle that, but repent, as if you never had repented. Do your first works. Do not take it for granted that you are a Christian, but go like a humble sinner and pour out your heart unto the Lord. You never can have the spirit of prayer in any other way.

You must understand this subject in order to be useful. Without the spirit of prayer, there can be no such sympathy between you and God that you can either walk with God or work with God. You need to have a strong beating of your heart with His, or you need not expect to be greatly useful. Understanding the spirit of prayer is important for your sanctification. Without such a spirit you will not be sanctified; you will not understand the Bible; you will not know how to apply it to your life or the situations you face. I want you to feel the importance of having God with you all the time. If you live as you ought, God says He will come unto you, make His abode with you, sup with you and you with Him.

If people know not the spirit of prayer, they are very apt to be unbelieving in regard to the results of prayer. They do not see what takes place, or do not see the connection, or do not see the evidence. They are not expecting spiritual blessings. When sinners are convicted, they think they are only frightened by such terrible preaching. And when people are converted, they feel no confidence and only say, "We'll see how they turn out."

Those who have the spirit of prayer know when the blessing comes. It was just so when Jesus Christ appeared. The ungodly religious leaders did

The Spirit of Prayer

not know Him. Why? Because they were not praying for the redemption of Israel. But Simeon and Anna knew Him (see Luke 2:25-38). How was that? Mark what they said; how they prayed and how they lived. They were praying in faith, and so they were not surprised when He came. So it is with such Christians. If sinners are convicted or converted, they are not surprised at it. They are expecting just such things. They know God when He comes, because they are looking out for His visits.

There are three classes of people in the church who are liable to error or who have left the truth out of view on this subject. *First*, there are those who place great reliance on prayer, and use no other means. They are alarmed at any special means and talk about your "getting up a revival." *Second*, there are those who use means, and pray, but never think about the influences of the Spirit in prayer. They talk about prayer for the Spirit, and feel the importance of the Spirit in the conversion of sinners, but do not realize the importance of the Spirit in prayer. And their prayers are all cold talk, nothing that anyone can feel, or that can take hold of God. *Third*, there are those who have certain strange notions about the sovereignty of God and are waiting for God to convert the world without prayer or means.

There must be in the church a deeper sense of the need of the spirit of prayer. The fact is that, generally, those who use means most assiduously, and make the most strenuous efforts for the salvation of people, and who have the most correct notions of the manner in which means should be used for converting sinners, also pray most for the Spirit of God, and wrestle most with God for His blessing. And what is the result? Let facts speak and say whether these people do or do not pray, and whether the Spirit of God does not testify to their prayers and follow their labors with His power.

A spirit very different from the spirit of prayer appears to prevail in certain portions of the Presbyterian church at the present time. Nothing will produce an excitement and opposition so quick as the spirit of prayer. If any person should feel burdened with the case of sinners, in prayer, so as to groan in his prayer, why, the women are nervous, and he is visited at once with rebuke and opposition. From my soul I abhor all affectation of feeling where there is none, and all attempts to work one's self up into feeling by groans. But I feel bound to defend the position that there is such a thing as being in a state of mind in which there is but one way to keep from groaning; and that is by resisting the Holy Spirit. I was once present where this subject was discussed. It was said that groaning ought to be discountenanced. The question was asked whether God could not produce such a state of feeling that to abstain from groaning was impossible? Some answered, "Yes, but *God* never does." If that answer were correct, then the Apostle Paul was egregiously deceived when he wrote about groanings that cannot be uttered. According to this answer, Jonathan Edwards was deceived when he wrote his book upon revivals. Revivals are all in the dark. Now, no man who reviews the history of the church will adopt such a sentiment. I do not like this attempt to shut out, or stifle, or keep down, or limit the spirit of prayer. I would sooner cut off my right hand than rebuke the spirit of prayer, as I have heard of its being done by saying, "Do not let me hear any more groaning."

I hardly know where to conclude this subject. I would like to discuss it a month, until the whole church could understand it and pray the prayer of faith. Beloved, I want to ask you if you believe all this? Or do you wonder that I should talk so? Perhaps some of you have had some glimpses of these things. Now, will you give yourselves up to prayer, and live so as to have the spirit of prayer, and have the Holy Spirit with you all the time? Oh, for a praying church! I once knew a minister who had a revival fourteen winters in succession. I did not know how to account for it till I saw one of his members get up in a prayer meeting and make a confession. "Brethren," said he, "I have been long in the habit of praying every Saturday night till after midnight for the descent of the Holy Spirit among us. And now, brethren," and he began to weep, "I confess that I have neglected it for two or three weeks." The secret was out. That minister had a praying church. Brethren, in my present state of health, I find it impossible to pray as much as I have been in the habit of doing and continue to preach. It overcomes my strength. Now, shall I give myself up to prayer and stop preaching? That will not do. Now, will not you, who are in health, throw yourselves into this work and bear this burden and lay yourselves out in prayer, till God will pour out His blessing upon us?****

The Spirit of Prayer

---

* Finney's revival lectures on prayer include: Lecture 4, "Prevailing Prayer;" Lecture 5, "The Prayer of Faith;" Lecture 6, "Spirit of Prayer;" Lecture 7, "Be Filled with the Spirit;" Lecture 8, "Meetings for Prayer." These lectures on prayer are compiled and edited into a devotional book of readings with daily prayers entitled, *Principles of Prayer*: Minneapolis, Bethany House Publishers, 1980. Compiled and edited by Louis Gifford Parkhurst, Jr.

**According to his autobiography, this was Finney's own experience.

***Hymn Number 630, Hymn 2, Book 2, "The Death of A Sinner" in *An Arrangement of the Psalms, Hymns, and Spiritual Songs of the Rev. Isaac Watts, D.D.*: Arranged by James M. Winchell, A.M., Second Edition, Boston: Lincoln & Edwards, and James Loring, Cornhill, James Loring, Printer, 1820.

****For Review: Answer the Study Questions on page 228, Cowles page 251.

Isaiah on Peace

For to us a child is born, to us a son is given, and the government will be on his shoulders. And he will be called Wonderful Counselor, Mighty God, Everlasting Father, Prince of Peace. Of the increase of his government and peace there will be no end. —Isaiah 9:6-7

You will keep in perfect peace him whose mind is steadfast, because he trusts in you. Trust in the Lord forever, for the Lord, the Lord, is the Rock eternal. —Isaiah 26:3-4

Lord, you establish peace for us; all that we have accomplished you have done for us. —Isaiah 26:12

The fruit of righteousness will be peace; the effect of righteousness will be quietness and confidence forever. —Isaiah 32:17

"There is no peace," says the Lord, "for the wicked." —Isaiah 48:22

How beautiful on the mountains are the feet of those who bring good news, who proclaim peace, who bring good tidings, who proclaim salvation, who say to Zion, "Your God reigns!" —Isaiah 52:7

But he was pierced for our transgressions, he was crushed for our iniquities; the punishment that brought us peace was upon him, and by his wounds we are healed. —Isaiah 53:5

"Though the mountains be shaken and the hills be removed, yet my unfailing love for you will not be shaken nor my covenant of peace be removed," says the Lord, who has compassion on you. —Isaiah 54:10

"Those who walk uprightly enter into peace; they find rest as they lie in death. —Isaiah 57:2

10

All Things for Good to Those That Love God

1847

And we know that all things work together for good to them that love God, to them who are the called according to his purpose.—Romans 8:28—KJV

And we know that in all things God works for the good of those who love him, who have been called according to his purpose.—Romans 8:28—NIV

In illustrating the subject presented in this verse, I shall show what the passage means, illustrate the manner in which this is accomplished, notice some particulars as illustrations of this truth, and show how we know this truth, as the text affirms that we do.

The Scripture text affirms a universal proposition.

The language of our text is universal. It affirms in an unqualified manner that all things work together for good to God's friends. Now it is a good rule of interpretation to understand scripture as it reads; that is, according to its most obvious sense—unless the nature of the affirmation or some circumstances pertaining to it seem urgently to demand a modification of this meaning. All sound-minded people follow this rule in interpreting both the Bible and all other books and documents.

There is nothing in the nature of the case to limit the meaning of this language. On this point especially there is ample room to enlarge very greatly—but my time will not permit. There is nothing in the context which demands any limitation, but much on the contrary which favors the universal construction. There is nothing anywhere in scripture that conflicts with this, understood as a universal truth. On the contrary, the Bible throughout teaches us that everything in the whole plan of God's universal government conspires to this result. All is adapted to befriend God's people and to promote their highest good. God is evermore controlling all things for the good of His children. He is their great and good Father.

The manner in which this result is accomplished.

The manner in which God accomplishes His purposes deserves special consideration, because there are many things affecting true Christians which in their present operation seem to work together for their evil and not for their good. It would require many sermons to investigate this subject thoroughly. At present I can only sketch a few leading principles.

The highest well-being of moral agents depends upon their holiness. This is perfectly obvious. Their holiness, moreover, is conditioned upon knowledge. There can be no holiness in an intelligent being without knowledge, and holiness can advance only as knowledge advances. In fact, *holiness is* nothing else but *conformity of heart to knowledge*, so that of course there must be knowledge or there could not be holiness. Therefore, knowledge is both the condition and measure of holiness.*

Obviously, then, everything that is a means of knowledge is also a means of holiness. If they are holy in character, whatever gives moral agents a knowledge of themselves will increase their holiness, for they would cease to be holy if they did not use their knowledge to increase their holiness.

All events that occur are providential; that is, they occur under the universal government of God, and occur as they do either because the hand of God controls and shapes them, or because His wisdom permits them to occur as they do rather than interpose to prevent them. Hence all events reveal God. No event can possibly occur which shall not teach moral agents something concerning God, or themselves, or something useful that they need to know. These events also teach us very much that reveals our relations to God and hence our duties toward Him. And these are precisely the things that are required to augment the blessedness of intelligent moral agents.

These remarks apply especially to all those events that fall directly within the range of our present knowledge. But things not within our present knowledge are so related to things that are as to have a remote bearing upon us, and hence will ultimately come to be known to us. It is probably not too much to presume that all events that ever did or ever shall occur in this world will ultimately be known to all the people of God, and hence will have an important bearing upon their holiness and highest well-being.

Some particulars which illustrate the doctrine of our text.

What we call *mercies* work for the good of those who love God. For if people love God, these mercies quicken their love and gratitude. Every real Christian knows this. It is a precious part of their daily experience. What we call *rebukes* also have the same tendency to good. Though they may seem evil, they are really among the good things that flow to us from the hand of our great Father. They serve to increase our knowledge of God. They show us His faithfulness and assure us that His heart is thoroughly set upon correcting all in us that is wrong—and strengthening all that is right. The rebukes of God's providence naturally serve to increase our virtue, and hence are often among the very best things God can give us.

The *crosses* of Christians work together for their good. Those very things that disappoint their plans and frustrate their schemes are often among the indispensable things for their real and highest welfare. They are the means by which God breaks them off from their own ways and shows them that they must not have any ways of their own at all. While people are in a state in which they can be crossed, they of course need more discipline. You may recollect the remark made by Dr. Payson that since he had given up his own will and quite lost it so as to have no will of his own, he had not known a single disappointment. He was perfectly satisfied with everything just as God arranged and ordered it, for he had no other will than God's will.** Now God is seeking to produce such a state of mind in His children that they will say, "I want only to do this or that according to the will of God. Nothing pleases me except what pleases Him. I want to learn His will before I have any special preference of my own. Then if His apparent will changes, I am perfectly pleased, for His will is always best." Now this state of mind should extend to all events wherein the special will of God is not known by revelation. Hence *crosses* are exceedingly well calculated for doing good to God's people and are most kindly and wisely designed for this end. We are not to suppose that it is agreeable to our Father to perplex and distress us; but it is agreeable to Him to discipline and chasten us, because He knows that the results are so precious. It often happens that people come to see the truth of this in their own case. Then they say, "Now I see how well it has been for me to be disappointed, and how good and wise my Heavenly Father has been in doing it." When I have seen people eagerly set upon some earthly good, I have said to myself, "They need to be disappointed, and God will doubtless do it. I shall think it strange if He does not. If they are real Christians and God loves and cares for them as His children, He will surely bring them under discipline to break off their hold upon the world and save their souls."

Afflictions should doubtless be accounted among our good things. The Bible teaches this truth in many passages. One says, "Before I was afflicted I went astray; but now have I kept thy word" (Psalm 119:67). Another verse testifies, "I know, O Lord, that thy judgments are right, and that thou in faithfulness hast afflicted me" (Psalms 119:75). *Afflictions,* therefore, are not to be regarded as evidences of peculiarly great guilt in those who experience them. The case of Job seems to have been designed to teach us this lesson. They rather evince the special faithfulness of God. Remember these truths: "For whom the Lord loveth he correcteth; even as a father the son in whom he delighteth" (Proverbs 3:12). And, "For whom the Lord loveth he chasteneth, and scourgeth every son whom he receiveth. If ye endure chastening, God dealeth with you as with sons; for what son is he whom the father chasteneth not?" (Hebrews 12:6-7).

All those *trials* which we call temptations are to be accounted among these good things. They very often establish our virtue and greatly develop and strengthen our graces. For this manifestly they were intended. Hence the apostle says, "My brethren, count it all joy when ye fall into divers temptations; knowing this, that the trying of your faith worketh patience" (James 1:2, 3).

The *responsibilities* which God throws upon His children are among the things that work for their good. We may perhaps be made to groan out under these things, and possibly stagger under their burden, yet shall they work out good at last. They are perhaps the very things that are needed to develop our powers. It may be that nothing less than these burdens would make us feel our need of God's daily support, and thus discipline us to daily dependence. Moreover, some perhaps are naturally so sluggish that God could not save them if He should not lay upon them almost crushing responsibilities.

Our own *infirmities* work out our good. How often do we see this! Physical infirmities and frailties teach us our dependence upon God, and bring us to walk softly with Him and before Him. They often compel us to exercise sobriety, temperance and self-control, and in this way often become our greatest blessings. Paul had a thorn in the flesh, a messenger of Satan sent to buffet him. What it was we are not told, but the result plainly shows that it was greatly useful to him. Now all such things are in certain points of view greatly trying and painful, yet in other respects they are exceedingly valuable. And when we shall ultimately come to see all their bearings, we shall see that Infinite Wisdom sent them, or at least permitted them, and then overrules them for our good.

Our very *mistakes* often work for our good. Said a pious man once who had fallen into a great error, "Now that is just like me—that is just like me! I see it now. I might not have seen myself as I am, if that had not happened." The same is doubtless true of the *sins* of those who love God. Peter's great sin in denying his Lord seems to have been greatly blessed—

that is overruled so as to work out good to him. So with the sins of the children of God generally. Yet they have no excuse for themselves and are none the less guilty for committing them, because God is so good and wise as to counteract some of their evil tendencies and bring good out of them instead of unmingled evil.

The *infirmities, mistakes, and the sins of others* are among the things that work for our good. Who does not know how much we are benefited by witnessing the sins of others! No thanks indeed to them that their sins are a warning to us, nor can this circumstance lessen their guilt. The *afflictions of others* often work out great good to us. The afflictions which we see others suffering may and often do have much the same beneficial result as if we endured them ourselves. So wonderfully has God framed the social economy of our nature and of society.

Plainly, all events that occur under the providence of God serve to promote the good of His people.

How we know this fact to be true.

The Apostle Paul says, "We know that all things work together for good to those that love God." Now, we cannot suppose he meant to say merely that all inspired people know this. He doubtless meant that all Christians *may* know it. Reason affirms that it must be so under the government of an infinitely wise and benevolent God. No one can take just views of the character of God without seeing that He must have had a plan for governing this world. He must have foreseen all possible and actual results. He must have provided that nothing should occur in vain. That is, *He must have determined to prevent the occurrence of all those events which He could not overrule for so much good as on the whole to justify Him in permitting their occurrence.* These conclusions are either the direct affirmation of reason, or they are arrived at by the plainest inferences from its intuitions.

That all things work for good is a truth of revelation, and Christians may know it because the Bible teaches it. The Bible everywhere directly or indirectly teaches that God is overruling all events for the good of the righteous.

All Things for Good to Those That Love God

Experience and observation universally teach the same thing. Who does not know that all real Christians can say this. Looking over their past history, they can say, "This and that; yea, all these things, have been made, through divine mercy and wisdom, to work out my good and fit me for more usefulness here, or, at least for more glory hereafter." It is instructive to see how many of the saints of God can set up here their *Ebenezer* (Stone of Help), and testify, "Hitherto has the Lord helped me!" (1 Samuel 7:12).

REMARKS

We may blame ourselves for that which upon the whole we do not regret. For example, a person may commit a sin, and of course, he is guilty and inexcusable for this, and ought most surely to blame himself for committing it. His intention is all wrong and he is entirely to blame for it. Yet on the whole it may not be a matter of regret that the sin viewed as an event occurred, because God has brought a vast amount of good from it. As a full illustration of this point, take the sin of Satan in tempting Judas and the sin of Judas in yielding to the temptation to betray Christ. This transaction in both Satan and Judas was all evil and nothing else but evil; and was none the less a sin and a great sin even though the Lord overruled it for so much good. Moreover, this good result has been infinitely great. The event therefore is not to be regretted on the whole, though Satan and Judas are none the less to be blamed, because the wisdom and the love of God have brought so much good from their sins.

You will all recollect the view given in the Bible of the sin of Joseph's brothers in selling him into Egypt. "Be not grieved," said he, "nor angry with yourselves that ye sent me hither, for God did send me before you to preserve life" (Genesis 45:5). They had sinned, but God had educed so much good from their sinful act that it was now fit that they should rejoice in those manifestations of wisdom and love.

God may blame us and often does, when perhaps *on the whole* He does not see cause to regret the occurrence of the event. Doubtless God blamed both Judas and Satan; yet, He does not regret *on the whole* that great event toward which their sin directly contributed. Referring to this event, Peter said, "Him, being delivered by the determinate counsel and foreknowledge of God, ye have taken, and with wicked hands have crucified and slain" (Acts 2:23). Their hands were none the less wicked for the good which the Lord brought forth as a result from their evil doing. And it surely may be that the event *as a whole* even, including the sins of Judas and of the wicked Jews, is not regretted by the Most High.

It does *not* follow from this that sin is the necessary means of the greatest good; or that God could not bring about a still greater good if all His creatures were perfectly obedient. It cannot be shown that in every instance where sin occurs, more good results than would have resulted if holiness had been in its stead. Indeed, we cannot conceive of any higher blessedness to the created universe than universal holiness and its consequent happiness. Now, if in every instance when sin occurs, holiness under the same circumstances had occurred, the result would of course be universal holiness, and a degree of blessedness, than which we can conceive of none higher. But it is not my intention now to enter at length into this often disputed subject.

I am aware that those who maintain that sin is the necessary means of the greatest good argue thus; "All holiness depends upon knowledge of God; many truths respecting the character of God could never have been revealed if sin had not occurred; therefore, sin is necessary to the greatest amount of holiness and consequently of real good." This reasoning would have weight if the case were such that creatures could not be holy without such knowledge of God as nothing can reveal but the occurrence of sin. But no one can suppose that such can be the case of moral agents under the government of God. The argument therefore only shows that sin having occurred, *the Lord makes the wisest possible use of it*; a fact which no one can reasonably doubt. The argument altogether fails to prove that the state of the universe is better now than it would have been if all had persevered in holiness under the light they had. But it is especially to my purpose to maintain that *God's overruling all things for good to His people forms no apology or excuse for sin*. No thanks to the guilty sinner that a God of infinite wisdom can and does manage to work good out of the sinner's intended evil. No thanks to the sinner, for he is altogether evil and wicked. He does not use it for good himself, nor mean it for good, no

All Things for Good to Those That Love God

more than the devil did in the case of Judas, or than Judas himself did.

Suppose Christ's death, and His death in precisely that manner, was the very best thing that could have occurred. No thanks to Judas or Satan for that; they meant only evil, and all the resulting good must be ascribed to God alone. Hence it does not follow that we should do evil that good may come. In fact, it is in the nature of the case impossible that a person should do evil for the sake of its resulting good. It is impossible that a person should sin for the sake of doing good thereby, and with this design.

Suppose a person said, "Let me sin on now for this is the way to do good!" Pause a moment and ask. "What is sin?" Surely, sin is not doing anything with the design of bringing about good; sin is mere selfishness, *sin is always a trampling down of the greater good for the sake of a far less good for oneself.* Sin, therefore, never can have the greatest good for its object. Every act that has the greatest good for its design, object or motive, is holiness, not sin.

I am fully aware that the doctrine of my text has been greatly abused. Some have said, "Because sin results in good, therefore let us sin on, and leave it with God to bring out the good which He needs sin in order to educe." But this is an outrageous perversion of this precious truth. The fact that God can overrule sin for good affords not the least mitigation of the guilt of any sinner. Every sinner is just as guilty as if all sin tended to evil only and as if God had no power or disposition to bring any good out of it whatever.

Very often, we are unable to see how the providence of God will result in our ultimate good. Events that affect us or our friends look utterly dark and we seem almost compelled to say with Jacob, "All these things are against me (Genesis 42:36). All this must be evil to me and mine, and cannot work out my good." But in such cases we are bound as believing children to dismiss the views which sight gives us, and fall back upon faith. We must now believe God, who says, "All things shall work together for good to those that love me. Let all my children believe that and trust their own kind Father!" In a world like this, framed for a state of trial, events should often assume such an aspect as this. It results in the trial of our faith. And here apply those most pertinent and consoling words of Jesus Christ, "What I do, thou knowest not now, but thou shalt know hereafter" (John 13:7). However much then the events of divine providence may make us smart, or throw us into perplexity, still let us fall back upon the unfailing promise: "All things shall work together for good to those that love God."

We see why we should give thanks for all things, and why everything that occurs is, in reference to God and His agency in it, a matter of gratitude. We see why we should thank Him for everything He brings about directly by His providence, and also for everything He allows to be done by moral agents and not preventing them from doing it. We should thank God for not preventing the murderous deeds of Judas and of Satan; for *He had wise and good ends in view in not preventing them*. Under the circumstances, the Lord did the very best thing He could in permitting those wicked beings to go on and consummate the murder of His own dear Son.

The same is true of every sin that occurs in the universe. So far as God has anything to do with it, we thank Him, because He does all things well; always doing even in respect to sin the very best thing that under all the circumstances of the case He can do. For this, then, we thank Him. But for what sinners do, we cannot thank them, for they intend only evil. They are to be cursed, not thanked, for their sins, and cursed none the less because *God always overrules their sin to make it result in just as much incidental good as He wisely can*.

We see why it is that we are required to rejoice always. Why should not Christians rejoice always in all that God is doing? Many of these things, I know, often seem for the present, not joyous but grievous. Yet, in their remote and ultimate bearings, they always work out great good, and the greatest good which under the circumstances God could effect. A person who is sick may need to resort to many unpleasant medicines. If maimed, he may have need for the best, but most painful, surgical operations. These things, though sad in many of their bearings, are yet good in their ultimate results; therefore, it is a cause of gratitude when they are skillfully and successfully performed. So with many of the events in daily life. They come mingled with sorrow, but good in their ultimate result; therefore, it would be a great mistake to estimate them only by their present evil, leaving out of view the greater resulting good.

All Things for Good to Those That Love God

Sometimes, people are in this state. "I know," say they, "that all things work together for good to those that love God; but I am thrown into such circumstances of perplexity and darkness that I cannot tell whether I am one of those who love God or not. The only emotions of which I am sensible are those of pain and agony. I am full of distress, and I can scarcely think of anything else. Especially I cannot feel on any other subjects but my own trials and sufferings." Now all such people should look at the attitude of their will and not of their emotions. If they would do so, they would see through this mist, and their perplexities would no longer harass them. I have often seen individuals in great distress, under deep trials and perplexities; but strengthening themselves in the Lord their God, they came forth from those scenes of tempest as the sun breaks out from an ocean of storms, all the more glorious for the long and fearful hiding of His beams. So the tried and believing Christian comes forth from his sorest trials having learned lessons concerning God unknown to him before. Now he sees that his trials are among the greatest blessings he ever received from the Lord.

Whatever befalls Christians is to be rejoiced in. Trials may befall our friends; perhaps our own children; but *if we have evidence that they love God, we may rejoice in everything that occurs to them.* What if afflictions come wave after wave; *all things shall issue in their ultimate good.* This is as sure as the word and the government of the eternal God. Even if we should see such a case as that of Job, and none perhaps ever looked more dark, yet even in view of such a case we should rejoice; for we might know that in every similar case as in that, *God prepares His afflicted child for a double blessing.*

So also in the trial of Abraham's faith in the matter of offering up Isaac. In this case some things are developed, not often noticed, things pertinent to the case of some Christians at the present day. You recollect, God commanded him to go and take his own son and put him to death, and then offer him as a sacrifice on an altar. "What!" Abraham might naturally have said, "What! God command me to kill my own son? The devil might do this, but how can it be that God should do it? Surely I never heard anything like this in the ways of God before! This contradicts everything I have ever seen or heard of the Lord Jehovah! He commands me to commit one of the most horrid crimes that ever can be committed. And then, this is my son of promise, and God has said that out of him He would make a great nation." Surely this was one of the most severe trials. It threw Abraham upon his naked faith. He had no resource but to fall back upon simple trust in the Lord, and say, "God has spoken—even the wise, the good, the just God, and now let me trust his name! He can raise my Isaac from the dead if need be in order to fulfill His promise." Thus Abraham stood his ground, and passed this great and fearful trial. Oh, how useful and blessed were the results of this trial to Abraham during all his future life and through all his glorious existence. How gloriously has this example of faith stood out before all the children of God from that day to this! How many have had their faith quickened, directed, edified, by this great example! And perhaps it is not too much to suppose that sooner or later all the angels of heaven will be blessed by the far-reaching influence of this example of trusting and obeying God.

It is a great mistake to overlook these future results of our trials. We ought ever to keep them full in our view. Doing so is indispensable in order to be able to rejoice continually in the Lord, and in all the events that occur under His all-pervading providence. If we fail to do so, how many things will disconcert us and make us stumble to the sore wounding of our peace with God and of our confidence in Him.

In continuing this subject, I shall show in the next lesson that the opposite to the doctrine of the text is true of the wicked; all things shall work together for their evil.**

---

* Editor's Note: I would add that holiness is also conformity of the heart to the truth, and Jesus is the way, the truth, and the life (see John 14).

** Edward Payson (1783–1827) was the pastor of the Congregational Church in Portland, Maine. His 3 volume *Works* had a great influence for subsequent generations of pastors and Christians.

*** *The Oberlin Evangelist*, January 6, 1847. The companion lesson follows this one (Lesson 11); to be followed by a later lesson on the same scripture text (Lesson 12). For Review: Answer the Study Questions on page 229, Cowles page 253.

11

All Events, Ruinous to The Sinner
1847

And we know that all things work together for good to them that love God, to them who are the called according to his purpose. —Romans 8:28—KJV

And we know that in all things God works for the good of those who love him, who have been called according to his purpose. —Romans 8:28—NIV

As we discuss this subject further, I shall attempt to show that *all events conspire to ruin the obstinate and finally impenitent sinner.* This fact is *not directly taught* in Romans 8:28, but *it is implied* in this text and in what the Bible teaches as a whole. Indeed, *this truth is abundantly taught in the Bible as a whole*, and it should serve as a warning to those who stubbornly remain unrepentant in their practice of sin.

I will show as a matter of fact that *all events* are ruinous to the sinner and that this is and must be a universal truth and applicable to all sinners, point out some particulars to illustrate this fact, show that we really know this to be true even as we know its opposite to be true of the people of God.

Principles of Peace — Finney's Lessons on Romans

This is and must be a universal truth.

Moral obligation is conditioned upon knowledge and is always equal to knowledge. Whatever increases knowledge increases guilt if moral obligation is not complied with and the individual continues to resist the light and its claims. Increasing guilt augments the sinner's ruin. The more guilty, the greater his punishment; therefore, whatever augments his guilt conspires and conduces to aggravate his ruin. It cannot be doubted a moment that all events that fall under the sinner's observation, or become known to him by any means whatever in this life, will increase his knowledge of God and of course his duty and obligation. All these will consequently conspire at once to augment his guilt and damnation.

All those events that remain unknown to the sinner during his present life may become known to him in the future life, and then may work out their legitimate results—increased knowledge—augmented guilt—more aggravated doom. This whole point may be rendered more plain and practical by some detail of illustration.

All the gifts of providence conspire to work out the sinner's ruin. Of these, the first is *the gift of existence*. The existence which God gives the sinner is a blessing to him if he uses it rightly, but a fearful curse to him if he abuses it. But he does abuse it in the worst possible manner as long as he lives in sin; just as long as he devotes the existence which God gives him to rebellion against his Maker—and what can be a greater and fouler abuse of existence than this! Every moment of life spent in sin must therefore prove a curse to the sinner. It goes to aggravate his guilt and of course his ruin. No sinner can avoid this fearful result, if he persists in sinning. Exist he must—he cannot prevent it—cannot put an end to his existence—for death only changes its place and mode— death does not bring it to an end. Live, then, each sinner must, and if he will go on in sin, he must go on augmenting his guilt and consequent ruin.

Reason is another gift of providence—a precious blessing if devoted to God—if used legitimately and faithfully according to its nature and design; but if trampled down, abused, set at naught; if its demands for right and for God are all repelled and denied, how fearful the guilt which its possession and abuse involves! In what respect do you differ from the

All Events, Ruinous to The Sinner

lower orders of created beings? They have understanding; they have will; but they lack reason; this then is your pre-eminence above them. And will you abuse this and bring yourself quite down to a level with them in your conduct? How can you do so without awful, shameful, damning guilt?

Conscience is one of the functions of the reason. Did your conscience ever stand up and accuse you? Did it ever set your sins in order before your eyes and make you see and feel their perfect guilt? If so, then you know something of that deathless worm of your future cup. You have had a little foretaste of the horrors of self-accusation and self-condemnation. Oh, there is nothing in your existence so terrible as this! If you allow yourself to trample down this law of God developed in your reason, you will arouse against your own soul a fearful power within your own bosom that you can never resist or appease! It will be heard—that dreadful tone of self-accusing—self-reproach—what can ever allay the pungency and anguish of its tortures!

Now consider the most commonly *desired gifts and bounties of providence*—the things on which you are prone to lay much stress. Suppose you have health and wealth, friends and education. What are they? Are they working together for your good—your real, highest, eternal good? This turns entirely on the question of whether they lead you to repentance, gratitude and love to God, or whether they only yield you the pleasures of sin for a season, augment your mercies, your ingratitude, your guilt and consequent damnation. You may call these things good, and if you would use them in serving God and let them lead your heart to Him in love and gratitude and sweet obedience, they would be truly a good to you; but if you remain a sinner, you are of course the greater sinner for having received and abused these greater mercies, and they can only work out for you a far more exceeding and eternal weight of damnation. You allow the Lord to load you down with His blessings here, and then abuse them so that they shall become only as millstones about your neck in the lake that burneth with fire forever. You know it must be so, and cannot be otherwise.

So it will be with all those *things by which you amuse yourself* and seek to augment your enjoyment in sin. You count yourself most happy if you can secure things; but oh! your final disappointment when you shall see how they are converted into curses to your soul! These very amusements may have diverted your attention from saving your soul. They may have fanned and fed the fires of unhallowed passion. They may have made you ten fold more the child of hell then otherwise you could have been, and thus they may have exceedingly augmented your final ruin.

Let us continue. What you deem your *good fortune* results in the same augmentation of guilt and damnation. You deem yourself most fortunate if you can secure earthly good; but oh! how do these things—abused—work out your deeper damnation! How they help to treasure up wrath against the day of wrath! Your Father sent that good fortune to turn your eye toward His kind hand—to touch your heart with gratitude, and lead you to repentance. You abuse and pervert everything, and swell the fearful measure of your awful doom!

Let the wicked go on his way according to his heart's desire, filling his cup with *earthly pleasures* and finding all things prosper in his hand; yet saith the word of Jehovah, "Woe unto the wicked! it shall be ill with him: for the reward of his hands shall be given him" (Isaiah 3:11).

Yet again, *the trials and the curses* that fall to the sinner's lot shall all have the same result. You complain of these things as if they worked out only evil and as if God designed them for no other end; but in this you altogether fail to comprehend the gracious designs of your Heavenly Father. He sends you earthly good to melt your heart and you abuse it and wax more hard in sin; then why should He not change His hand and at least make trial, if possibly reverses and disappointments will not bring you to reflection; or to see whether He cannot tear you away from your idols and make you search for the living God. He does so; but all is of no avail; you only fret and complain. Not so do Christians. If God sends them mercies they are grateful. If He sends chastisements, they are submissive. But how different is it with you! If God sends you mercies, you are thankless. You sit every day at the table which your Heavenly Father spreads and loads down for you; but you can do it each day with a heart as cold as a stone. It seems to be entirely out of the question for you to think of recognizing your Father's hand, or your own augmented obligation to serve and please Him. If on the other hand He sends afflictions upon

All Events, Ruinous to The Sinner

you, you complain and harden, not humble, yourself under His chastising hand. Oh, you ought to understand that these trials are a part of the discipline with which God seeks to subdue your soul to His scepter. And you ought to know that if His efforts fail, it is all evil to you, utterly and infinitely evil. Oh, indeed! If all the resources of infinite power, wisdom and love fail to change you, what can be more desperate than your case or more guilty than your heart? Your whole life of impenitence is filled up with such results. Does the Lord take away your friend? Then you repine; you feel that there never was a case so aggravated as yours, and you will not bow under the hand that chastises you. How unlike the Christians who when smitten look up to their own Father's hand, and bow beneath it; smile, love, trust, adore. But not so do you accept the punishment of your iniquity. Every effort the Lord makes to reclaim you renders you only more hardened, more guilty, more fitted for destruction.

It is indeed grievous beyond expression to see how these things work and what results are produced by all the *varied discipline* which the Lord employs to save your soul. It is painful to see that all these efforts only serve to harden your heart, until the Lord is forced to say of you, as He said to the ancient Jews: "Why should ye be stricken any more? ye will revolt more and more. The whole head is sick, and the whole heart faint. From the sole of the foot even unto the head, there is no soundness in it; but wounds, and bruises, and putrifying sores" (Isaiah 1:5-6). The original in this passage seems to convey the idea that they had been chastised till from the crown of the head to the soles of the feet there was no longer a sound spot where another blow could be inflicted. *The resources of chastisement were exhausted, and still no good result followed.* So it sometimes happens that a parent will chastise his child until he has no hope that more chastisement can do any good. This seems to be the state of mind which the Lord expresses respecting the Jews. And He often has occasion for this state of feeling toward impenitent sinners. He watches all round their path, searches out all the avenues of their heart; tries now mercies and then afflictions, and follows up the alternations perhaps year after year through a long life—but all in vain. Ah, worse! Often infinitely worse than in vain, for it only serves to augment the sinner's fearful guilt and final condemnation. Strange that sinners do not see that this is true and in the nature of the case must be. Strange you do not see that sickness, losses, judgments of every kind are designed to subdue your refractory spirit, and of course if they only serve to make you the more refractory, the result can be nothing less than a fearful aggravation of your guilt and ruin. Thus all your sins, instead of being overruled for your good, serve only to heap up a mountain load of guilt and swell the miseries of your doom.

The *deeds of others*, good, or bad, only enhance your guilt. I beg of you to look a moment at this fact. You live among professed Christians. If they are faithful to God and to your soul, and adorn the gospel by their life, this only hardens your heart, for you resist all the influences of their entreaties, prayers, tears, and godly life. On the other hand, if they dishonor the gospel, you take offence—you stumble over them, and become the more bold and hardened in your sins.

Now you know it would not be thus in either case with Christians. If they fell in with truly pious brothers and sisters in Christ, their hearts would be refreshed and their piety quickened. If with bad behaving church members, the result would be to quicken them to pray, to revive their own love for the Church, and their sympathy for the cause of Jesus Christ. So also, if Christians are persecuted, it only works good to them, teaching them forbearance and forgiveness of injuries; training them to love their enemies and bless those that curse them. Far otherwise with you, sinner. In fact, you never know what it is to be benefited by any conduct, good or bad, of others. All works only evil to you. Indeed, everything works out evil and only evil to you. The law of God—the gospel of God—the smiles of providence or its frowns; all possible conduct of others and all possible varieties in the course of the Lord toward you—rain or sunshine—storm or calm—prosperity or adversity—each and all serve only the one dreadful end with you—that of augmenting your guilt, and of course your final doom of misery.

Dreadful consideration! That your character should be such that all possible events work evil and evil only to your soul! If you had a full and a just view of your case as it is, you might truly say, "Whatever happens is all evil to me. Whatever the times are—times of revival, or times of declension—all is evil to me; times of plenty, or times of famine—all is

All Events, Ruinous to The Sinner

evil to me; times of health, or times of pestilence—all is alike, evil to me. All conspire to fill up the measure of my guilt and aggravate my eternal doom."

In looking at this, I have often felt as if I should sink—the view is so saddening, so awful. Sinners seem so stubborn and so refractory, and it is so obvious and sure that everything that occurs to the sinner must work evil and evil only to his guilty soul.

All those providential circumstances that befall others result alike in evil to the sinner. If his neighbors are sick, or if they are well, the sinner will abuse the warning voice of God through His providence. Perhaps the sinner thinks that such things as these are not going to have any effect on his own case, but they surely will and inevitably must. They are the voice of God to him, and he must hear or refuse. Continuing in sin, he does the latter, and of course augments his own guilt and damnation.

It matters not how these *events may affect your neighbor*, whether for good or for evil; they are in either case evil and only evil to you. The same event may work good to another; yet shall it be only evil to you. Consider the funeral we attended this morning when a dead child of God was laid in the grave as a true Christian. It may have touched your sympathies, and you may have been moved to pity over so early a death, but you might much more reasonably pity yourself. When I see sinners at a funeral, I know they are often saying to themselves, "I am glad that I am not there in the place of the dead;" and yet it may be better far that you should die now than that you should be spared any longer. Beyond all question it is better for you to die and be laid in the grave in the place of the first death that occurs rather than that you should live longer to make every death you hear of only an augmented curse to yourself. Oh, how horrible is this!

So also *to live in a land of Bibles and Sabbaths* and enjoy Christian instruction and choice influences enough to make you an angel of light: and yet abusing and perverting them all! You convert them into the worst form of curses. All the means God uses to save you are working evil to you. God means them for good, but you pervert them into evil. God would bless you, but you will curse yourself by the very means He uses for blessing you.

He would happily make all the events of His providence work out for you a far more exceeding and eternal weight of glory, but in spite of the endeavors of infinite love, you persist in working out of all these things your own deeper damnation.

All things work out evil to the sinner.

Though our text does not affirm this specifically, *the Bible does, along with reason, experience and observation.* That all things work out evil to the sinner is a truth that everyone's reason must affirm. Everyone knows that the occurring events of God's providence increase his knowledge of God and hence his obligation to love and obey God. Of course with this increase of light comes also increasing guilt in resisting its claims, and in the train of increasing guilt comes augmented ruin. Every sinner must know all this to be true. There is not a sinner in this house whose reason does not affirm each step in this process of argumentation to be true, and true as to himself.

Furthermore, this leads me to say that everyone's own experience will testify that until he turns from sin by real repentance, all the course of divine providence serves only to harden his heart. He knows that the longer he resists and the more light he has to oppose, the more hardened he becomes. All our observation of others testifies that this is true. We see the sinner growing old in his sins—resisting one call of God after another, breaking through every restraint, setting at naught the repeated warnings of divine providence. We always see such a sinner waxing fearfully hard of heart against God and the voice of his own conscience. I have often been shocked to see how fearfully hardened sinners sometimes become by resisting a long succession of means and influences adapted to bring them to repentance.

The truth we have been illustrating is evinced also by ample testimony from the word of God. The Bible seems everywhere to assume that all things do and shall work evil to the sinner who will not repent. The Bible solemnly warns, "He, that being often reproved hardeneth his neck, shall suddenly be destroyed, and that without remedy" (Proverbs 29:1).

All Events, Ruinous to The Sinner

REMARKS

Christians sometimes blame themselves for things the occurrence of which upon the whole they do not regret; so wondrously will God overrule those evil deeds of theirs for great good. Thus God will not leave them to bitter and eternal regret over the consequences of their failures or their sins, though they must forever condemn their own sins and blame themselves for sinning. It is one of the great mercies of the Lord toward them that He does not leave them under the pang of everlasting regret in view of unmingled evil resulting from their misdeeds.

On the other hand, sinners are left to the double anguish of everlasting self-blame and eternal regret over the utterly ruinous results to themselves of all their sins. Every event of their lives has been sin and only sin, and all have worked out the legitimate results of sinning, all evil to them and evil only and continually. Since they would not repent and would not open their hearts to the healing and restoring influences of God's providence and Spirit, the Lord could not counteract the natural tendency of sin on their heart to augment its moral hardness and consequently their own eternal ruin.

Sinners never have any good reason to rejoice with respect to their own prospects. In fact, remaining in sin, they have nothing in which they can reasonably rejoice. Those very events of their lives in which they are most apt to rejoice will probably be those which above all others will fill them with anguish hereafter. Those very seasons of prosperity in which you rejoice most now may be your bitterest grounds for regret and sorrow when you shall come to see all their legitimate results upon your character and doom. So long then as you continue in sin, so long you have absolutely nothing to rejoice in. The more you rejoice and deem yourselves prosperous and happy in earthly good, the more will these very things pierce and sting your soul through all your future existence.

As long as you remain an unrepentant sinner, others have no good reason to rejoice in anything that befalls you. The only valuable hope they can have is that it may lead you to repentance. This failing, all will work for evil and only evil to the sinner. It often happens that parents rejoice in events that befall their ungodly children. They rejoice perhaps to see them well settled in life, or peculiarly fortunate in business. But none of these things are ever looked upon on their true light except through the medium of the great truth we are now considering. Whatever leaves them still in their sins works fearful ruin to their souls, and the more joy it seems to bring, the more fearful will be its power to curse and embitter all their future being.

While it is true that no event, however grievous in itself, can befall a Christian which should make us grieve for him, it is equally true that no event can befall the sinner in which we are not compelled to grieve for its results upon him. Nothing can happen to him that will not fearfully curse him, if he still persists in sin. It may be ever so well adapted for his improvement, for his best good, for his happiness; yet shall he pervert it all to the greatest of evils to his soul. Think about a young man, an unrepentant sinner, going to college. It might prove a blessing to him, but it will prove to him only a curse. It will increase his knowledge, and thus augment his guilt. It will give him greater pre-eminence and influence; but if he improves this for greater sin and mischief, it will curse him at the last with tenfold destruction.

Think of an unrepentant married man with a beautiful, accomplished, pious wife—so much the worse for him. It only serves to swell the sum of his guilt and ruin. He may live in a land of Sabbaths, and in the midst of revivals; so much the worse; he may have pious, praying parents; so much the worse.

Sinners need not stumble at the trials of the people of God. No more or greater trials shall befall the Christian than are indispensable as means to work out for him a far more exceeding and eternal weight of glory. The truth is, God's people need these trials. They must be carried through many a fiery ordeal. What then? Let them rejoice, for all shall work out their good. Let them be made to weep; it shall work for their good. Let them be sick; it shall do them good. Let them lose their property; it shall be for their good. Let their friends die; all shall augment their good. Every Christian may say, "Whatever befalls me, the Lord will cause it to result in my greater good." Let a mighty wave dash over him, lifting high its crest and sweeping him along with torrent power; it does him good. Let another come with mighty force; it does him good. Another still; all

All Events, Ruinous to The Sinner

is good. There he stands amid those mountain-waves, happy in his God, for he believes that all shall work out good to his soul. This is only the discipline his Father sends him, and why should it not cheer his soul to think how all shall work out his eternal good.

Right over against this, everything is occasion of grief and dismay to the sinner, no matter how joyous his soul in its approach. "Whatever befalls me," he must say if he sees rightly, "all is evil to me. Be it storm or sunshine; whether I lie down in peace, or take my bed of pain and languishing, all is prospectively evil to my soul!" How awful this condition! But it is even so; and the intelligence of every being in the universe affirms that these results are all right and as they should be.

All events to all eternity will make the impassable gulf between Christians and sinners only the more deep and broad. The fact is, these two classes are oppositely affected by all the providences of God, and doubtless will be so, by all that shall occur to them throughout eternity. God has so constituted the human mind that in its selfish state, all right events shall work out only evil; while in its renewed state all shall work out good. Difference of character lays the foundation for this wide contrast in the result. Only the sinner himself is ultimately to blame that all things work evil to him. If he will do evil, then shall all things be converted into evil in their results to him.

It is infinite folly for anyone to estimate events only according to their present and most obvious bearings and relations. The result of this course is and always must be that people will constantly and fatally deceive themselves. If every sinner in this house could see all the final results of the events that are transpiring now, he would stand amazed and transfixed with horror. "What!" he would say, "Is untold anguish and horror coming out of this cup of my earthly joy?" Oh, if sinners could clearly see these things, they would not so often bless themselves for their good fortune.

The arrangements of providence in respect to both Christians and sinners are made with a design to illustrate the character of God. All the events of this life, and all that occur throughout eternity also, will all serve to illustrate the perfections of God. Not to have arranged all things for this end would have been a great mistake, but God never makes such mistakes. A wise and glorious end in view characterizes all God does.

It is the perverse course of the sinner and nothing else but this that makes the providences of God work out evil to him. Sinners are prone to pity themselves, and say, "Alas for me, for God has made my lot such that all things work only evil to me!" Let all sinners know that the fault is wholly and only their own, and that God has made the best possible arrangements for their good. It is only their perversion that makes the best things become to them the worst. And sinners cannot help knowing this. After all their complaining and fault-finding, they know that they have no plea to make against God. You know, sinners, that it is all your own fault that every day is not a blessing to you—that every sun-rising and sun-setting does not come fraught with mercies to your soul. You know that you might place yourself in such an attitude toward God that all His providences should work out your real and highest good. You are now an enemy of God; but you know you may at once become His friend. I can make the appeal to every sinner's own conscience. You know that if you would not harden your own heart, all the events of divine providence would result in your good. They would bring admonitions that you would give heed to with the greatest profit to your soul, and would throw you into scenes of discipline which could not fail to prove a blessing to you. Only yield your heart to the providences, the truth, and the Spirit of God, and you would become a child of God, and all things would work your good.

I can well remember how it seemed to me before my conversion. I then saw most clearly that all was good to the Christian. If he was sick, all was well to him. If in health, it was a real blessing. If he lived, it was to enjoy the friendship of God. If he died it was to enter upon his eternal reward. Being himself a friend of God, evil could no sooner befall him than it could befall his Great Friend, God himself. Nothing could be an evil to him, for if he were ever so much afflicted, it would only make him the more self-denying, meek, patient, heavenly.

But right over against this, the opposite in every respect, is the case of the self-hardening sinner. He puts on an air of self-confidence and enjoyment. He would be pleased to make you think that sinners are the only happy people on earth. He dances along his way for a brief season, but it

All Events, Ruinous to The Sinner

is on slippery places—and suddenly his feet slide—and he is in hell! So transient is all the bliss that sin and Satan give. It is only a lure to endless woe. If sinners only appreciated their real condition, they could not rest in sin one moment. All their levity would appear infinitely shocking to themselves. I recollect to have seen several cases in which sinners were in such a state of mind that they could not rejoice in any possible event. There is one lady among you today who could tell you a great deal about this state of mind—a state of darkness, despair and anguish, in which everything was clearly seen to be evil and only evil, and all things however apparently prosperous were working out evil and nothing else to her soul and her eternal state. If the sun shown sweetly, all was gloom, for that God who smiled through those sunbeams was her enemy. Each storm only reminded her of God's wrath against the sinner. If friends loved her and sympathized with her, all was evil—she had no friends above, and deserved none here below. So of everything that could occur. All was evil, undiluted, unassuaged. But when her soul came into the light and glory of the gospel, and found peace and joy in God, the whole scene was at once perfectly changed. Her husband has told me that he never knew her to fret or repine since that blessed hour. I asked her once what was the secret of her remarkable equanimity. She replied, "I escaped from the jaws of hell—from the dark iron castle of Giant Despair.* Ever since I have looked upon myself as a miracle of grace, and I cannot regard any of the little troubles of life as anything to be compared with those indescribable agonies. I am often amazed to see how small a thing can disturb the equanimity of true Christians or raise the mirth of the sinner."

If sinners are going to continue in their sins, they may as well bid farewell at once to all peace and joy; and welcome anguish and black despair to their souls. Let them say at once, "All things are evil and nothing but evil to me." Let them give themselves up to universal mourning, no matter how soon, or how utterly. "Hail everlasting horrors, hail!"

There is only one way of escape—open yet a moment longer. Turn to God; yield your whole soul to God; accept His Son, Jesus Christ, your Savior, and His service as your choice for life; then you are a child of God and His foe no longer. Then all things are yours—and you are Christ's, and Christ is God's. You are welcomed at once to the bosom of that glori-

Principles of Peace — Finney's Lessons on Romans

ous family above, and the possession of the riches and joys of heaven is all your own.

On the other hand, if you remain in your sins, as from present appearances you are likely to do, all events and all agencies possible will work out your destruction. Every step you take brings you nearer the vortex of that awful whirlpool—the great maelstrom of perdition. Your steps take hold of hell.**

---

* In *Pilgrim's Progress* by John Bunyan, Christian and Hopeful leave the highway for an easier, but forbidden, route through By-Path Meadow. They are caught by Giant Despair and imprisoned in Doubting Castle. Christian finally found the way of escape for them both.

** *The Oberlin Evangelist*: January 20, 1847. *Principles of Liberty*, 119-127. For Review: Answer the Study Questions on page 230, Cowles page 253.

12

All Things for Good to Those That Love God

1852

And we know that all things work together for good to them that love God, to them who are the called according to his purpose. —Romans 8:28—KJV

And we know that in all things God works for the good of those who love him, who have been called according to his purpose. —Romans 8:28—NIV

You will observe that the Apostle Paul speaks with all confidence. He does not say, "We *expect*, or we *believe*, or we *conjecture* that all will be well for God's friends." Rather, he declares, "*We know*." There is no doubt about the fact that in all things God works for the good of those who love Him.

We will consider what his language means, show how the result of good to all that love God is secured, illustrate some particulars of this general truth, and show how we know it to be true.

What the Apostle Paul means.

Regarding this verse, the great question is, "Shall his language be interpreted as strictly universal?" In terms, he announces a universal proposition. *All things*, he declares, work together for good to those that love God. But does he mean to affirm a proposition strictly universal? Not all universal language should be taken in a strictly universal sense. In the scriptures, we frequently find it necessary to modify universal language. There may be things in the text or context which forbid the universal sense; or there may be declarations in other parts of the Bible which preclude it, or the nature of the case may render the universal sense either violently improbable, or perhaps absurd, and hence may demand some modification. Remember, the language of the Bible is the language of common life, and everybody knows that in the language of common life we often affirm something in the form of a universal proposition when we really mean something much short of this. For example, it is common to say of a well known fact: "Everybody says so;" but by our "everybody," we do not intend to mean every single person in the world.

Regarding the language of our text, I understand Paul to be speaking in the strictly universal sense. He means that absolutely *all things*, present and future—all things, above and beneath—in heaven, earth, and hell—do and will conspire to the ultimate blessedness of God's people. The Bible obviously teaches this doctrine, and I know of no facts in the universe that militate against its universal application.

How true Christians secure this result.

In order to see this matter in its true light, we need to consider that the happiness of moral agents is conditioned on their holiness and results from it. Those who live holy will of course be happy and have real enjoyment in proportion to the degree in which they are holy. Still further, remember that the holiness of moral agents is conditioned upon their knowledge. Every moral agent is more or less holy according to what he knows more or less and is more or less conformed in heart and life to what he knows. I speak now particularly of the knowledge of God, whether obtained through His word or through His works. Now, all events are matters of knowledge, and not only all events that occur under God's government, but God himself is also an object of knowledge. According to the Bible, all events will ultimately be known to true Christians, for the judgment day will bring them all to light. Hence we learn that ultimately the entire history of all God's doings will be known to all His creatures. All God has ever done or shall ever do—whether in this world or in other worlds—will be open subjects of knowledge to His creatures, and will be known as fast and as far as their limited capacities will admit.

Plainly, if all things embracing all events and all the works of God are matters of knowledge, and if knowledge is a condition of real holiness, then all the knowledge which true Christians attain will be at once available to their happiness. It will go to enhance their real blessedness. Especially will this be true of all their knowledge of God and of His countless works and various ways. *All things*, true Christians will then see, are parts of one great plan—both those which God himself performs by His direct agency, and those which are done through His permissive agency by His creatures. It will then be seen that all things are arranged and planned for the good of His obedient children, and when this great all-controlling principle in God's administration comes to be seen in all its bearings, the knowledge of this truth cannot fail to be a source of ineffable blessedness to all who live holy. God's infinite grace, as the great and good Father of all His loving children, will be so revealed as to show that He makes all things work together for their good.

Some particulars that illustrate this general truth.

In general, what we call mercies and blessings, and what we recognize by name as God's good gifts, are really good things to those that love God. We can see that they are, and people universally recognize them as good. The same is equally true of what we call judgments and chastisements—the rebukes of God; for all these too are means of grace, and are blessed of God for the spiritual good of His children. Their only design as they come from our Father's hand is that they may work out good to His children. He does not afflict willingly nor grieve His children from caprice or from any pleasure in their pain, but only and wholly for their profit, that they may the more deeply partake of His holiness. Under this broad principle, we know that all the losses and crosses which befall true Christians—all their burdens of care and responsibility and all their infirmities—shall be overruled for their good. All these things will conspire to teach true Christians more of God and more of themselves. By the aid of such revelations they will be able the better to appreciate God's character and plans of discipline and their own infinite obligation to His manifold grace.

We cannot exclude from the "all things" of our text the sins of God's people. Sinners are indeed altogether blameworthy for all their sins and not the less so for the good which God educes from them by His overruling agency. The sin of Peter was overruled by God for his good. He was a more humble and a better man as long as he lived. He better knew his own weakness, and better appreciated Christ's tender compassion. He felt the force of Christ's admonition, "When thou art converted, strengthen thy brethren" (Luke 22:32). There was not one among all the original twelve disciples to whom Christ said more emphatically, "Feed My sheep; Feed My lambs" (John 21:14-17). The sin of Peter brought him into great peril; for Jesus warned him, "Simon, Simon, behold, Satan hath desired to have you, that he may sift you as wheat" (Luke 22:31). If Christ had left Peter to himself, he would doubtless have fallen fatally into the snare of the devil. But Christ did not leave him in this hour of his need. He encouraged him with the words: "But I have prayed for thee, that thy faith fail not: and when thou art converted, strengthen thy brethren" (Luke 22:32). Christ kept His hand and eye on him, and soon plucked him from the destroyer's grasp. In this situation, Peter learned more of the length and depth of his Savior's grace than he had ever known before. This is only a single case, yet it was by no means a peculiar case, and therefore it serves to illustrate the general law of God's administration over His people.

The case of King David was similar. No thanks to David, but all thanks to God, that his sin was overruled so as to make him a more meek, humble, penitent, and holy man.

Not only are the sins of true Christians overruled to their good, but the sins of others, of unrepentant sinners, and even of the most wicked, are overruled for the good of those who love God. All the mistakes of our associates, all their infirmities, and all the thousand nameless things that try us among the "all things," God makes subservient to the good of His people.

There is a woman whose husband is a bad man. His will not control his temper. His ways are adapted to make his intimate associates unhappy, and hence he causes his wife many sore trials. Yet if she loves God and makes Him the Refuge of her soul, all these little trials shall certainly work out for her good both in this world and the next. Not less so of the husband who has a bad wife. Not less so of those unhappy families in which the husband and the wife are great trials to each other. So of parents and children. Parents may be a source of trial to their children, and it often happens that children are a source of the greatest trial to their parents. But howsoever the trials occur, the great principle of our text applies to them all. To those that love God, they shall all work together for good.

The principle also reaches and applies to all the temptations of the devil. Let him poison his darts with demoniac skill and hurl them with hellish malice, they will not ultimately harm those who sincerely love God. "The name of the Lord is a strong tower into which the righteous run and are safe" (Proverbs 18:10). The Christian has a panoply complete, wherewith he may be able to withstand all the fiery darts of the devil. And what is more to our present purpose; though wounded by these darts, he shall not be slain, though cast down he shall not be destroyed, for there is a healing, overruling hand under whose agency even the wounds that Satan inflicts shall be wrought into better health and more spiritual vitality than true Christians enjoyed before. God knows how to foil Satan with his own weapons and make even his apparent temporary success react in terrible defeat and disgrace upon his own head. God knows how not only to rescue His children but to do much more than simply to rescue them: He imbues them with new vigor and sanctifies to them their most bitter and humiliating experience.

Yet further, "all events" are designed to illustrate God's true character. The whole creation is only a revelation of God, and all events that occur in it only serve to reveal more and more of God to intelligent beings. "The heavens declare the glory of God; the firmament showeth his handiwork" (Psalm 19:1). How many lectures upon God are read to us by the silent stars! How many lessons are repeated to us day by day by His rising suns and nightly dews and timely showers! Where in all the works of God, whether in nature or providence, is there a thing that does not speak His praise and bear some testimony which He can bless to the souls of true Christians?

How we know all things work together for good to true Christians.

Paul says so. How did he and his brethren know this to be true? Perhaps they knew it by revelations already made in God's word. Or, maybe Paul's mind rested on this truth because of his general knowledge of God. It is a matter of revelation: the Bible amply affirms this truth. It is also a plain dictate of reason: when we come to understand what God's attributes are as affirmed by the reason, we see that such a God can allow nothing to occur which shall not in some way result in good to His friends. This must be so, if it be true that God loves His friends, studies to promote their highest good, has all events under His control, had His choice in the depths of a past eternity among all possible events and could determine to cause and allow to exist such only as should serve the ends that lay near His heart.

We often experience and observe in this world that things which seem freighted with destruction turn out to be full of life and salvation. For a time, all looked dark and desolate, but light and joy came out at last. Look at the case of Job. You can scarcely think of one form of grief and sorrow which did not blend in the sufferings that rushed upon him as if to crush him: but he lived to see all these things work together for good to himself both for time and eternity. So in general, I remark that observation and experience will often show that this doctrine applies even to the present life and has its exemplification even here. *Still, the apostle did not mean to affirm that God's plans have their full development in the present world. His affirmation contemplated a future world in which results but partially unfolded here can have their full and everlasting development.*

All Things for Good to Those That Love God

REMARKS

In eternity, true Christians will blame themselves for what they cannot *on the whole* regret. Seeing the results which God has educed by His overruling agency, they cannot wish they had never done those wicked things; yet surely they will none the less blame themselves for their own sins. As to the blame of sin, no matter how much good may come from our wrongdoing, it never can affect the question of our guilt or its measure. Take the case of Judas. No thanks to him that his infamous treason was one of the agencies which provided a Savior for a ruined world. The good which accrued from the death of Christ changes not the intrinsic character of his sin; cannot in any measure make it less mean, less sordid, less revengeful. Hence, he must blame himself as much as if no good but only evil had resulted from his betrayal of Christ. God alone, by His own infinite wisdom and power, overruled this sin to great good. All praise therefore to God, and none the less blame to Judas the traitor.

Our subject shows how true Christians can be perfectly happy in heaven to all eternity. For there is in many minds a point of obscurity in this matter which needs explanation. God's children will see all their past sins in heaven's clear light, and they cannot but blame themselves for every sin they ever committed. How then can they be perfectly happy? The answer is, they will see how their sins have been overruled for good, and they will rejoice in this good which God brings out of their iniquities. In this exercise of joy, they will be deeply humble, as indeed they will have all reason to be, and their joy will be purely a joy in God, blended with everlasting adoration and praise that He had both the power and the heart to bring much good out of their own wrong doings. Every view taken by a Christian in heaven of his past sins will redound in praise to God and in deeper humiliation to himself. Yet this humiliation will by no means conflict with the Christian's happiness—for he enjoys being humble—he enjoys giving all glory and praise to God.

God blames a multitude of things, but has no regrets. He has often expressed himself as we do when we feel regret, but these forms of expression are shaped in accommodation to our modes of speaking, and when used by God should be interpreted in accordance with His known character and known relations. It cannot be that *on the whole*, under all the circumstances of the case, that He really regrets the occurrence of anything that takes place. He blames the guilty sinner; He condemns the sin; but it has not taken Him by surprise; it is no new thing to Him, and it has not in any way frustrated His purposes and plans for the government of the universe. Before any sin was committed or the sinner existed, God saw how He could overrule it for good; and for so much good that *on the whole* He judged it better to let its author come into existence and commit this sin rather than prevent either the one or the other. Yet, He blames every sin as much as if no good could be educed from it. The sinner is none the better for this development of good through God's overruling agency. To God alone belongs all the praise, because both the good intention and the good results are His alone. Except for His good hand interposing, all the results would have been evil, and the sinner's intention is of course all evil and only evil continually.

Still, while God blames both sinners and true Christians for all their sins, He freely forgives those who believe and repent; and He accepts them as His children. Then, He so overrules their sins so as not to be agonized by anything that occurs. We sometimes see results corresponding to this in the earthly discipline which parents exercise over their children. The parent sees that his child has sinned; at first he regrets the thing exceedingly; but having in the fear and help of God done his utmost to reclaim and improve his child, he sees his efforts crowned with the divine blessing, and he says. "That sin of my dear child almost killed me, but now I see him so much changed for the better that I can no longer regret the means which have resulted in so much good."

From closely examining this subject, remember this: it does not follow that sin is the necessary means of the greatest good. For, if under the very circumstances in which they sin, people would obey rather than disobey, do right rather than wrong, then yet greater good might accrue than accrues from God's overruling of their sin. But God prefers His own course to any other which He can take. Under the circumstances, He always does the wisest and best thing possible to Him, and hence He has no occasion for regret. He brings out the greatest good possible to himself. If His creatures who do in fact sin would be persuaded to do right instead of wrong, their agency for good concurrent with His would educe a still augmented good.

All Things for Good to Those That Love God

Consider this illustration: a father commands his son to perform some certain work. But he has good reason to believe that the son will not do it unless he himself stays at home to control the son by his presence. Yet it is so important for him to go away that he decides to go, though at the hazard of his son's disobedience. In case the son disobeys, he trusts he can subject him to such discipline as shall bring out some good, and the good to be secured by his own presence elsewhere is too great to be sacrificed. The greatest good possible can be secured only by the concurrent agency of father and son. The father can secure the greatest good possible to himself by going away, even though his son should disobey in his absence.

If God so overruled sin, so that in the end sin became the means of the greatest good, no thanks to the sinner. Suppose it were the case that the whole world would have been damned if Judas had not betrayed Christ, so that his sin secured the salvation of the world—no thanks to Judas for such a result, for Judas did not mean to secure the salvation of the world, neither did his heart think so. He intended no good to the world, nor to any being in it except himself. His act of betraying his friend would be none the less mean, sordid, and revengeful, for the good which in the case supposed would ensue. The good wrought out would be wholly attributable to God.

It is naturally impossible to sin benevolently. There can be no such thing as a benevolent sin. To sin with design to do good is an absurdity in terms; therefore, to say that we do evil that good may come is absurd and impossible. To do evil for the sake and with the motive of securing real good is a self-contradiction. Doing evil implies a wicked intention. Having a good end in view implies a good intention. But to have both a good intention and a bad intention at the same instant, each determining the same act, is surely a self-contradiction. If a man intends good by his act, it is not sin. No man ever sinned in order that it might redound to the glory of God. No tyrant ever persecuted the children of God that it might do them good. Suppose a wicked man said, "My wife is a good woman; let me plague her now for her good. It will only make her a better woman, so let me torment her all I can. There is no way in which I can do her so much good." He can't do any such thing! It is naturally impossible that a man should be honest in trying to do good by wickedness. This sinning benevolently is a natural impossibility.

True Christians should always be in a position to fall back upon God in all their trials in this life. They should stand in such relations to God that they can rationally and naturally trust Him to shape and control all events even here so as to make them work out good in the highest degree. If they walk humbly before God, they may know that all things shall be made to conspire for their good. Only let them truly love God and trust Him; then they need not fear the issues of any events whatever that may occur. None can occur without God's permission, nor independently of His direction. They may therefore be assured that God will shape all their bearings for the good of those that love him. However, if those who profess to be Christians are living in sin, they have no claim on this promise and no right to expect its fulfillment to themselves. But if they are not in sin, they may like Micah cry out triumphantly, "Rejoice not against me, O mine enemy; when I fall, I shall arise; when I sit in darkness, the Lord shall be a light unto me" (Micah 7:8).

The "all things" truth will afford a ground for strong consolation to all true Christians. Why should they ever be sad? Suppose all things do not apparently work out well in this present life. Let them still have faith in God and rest in His promises. Has He not said that all things shall work together for good to His loving friends? No wonder God's children are often seen smiling through their tears, for joy lies deep in their souls, though sadness may over-cloud their face. Joys and sorrows are often strangely blended in their bosom. Calamities, disappointments, bereavements befall them as they do others, and these things are not for the present joyous but grievous; however, their faith in God assures them that all will yet be well. Many things will befall them in life that burn and agonize their sensibility; but deep within are trust and faith in God and a sweet leaning upon His promises—for they know that the ground of their consolation is as firm and as strong as the pillars of the universe!

We may rejoice in whatever befalls any of God's real children; whether ourselves or others. Parents may rejoice in whatever befalls their godly children or friends. Many things may occur which cause tears now; yet, as Christians, our watchword should be, "It will surely be well for them in the latter end." The things which give the severest shock will do most good, and those which seem most afflictive, when God has brought out all their results, may be found to be most blest to His children. Those fearful events which seemed to come with a crash as if they would break down all the pillars of your foundation—Oh how sweet to see even those strange things so strangely overruled for the good of true Christians!

Very few Christians can live a single week, or even a day, without needing the consolation which this truth affords. Hence they ought to hold it fast, keep it treasured in their memory—lying near their hearts—ready to be applied for consolation and for strength in every emergency.

This truth may well reconcile God's people to any and all events of divine providence. They can afford to be submissive, while they know that their Father will make all things work together for their good. They can afford to have travail and suffering, for even their most intense sorrows shall all conspire to work out good to their souls Therefore, let not unbelief deprive us of this consolation. Apart from the light of faith many things will occur that are inexplicably dark, but faith illumines and explains all.

How wonderful are God's marvellous works. Well may it be said of Him: "He is wonderful in counsel and excellent in working" (Isaiah 28:29). Results may lie hidden long, but they will come out at last in glorious sunlight, showing that God's hand has guided events to their results with unerring wisdom. In the light of eternity if not in the light of time, they shall see it all, and seeing it shall wonder and adore. "God," they will shout aloud, "hath done all things well!" (Mark 7:37). Then, do not allow yourselves now to be deprived of this great consolation.

Now, do you say, "Ah, if I only knew that I am a child of God, if I only knew that I really love God, then I could receive this consolation legitimately. Then I could feel that it belongs to me. Then I could say, 'Let come anything that God is pleased to send, for I am anchored in His love and on His promise.'" You may be guilty of having these doubts, for surely you may be free from them altogether; but still, if with all your doubtings, you are really God's child, they shall all be overruled for your good, so that in heaven you will have it to say, "How wonderful are God's ways! That He should bring me out of a region, so dark and desolate, and then make all my doubts and darkness serve some useful ends to my own soul and to His glory—that out of such materials God should bring out any good at last! How wonderful!"

Finally, we can see that the volumes of glory and praise to God must be to all eternity continually accumulating. Fresh revelations each hour of God's wonderful wisdom and love must evolve from humble and holy hearts fresh accessions of praise and honor to His blessed name. Is is not delightful to think that such a God shall be thus praised and honored through eternity!*

The Oberlin Evangelist: July, 7 1852; *Sermons on the Way of Salvation*, 217-233; *Principles of Victory*, 128-136. For Review: Answer the Study Questions on page 231, Cowles page 253.

13

Religion of the Law and the Gospel
1837

What shall we say then? That the Gentiles, which followed not after righteousness, have attained to righteousness, even the righteousness which is of faith. But Israel, which followed after the law of righteousness, hath not attained to the law of righteousness. Wherefore? Because they sought it not by faith, but as it were by the works of the law. For they stumbled at that stumblingstone; As it is written, Behold, I lay in Sion a stumblingstone and rock of offence: and whosoever believeth on him shall not be ashamed. —Romans 9:30-33—KJV

What then shall we say? That the Gentiles, who did not pursue righteousness, have obtained it, a righteousness that is by faith; but Israel, who pursued a law of righteousness, has not attained it. Why not? Because they pursued it not by faith but as if it were by works. They stumbled over the "stumbling stone." As it is written: "See, I lay in Zion a stone that causes men to stumble and a rock that makes them fall, and the one who trusts in him will never be put to shame." —Romans 9:30—NIV

Principles of Peace — Finney's Lessons on Romans

In the *Epistle to the Romans*, the Apostle Paul pursues a systematic course of reasoning to accomplish a particular design. In the beginning, he proves that not only the Gentiles, but also the Jews, were in a state of entire depravity; and that the Jews were not, as they vainly imagined, *naturally holy*. He then introduces the Moral Law, and by explaining it shows that by works of law no flesh could be saved. His next topic is "Justification by Faith" in opposition to "Justification by Law." The next subject, with which Paul begins chapter 6, is to show that sanctification is by faith; or that true Christianity, all the acceptable obedience there ever was in the world, is based on faith. In the eighth and ninth chapters, Paul introduces the subject of divine sovereignty; and in the last part of the ninth chapter, he sums up the whole matter, and asks, "What shall we say, then? What shall we say of all this? That the Gentiles, who never thought of the law, have become pious, and obtained the holiness which is by faith; but the Jews, attempting it by the law, have entirely failed. Wherefore? Because they made the fatal mistake of attempting to become pious by obeying the law, and have always come short, while the Gentiles have obtained true religion by faith in Jesus Christ." Jesus Christ is here called "that stumbling-stone," because the Jews were so opposed to Him. But whosoever believes in Him shall not be confounded.

I propose to point out as distinctly as I can the true distinction between *the religion of law* and *the religion of faith*. I shall proceed in the following order: show in what the distinction does not consist; show in what the distinction does consist; bring forward some specimens of both to show more plainly how they differ.

In what the distinction between the two does not consist.

The difference between *the religion of law* and *the religion of faith* does not lie in the fact that under the law people were justified by works without faith. The method of salvation in both dispensations (in the Old and New Testaments or in the Old and New Covenants) was the same. Sinners were always justified by faith. The Jewish dispensation pointed to a Savior who was to come, and if people were saved at all, it was by faith in the Messiah who was to come. Today, sinners are saved by faith in Jesus

Religion of the Law and the Gospel

Christ, who has come and will come again.

Furthermore, the difference between *the religion of law* and *the religion of faith* does not lie in the fact that the gospel has cancelled or set aside the obligations to obey of the moral law. It is true that the gospel has set aside the claims of the ceremonial law or the law of Moses. The ceremonial law was nothing but a set of types pointing to the Savior; therefore, it was set aside when the great ante-type, Jesus Christ, appeared. All true believers now admit that the gospel has not set aside the moral law of God, and that doctrine has been maintained in different ages of the church. Unfortunately, many have maintained that the gospel has set aside the moral law so that believers are under no obligation to obey it. Such was the doctrine of the Nicolaitans, so severely reprobated by Christ. Antinomians, in the days of the apostles and since, believe that they are without any obligation to obey the moral law. They believe that Christ's righteousness was so imputed to believers, and that He so fulfilled the law for believers, that they are under no obligation to obey the law themselves.

In these days, there are many called Perfectionists, who believe that they are not under obligation to obey the moral law. They suppose that Christ has delivered them from the moral law and given them the Spirit, so the leading of the Spirit is now to be their rule of life instead of the moral law of God. Where the Bible says that sin shall not have dominion over believers, these Perfectionists understand by it that the same acts which would be sin if done by an unconverted person are not sins for them. Other people, they say, are under the moral law and so are bound by its rules; however, they themselves are sanctified and are in Christ; therefore, if they break the moral law it is no sin. But all such notions must be radically wrong. God has no right to give up the moral law. He cannot discharge us from the duty of love to God and love to others, because this is right in itself. Unless God alters the whole moral constitution of the universe so as to make that right which is wrong, He cannot give up the claims of the moral law. In addition, this doctrine of Perfectionism represents Jesus Christ and the Holy Spirit as having taken up arms openly against the government and moral law of God.

The distinction between *law religion* and *gospel religion* does not consist in the fact that the gospel is any less strict in its claims or allows any greater latitude of self-indulgence than the moral law. Not only does the gospel *not* cancel the obligations of the moral law, but it does in no degree abate them. Some people talk about *gospel liberty* as though they had received a new rule of life, a way of living less strictly and that allows them more liberty than the moral law allows. I admit that it has provided a new method of justification, but it everywhere insists that the rule of life is the same with the law. The very first sentence of the gospel, the command to repent, is in effect a re-enactment of the law, for it is a command to return to obedience. The idea that the liberty of the gospel differs from the liberty of the law is erroneous.

Neither does the distinction consist in the fact that those called legalists (or those who have a legal religion) do either by profession or in fact depend on their own works for justification. It is not often the case, at least in our day, that legalists do profess dependence on their own works, for there are few so ignorant as not to know that this is directly in the face of the gospel. Nor is it necessarily the case that they really depend on their own works. Often they really depend on Christ for salvation. But their dependence is false dependence, such as they have no right to have. They depend on Christ, but they make it manifest that their faith, or dependence, is not that which actually "worketh by love," or that "purifieth the heart," or that "overcometh the world." It is a simple matter of fact that the faith which legalists have does not do what the faith does which people must have in order to be saved; therefore, it is not the faith of the gospel. They have a kind of faith, but not that kind that makes people real Christians and brings them under the terms of the gospel.

Some of the particulars in which these two kinds of religion differ.

There are several different classes of people who manifestly have a *legal religion*. There are some who really profess to depend on their own works for salvation. Such were the Pharisees. The Hicksite Quakers formerly took this ground, and maintained that people were to be justified by works; setting aside entirely justification by faith. When I speak of works, I mean *works of law*. And here I want you to distinguish between *works of law* and *works of faith*. This is the grand distinction to be kept

Religion of the Law and the Gospel

in view. It is between works produced by *legal considerations*, and works produced by *faith*. There are only two principles on which obedience to any government can turn: one is the principle of hope and fear, under the influence of conscience. Conscience points out what is right or wrong, and the individual is induced by hope and fear to obey. The other principle is confidence and love. You see this illustrated in families where one child always obeys from hope and fear; and the other child obeys from affectionate confidence in their parents. So in the government of God, the only thing that ever produced even the appearance of obedience is one of these two principles.

A multitude of things address our hopes and fears; such as character, interest, heaven and hell, etc. These may produce external obedience, or conformity to the law. But *filial confidence leads people to obey God from love*. This is the only obedience that is acceptable to God. God not only requires a certain course of conduct, but He also requires that this course of conduct spring from love. There never was and never can be in the government of God any *acceptable obedience* but the *obedience of faith*. Some suppose that faith will be done away in heaven. This is a strange notion! As if there were no occasion to trust God in heaven, or no reason to exercise confidence in Him. Here is the great distinction between the *religion of law* and *gospel religion*. Legal obedience is influenced by hope and fear, and is hypocritical, selfish, outward, constrained. *Gospel obedience is from love*, and is sincere, free, cheerful, true. There is a class of legalists who depend on works of law for justification, who have merely deified what they call a principle of right, and who have set themselves to do right. Their obedience is not from respect for the law of God or out of love to God, but just because it is right.

There is another distinction here. The *religion of law* is the religion of purposes or desires founded on legal considerations, and not the religion of preference or love to God. The individual intends to put off his sins; he purposes to obey God and be religious; but his purpose does not grow out of love to God, but out of hope and fear. It is easy to see that a purpose founded on such considerations is very different from a purpose growing out of love. But the *religion of the gospel* is not a purpose merely, but *an actual preference consisting in love*.

Principles of Peace — Finney's Lessons on Romans

Another class of legalists depends on Christ, but their dependence is not gospel dependence, because the works which their dependence produces are works of law; that is, from hope and fear, not from love. Gospel dependence may produce, perhaps, the very same outward works, but *the motives are radically different.* The legalist drags on a painful, irksome, moral, and perhaps, outwardly, religious life. The gospel believer has an affectionate confidence in God, which leads him to obey out of love. His obedience is prompted by his own feelings. Instead of being dragged to do his duty, he goes to it cheerfully because he loves God and doing his duty is a delight to his soul.

There is another point. The legalist expects to be justified by faith, but he has not learned that he must be *sanctified by faith*. I propose to examine *sanctification by faith* another time in full.* Modern legalists do not expect to be justified by works; they know these are inadequate—they know that the way to be saved is by Christ. But they have *no practical belief* that justification by faith is as true as sanctification by faith is true, and that people are justified by faith only as they are first sanctified by faith only. And therefore, while they expect to be justified by faith, they set themselves to perform works that are works of law.

I wish you to observe that the two classes may agree in these points; the necessity of good works, and, theoretically, in what constitutes good works; that is, obedience springing from love to God. And further, they may agree in aiming to perform good works of this kind. But the difference lies here; in the different influences to which they look to enable them to perform good works. The considerations by which they expect their minds to be affected are different. They look to different sources for motives. *The true Christian alone succeeds in actually performing good works*. The legalist, aiming to perform good works, influenced by hope and fear, and a selfish regard to his own interest, obeying the voice of conscience because he is afraid to do otherwise, falls entirely short of loving God with all his heart, and soul, and strength. The motives under which he acts have no tendency to bring him to the obedience of love. The true Christian, on the contrary, so appreciates God, so perceives and understands God's character in Christ as begets such an affectionate confidence in God that he finds it easy to obey from love. Instead of finding it as a

Religion of the Law and the Gospel

hymn has strangely represented, "Hard to obey, and harder still to love," he finds it no hardship at all. The commandments are not grievous (1 John 5:3). The yoke is easy and the burden is light (Matthew 11:30). And he finds the ways of wisdom to be ways of pleasantness, and all her paths to be peace (Proverbs 3:17).

Is it so with most who profess to be Christians? Is it so with YOU? Do you feel in your religious duties constrained by love? Are you drawn by such strong cords of love, that it would give you more trouble to omit duty than to obey? Do your affections flow out in such a strong current to God that you cannot help but obey? How is it with those individuals who find it "hard to obey, and harder still to love?" What is the matter? Ask that wife who loves her husband if she finds it hard to try to please her husband? Suppose she answers in a solemn tone, "O yes, I find it hard to obey and harder still to love my husband," what would the husband think? What would any one of you who are parents say, if you should hear one of your children complaining, "I find it harder to obey my father, and harder still to love?" The truth is, there is a radical defect in the religion of those people who love such expressions and live as if they were true. If any of you find religion a painful thing, rely on it, you have the religion of the law. Did you ever find it a painful thing to do what you love to do? No. It is a pleasure to do it. The religion of the gospel is no labor to those who exercise it. It is the feeling of the heart. What would you do in heaven, if religion is such a painful thing here? Suppose you were taken to heaven and obliged to grind out just so much "religion" every week and month and year for eternity. What sort of a heaven would it be to you? Would it be heaven, or would it be hell? If you were required to have ten thousand times as much as you have here, and your whole life were to be filled up with this, and nothing else to do or enjoy but an eternal round of just such duties, would not hell itself be a respite to you?

The difference lies here. One class strives to be religious from hope and fear, and under the influence of a conscience which lashes them if they do not do their duty. The other class acts from love to God and the impulses of their own feelings, and know what the text means which says, "I will put my law in their inward parts, and write it on their hearts, I will be their God, and they shall be my people" (Jeremiah 31:33).

Some specimens of these two classes by way of illustration.

For the first example, reconsider that of the Apostle Paul as he recorded it in the Seventh Chapter of Romans (see Lesson 1: *Legal Experience*) where he exhibits the struggle to obey the law under the influence of law alone. He struggled and labored under the motives of the law until he absolutely despaired of help from that quarter; and then, when the gospel was brought to view, the chain was broken and he found it easy to obey.

You may see the same in the experience of almost any convicted sinner after he has become truly converted. He was convicted, the law was brought home to his mind, he struggled to fulfill the law, he was in agony, and then he was filled with joy and glory. Why? He was agonized under the law, he had no rest and no satisfaction, he tried to please God by keeping the law, he went about in pain all the day, he read the Bible, he tried to pray; but the Spirit of God was upon him, showing him his sins, and he had no relief. The more he attempts to help himself the deeper he sinks in despair. All the while, his heart is cold and selfish. But now let another principle be introduced, and let him be influenced by love to God. The same Holy Spirit is upon him, showing him the same sins that grieved and distressed him so before. But now he goes on his knees, his tears flow like water as he confesses his guilt, and his heart melts in joyful relentings, such as cannot be described, but easily understood by them that have felt it. Now he engages in performing the same duties that he tried before. But, O, how changed! The Spirit of God has broken his chains, and now he loves God and is filled with joy and peace in believing.

The same thing is seen in many who profess to be Christians and find obedience and the practice of Christian principles a painful thing. They have much conviction, and perhaps much of what they call religion, but their minds are chiefly filled with doubts and fears, doubts and fears, all the time. By and by, perhaps, that same person will come out, all at once, a different character. His Christianity is now not all complaints and sighs, but the love of God fills his heart and he goes cheerfully and happily to do his duty. His soul is so light and happy in God that he floats in an ocean of love, peace, and joy that fills him like a river.

Here, then, is the difference between *the slavery of law* and *the liberty*

Religion of the Law and the Gospel

of the gospel. The *liberty of the gospel* does not consist in being freed from doing what the law requires, but in a person's *being in such a state of mind that doing what the moral law requires is itself a pleasure* instead of a burden. What is the difference between slavery and freedom? The slave serves because he is obliged to do so, the freeman serves from choice. The person who is under the bondage of the law does his duty because his conscience thunders in his ears if he does not obey, and he hopes to go to heaven if he does. The man who is in the liberty of the gospel does the same things because he loves to do them. One is influenced by selfishness, the other by disinterested benevolence [love without self-centered concern or selfishness].

REMARKS

If we believe the words and actions of most who profess to be religious, they have made a mistake; they have the religion of law and not the gospel religion. They are not constrained by the love of Christ, but are moved by hopes and fears and the commandments of God. They have gone no further in religion than to be convicted sinners. Within the last year, I have witnessed the regeneration of so many who thought they were Christians but were deceived that I am led to fear that great multitudes in the church are still *under the law*; and although they profess to depend on Christ for salvation, their faith is not the faith which works by love.

Some people are all faith, without works. These are Antinomians. Others are all works, but no faith. These are Legalists. In all ages of the church, some people have inclined first to one of these extremes, and then over to the other. Sometimes they are settled down on their lees, pretending to be all faith and waiting God's time. Then they get roused up and dash on in works without regard to the motive from which they act.

You see the true character of those who profess to be religious who are forever crying out "Legality!" just as soon as they are pressed up to holiness. When I first began to preach, I found this spirit in many places; so that the moment Christians were urged to do their duty, the cry would rise, "This is legal preaching, do preach the gospel; salvation is by faith, not by duty; you ought to comfort Christians, not to distress them." All this was nothing but rank Antinomianism.

On the other hand, the same class of churches now complain if you preach faith to them and show them what is the true nature of gospel faith. They now want to do something, and insist that no preaching is good that does not excite them, and stir them up to good works. They are all for doing, doing, doing, and will be dissatisfied with preaching that discriminates between true and false faith, and urges obedience of the heart out of love to God. The Antinomians wait for God to produce right feelings in them. The Legalists undertake to get right feelings by going to work. It is true that going to work is the way, when the church feels right, to perpetuate and cherish right feelings. But it is not the way to get right feeling in the first place, to dash right into work without any regard to the motive or ultimate intention of the heart.

Real Christians are a stumbling block to both parties; to those who wait God's time and do nothing, and to those who bustle about with no faith. The true Christian acts under such a love to God and others, and he labors to pull sinners out of the fire with such earnestness, that the waiting party cry out, "O, he is getting up an excitement; he is going to work in his own strength; he doesn't believe in the necessity of divine influences; we ought to feel our dependence; let us wait God's time, and not try to get up a revival without God." So they sit down and fold their hands, and sing, "We feel our dependence, we feel our dependence; wait God's time; we don't trust in our own works."

On the other hand, the legalists when once they get roused to bustle about will not see but their religion is the same with the real Christian. They make as strenuous outward efforts and suppose themselves to be actuated by the same spirit. You will rarely see a revival in which this does not show itself. If the members of the church are awakened to duty and have the spirit of prayer and zeal for the conversion of sinners, there will be some who sit still and complain that these church members are depending on their own strength. Others will be very busy and noisy but without any feeling. While others will be so full of love and compassion toward sinners that they can hardly eat or sleep, and yet so humble and tender that you would imagine they felt themselves to be nothing. The legalist, with his dry zeal, makes a great noise, deceives himself, perhaps, and thinks he is acting just like a Christian. But mark! The true Christian

Religion of the Law and the Gospel

is stirring and active in the service of Christ, but moves with the holy fire that burns within his own bosom. The legalist depends on some protracted meeting, or some other influence from without, to excite him to do his duty.

You see why the religion of some is so steady and uniform, while the religion of others is so fitful and evanescent. You will find some individuals who seem to be always engaged in religion. Talk to them any time on the subject and their souls will kindle.

Others are awake only now and then. Once in a while you may find them full of zeal. The truth is, when one has the anointing that abides he has something that is durable. But if his religion is only that of the law, he will have only just so much of it as he has of conviction at the present moment, and his religion will naturally be fitful and evanescent.

You see why some are so anxious to get to heaven, while others are so happy here. There are some who have such a love for souls, and such a desire to have Christ's kingdom built up on earth, that they are perfectly happy here and willing to live and labor for God as long as He chooses to have them. Nay, if they were sent to hell and permitted to labor there for souls, they would be happy. Others talk as if people were never to expect true enjoyment in this life; but when they get to heaven they expect to be happy. One group has no enjoyment but in hope. The other group has the reality already, the very substance of heaven begun in their souls.

Now, beloved, I have as particularly as I could in the time pointed out to you the distinction between the *religion of the law* and the *religion of the gospel*. And now, what religion have you? True Christian faith is always the same and *consists in disinterested love to God and others*. Have you that kind of Christianity? Or, do you have the kind of religion that consists, not in disinterested love, but in the pursuit of your own personal happiness as the great end and goal of your life? Which religion do you have? The fruit of the Holy Spirit includes love, joy, and peace. There is no condemnation of such faith (Galatians 5:22, 23). But if you do not have the Spirit of Jesus Christ, you are not of Him. Now, don't make a mistake here and allow yourself to go down to hell with a lie in your right hand because you have the religion of the law and are under the law. The Jews failed here, while the Gentiles attained true holiness by the gospel.

O, how many are deceived and acting under legal considerations, while they know nothing of the real experience of Christians under the gospel of Jesus Christ!**

---

* See especially Finney's lesson *Sanctification by Faith* on Romans 3:31, in *Principles of Righteousness*, pages 67-78.

** Charles G. Finney, *Lectures to Professing Christians* (1880), 270-282, *Principles of Victory*, 137–145. For Review: Answer the Study Questions on page 233, Cowles page 255.

Study Questions for Individuals and Groups

The study questions in *Principles of Peace* will serve as a review and help you focus your thoughts on some of the main teachings in each of Charles Finney's sermons or lessons on Paul's *Letter to the Romans*. You can use these questions for personal enrichment and for small group study. Experience indicates that probably no more than five questions can be discussed fully in one hour, so you may want to omit some questions, hold a longer discussion, or cover each lesson in two meetings (encouraging people to read the lesson again before your next meeting). The study questions that are obviously phrased for a group discussion can be thought about and answered individually. All of your answers could be written in a personal journal. For additional help in the interpretation of Finney's lessons on Romans, refer to the commentary on the various verses by Henry Cowles which follows these questions, beginning on page 235.

Principles of Peace — Finney's Lessons on Romans

1. Legal Experience

1. What seems to be the prevailing view or interpretation in the church today regarding Romans, Chapter Seven?

2. Did Finney's lesson influence you to make any changes in your views? If so, what were these changes? Did Finney's lesson reinforce any of your views? If so, how were your views reinforced by his teaching?

3. What did you learn from Finney's lesson on Chapter Seven that you could use in a discussion with someone about the prevailing view in the church today regarding this chapter?

4. How does Romans Chapter Seven describe a sinner under conviction of sin or a person who professes to be a Christian, but is acting under the motives of the law instead of the motives of the gospel? How does Finney define a backslider?

5. What would you tell a person who thinks he is a good Christian, if in fact he describes his spiritual experiences as being those of a person acting under the motives of the law instead of the motives of the gospel?

6. How does Finney define and distinguish, compare and contrast, these two terms: "desire" and "will"? What is the difference between "would not" and "could not." Explain the difference in regard to the sinner. Why does Finney find it so important to define his terms and give rules of interpretation?

7. Define regeneration or conversion in one sentence. Now, write a a one page explanation of that sentence and how one is regenerated or converted.

8. Describe the character of a converted person and how it differs from the unconverted person.

9. Explain "the constitutional approbation of truth and the law of God." How can you use this concept in talking to the unconverted sinner?

10. Define and describe the real condition of the true Christian and contrast this with the real condition of the sinner under conviction of sin and the sinner prior to being under conviction of sin. Why do people need to know these definitions?

2. *Christ the Husband of the Church*

1. In what ways might Christians help others understand the true nature and function of marriage and the family by teaching about Christ as the Husband of the church?

2. How might the world's changed or changing concept of marriage, what constitutes marriage, and the nature of the family have an effect upon people's understanding of Christ as the Husband of the Church?

3. How has the understanding of the relationship between a husband and a wife changed since Finney's day, as Finney describes marriage in this lesson? If you are in a class, discuss this changed understanding with others in the class and how this change has had an effect on the church and society. Do you think this changed understanding is for the better or for the worse? Explain your reasons.

4. If you think this changed understanding is for the worse, what do you think the church and others might be able to do to "turn things around"? What do you think the consequences will be in the church and world, if the state of marriage and the family continues to decline as it has in the past?

5. How would you recognize whether or not your church or fellowship is governed by Christ's will? What are some things believers in a church can do to make certain their church is governed by Christ's will or continues to be governed by Christ's will?

6. Give some reasons why every believer in Jesus Christ is kept safe from all attacks by any earthly or demonic powers?

7. Explain what Finney means by this statement: "Jesus Christ holds himself responsible before God for all the conduct of His church. Every believer is so a part of Jesus Christ, and so perfectly united to Him, that whatever sins any of them may be guilty of, Jesus Christ takes upon himself to answer for. This is abundantly taught in the Bible." Do you agree or disagree with Finney? Explain your answer. If you agree with Finney, how does this make you feel? How does it have an effect on your thinking, on your worship, on your prayers, on your service of Christ and His Church?

8. What are two of the most important reasons you can think of for the Bible (and Finney) teaching about Christ's relationship to the Church as a marriage relationship? How does the Church benefit from this marriage relationship?

9. In what ways do churches today behave as an unfaithful wife to Jesus Christ? In what ways can churches be encouraged to become faithful to Christ again?

10. As the bride of Christ, what are some of the consequences of our sins? Can you think of some consequences that Finney has not discussed in this lesson? How can understanding the consequences of sin help believers in the future? What solutions or resources does Finney discuss to help the believer live free from sin?

3. Revival of Sin and the Law

1. Paul had been taught the law from his childhood, what does Finney say Paul did not understand about the law or was ignorant of as a Pharisee?

2. Define and describe what it means to be *objectively just*, but *subjectively unjust*; to be *objectively obedient* and *subjectively obedient*, according to

Finney. Do you agree or disagree with his definitions and distinctions? Explain your answer.

3. What is a *natural consciousness*, a *moral consciousness*, and a *spiritual consciousness*? Why are these distinctions important?

4. Define *self-righteousness* and explain how Finney used the example of Paul prior to his conversion as a example of a self-righteous person. What is the opposite of being self-righteous?

5. What does the truly converted person understand by "divine grace"?

6. What things happened to Paul when "the commandment came" to him? Compare the example of Paul with your own spiritual experience.

7. Describe some of the conversion experiences that Finney speaks of in this lesson. What struck you as most amazing or profound about these conversion experiences?

8. What is a Pharisee in heart? How would you recognize such a person today?

9. What things can happen to people, perhaps even church members or leaders, if they reject, or do not follow through and repent, when the light of the Holy Spirit shines upon their hearts in their unconverted state?

10. What does Finney mean when he talks about being slain by the law prior to conversion? Why does this seem important? Why does Finney say the Holy Spirit must be involved in this process?

4. *Thanks for the Gospel Victory*

1. How would you define the terms *morally dead* and *spiritually dead*? Do you agree with the way Finney defines these terms? Why or why not? How can a person know if he is morally and/or spiritually dead?

2. Compare, contrast, and define *natural weakness* and *spiritual weakness*. What is the cause of *spiritual weakness*? What are some indications that a Christian is spiritually weak? What is the solution for overcoming *spiritual weakness*?

3. Why did Finney at one time doubt whether anyone could be saved?

4. Where can we find victory over sin? What is this victory?

5. How can one know the love of God and love God? What is the difference between knowing that God loves you and knowing by experience that God loves you?

6. What are some of the consequences of knowing the love of God by experience?

7. How does the sinner feel? Why does he feel this way?

8. What is the evidence of a saving change to ourselves? What is the evidence of a saving change to others?

9. Compare and contrast faith and love. Why is faith important? Why is love important? Which must come first in the experience of a person becoming a true Christian? Why must this be so?

10. At what point in his experience is a sinner ready to trust Christ for salvation? What must the church become to help sinners come to saving faith in Jesus Christ?

5. Justification

1. What does Finney mean by "perpetual justification"? In what ways do you see this doctrine taught and promoted today? What effect do you think this doctrine has had in churches, among Christians, and in your country's culture? What effect might it have on continuing a revival?

2. Why do you think some people have the opinion that those who oppose the doctrine of "perpetual justification" are heretics? What might an appropriate response be to those who think "perpetual justification" is the only valid interpretation of the doctrine of justification?

3. If possible, read John 15:4-7 in 3 or 4 different translations of the Bible. Look up the word "abide" in a dictionary. What does it mean to abide in Christ? Read 1 John 3:5-6 in some different translations. What can happen to us in those times when we choose not to abide in Christ?

4. Why is there *now* no condemnation for the person who is in Christ Jesus?

5. Of what value is Christ's atoning death on the cross? What does Christ's death accomplish for believers?

6. Compare and contrast what the law requires and the fruit of the Spirit? What does the law do for us? What does the Spirit do for us?

7. What is the difference between walking after the flesh and walking after the Spirit? Who will walk after the Spirit and who will not?

8. How does Finney define "repentance"? Do you agree or disagree with his definition? Why or why not? Why does God require believers to repent?

9. How does Finney define "sanctification"? How does "sanctification" differ from "permanent sanctification"? What is "consecration"?

10. What is antinomianism? Why is it dangerous for someone who calls himself a Christian to live as an antinomian or think it is okay for Christians to live as antinomians? Do you think antinomianism is present in churches today? Can you give some examples of antinomianism in today's churches and in the preaching of today?

6. Total Depravity

1. Why does Finney carefully distinguish between moral depravity and physical depravity? Why are we not blameworthy for physical depravity? Why are we blameworthy for moral depravity?

2. List some ways that sinning (or even committing a single sin) may result in physical depravity. How might physical depravity (or a disease) influence someone to sin? Why would they still be blameworthy?

3. List two misconceptions about total depravity. How does Finney define total depravity? Do you agree with his definition and his interpretation of Genesis 6:5? Why or why not?

4. When trying to convince totally depraved people that they are totally depraved, why does Finney not rely only on quoting Jesus and the Scriptures to prove his conclusions? What facts does Finney choose to use in his arguments? Do you think he was successful in his endeavor? Do you agree with his approach? Why or why not?

5. What are some consequences for Christians when they love and seek to please God? What are some of the things love will motivate people to do? How does Finney use love to argue by analogy with sinners that they do not love God, even if they say they do?

6. What does it mean to think of God the Father and Jesus Christ as objects of affection or persons that we love? What are some of the consequences of thinking of them as objects of affection or persons that we love? What does Finney mean by "natural consequences"?

7. How do you feel or what do you think when you are with a group of sincere Christians who are discussing their faith and how they might be more effective in sharing the gospel with others? What does your feeling or thinking tell you about yourself? Do you need to make any changes?

8. What is the difference between selfish gratitude to God and true love for God? Why do you think sinners mistake these two? What are some of the consequences of mistaking selfish gratitude and true love for God?

9. What gods or idols do sinners make for themselves, or find, to serve today? Why do they fall in love with these false gods? Why is it difficult to turn them from idolatry to the true God? What are needed to do change them and their perspective?

10. What is the carnal mind? What does the carnal mind prefer? Why do some people think a person can have a carnal mind and also be a Christian who is saved, who will go to heaven with they die? How dangerous is carnal Christianity to individuals and the churches?

7. Moral Depravity

1. Compare this sermon "Moral Depravity" with Finney's previous sermon "Total Depravity." When was each sermon preached (or first published)? What type of people do you think Finney was speaking to in each sermon? Which sermon would be most likely to be a revival sermon? Why?

2. Which sermon seems to most clearly define terms or words? Why do you think one sermon was better than the other in defining terms? Which sermon would be the most effective with someone in college? Why?

3. What is Finney's definition of "moral manners"? What are *outward* or *bodily* manners? What does Finney mean by "a state of mind"? What state of mind is characteristic of the sinner? What state of mind is characteristic of the true Christian?

4. Why does Finney teach that a state of mind can be instantly abandoned? What state of mind does he insist ought to be abandoned? Why does Finney argue against the idea of the inability of a person to change their state of mind?

5. What is "physical depravity"? Why can't a physical depravity be against the law of God? What is the danger of confusing physical depravity with moral depravity? Would Finney teach that sin is a disease? Give a reason for your answer.

6. Define and describe temptation. What are some causes or sources of temptation? Why does Finney say we should not confuse a temptation with moral depravity? Is temptation a sin? Why or why not?

7. What is a "sin" according to the Bible? What is a "sin" according to Finney? How are these definitions of sin the same or different? Why does Finney teach that sin is not physical or cannot have a physical cause?

8. What is the difference between a *cause*, an *occasion*, and an *influence* with regard to morals and the choices people make and the state of mind that people commit themselves to adopt? Using each of these terms or words, write three or more sentences regarding sin and how we can account for a person committing a sin or living in a state of sin.

9. What does Finney mean by ultimate choice? Explain ultimate choice in a way someone would understand today; give an example. What is the ultimate choice of a sinner? What is the ultimate choice of a Christian? Why is our ultimate choice important to God and to us us?

10. What is a "carnal mind"? What are some of the evidences that someone has a carnal mind? What would you say to someone who claims to be a Christian and who demonstrates by their behavior and choices that they have a carnal mind?

8. *License, Bondage and Liberty*

1. How would you describe a mercenary servant of the Lord Jesus Christ? Can you think of any examples of this spirit today? In your opinion, how many who think they are true Christians have been led to "accept Jesus" or go to church for mercenary reasons? What must Christians do to pre-

vent this from happening today?

2. How does Finney define license? What does it mean to say that a person' state is one of license? How does some preaching lead some people to develop a spirit of license and also sear their conscience?

3. In your opinion, what are some things today that contribute to many children, young people, and adults having an undeveloped conscience? In what ways do some churches and preachers contribute to the problem of an undeveloped conscience? How can preachers and teachers solve this problem

4. In what ways do some churches and preachers contribute to worldly-mindedness? How can preaching worldly-mindeness promote church growth? What does Finney say are some consequences and dangers of worldly-mindedness?

5. In what ways does the conscience work differently in a person with a spirit of license from the way the conscience works in a person with a spirit of bondage?

6. Describe the state of heart of a person with a spirit of bondage. Why does a person with a spirit of bondage seem like a Christian to some observers? How does the spirit of bondage differ from the spirit of a true Christian?

7. How do those with a spirit of bondage often pray? Why are they unsuccessful in achieving gospel rest and peace from the way they pray?

8. How do some confuse gospel liberty with the spirit of license? What is liberty according to Finney? Do you agree with his definition? Why or why not? What is liberty and the spirit of liberty in the Christian?

9. How does a child of God serve God differently from one who serves God with a spirit of bondage? How does a person become a child of

God? How does the conscience of a person with gospel liberty influence a child of God? How does the conscience influence a person with a spirit of bondage?

10. Describe the full idea of Christian liberty. How might you begin to lead someone in a spirit of bondage to full Christian liberty?

9. *The Spirit of Prayer*

1. What does the word "intercede" mean? What does the word "intercession" mean? What kind of a person could be called an "intercessor"? Why does the Holy Spirit intercede for Christians? Why do Christians need to intercede for sinners?

2. What "new thing" or "amazing thing" did you learn about how the Holy Spirit intercedes for Christians that you did not know before? How will this new knowledge help you pray more effectively in the future?

3. How does the Holy Spirit make the Christian feel about sinners? How do Christians normally feel about sinners based on what you hear Christians say about them? Why do Christians need the Holy Spirit to help them feel right about sinners? How do your feelings influence your praying?

4. What can we infer when the Holy Spirit leads us to pray for someone? What effect does this inference have on our faith when we respond to the Spirit's leading?

5. How does discerning the signs of the times and God's providences influence the prayers of sincere Christians? In what ways can God's providences be recognized by Christians today?

6. How can you discern the Holy Spirit from other spirits so you will not be misled or misguided in your thinking, praying, and behaving?

7. How do you seek and receive the Holy Spirit's influence? What problems might keep someone from receiving the Holy Spirit's influence?

8. What effect can practicing any sin have on the prayers of someone who professes to be a Christian? How can this also have an effect on a church? At what should a person aim when he wants to draw near to God?

9. What is essential for a Christian to pray right?

10. Explain the relationship between a specific promise in the Bible and praying with faith. Explain the relationship between a general promise in the Bible and praying in faith. How can Bible study with the Holy Spirit's influence help you pray more effectively?

10. *All Things for Good to Those That Love God*

1. Can you think of anything that has happened to you that you thought was something totally bad or evil that you later saw God turn around for your good or the good of others? If so, thank God now for working that event out for good.

2. What is one condition that Finney insists on for holiness in someone? In other words, without this condition being met, a person cannot be holy. Why is this condition essential to holiness? How can this condition be used by someone to increase holiness? What are some ways that God uses this condition with people? Can you think of other conditions?

3. Do you agree or disagree with Finney that "All events that occur are providential"? Give a reason for your answer.

4. What does a rebuke show us and what is the value of a rebuke? How does God sometimes rebuke His children? What might this teach us about how to rebuke others or accept rebuke from others?

5. What does it mean to have your way crossed? If we have our was crossed

sometimes, what does Finney say we need in our lives? Do you agree or disagree with Dr. Payson's attitude and beliefs? Why or why not.

6. In what ways do Finney's teachings on affliction differ from some of the ideas that are common today about the causes of afflictions? Do you agree or disagree with Finney? How does Job's experience help us understand the causes of affliction and how we should respond to them?

7. What opportunities do our infirmities and frailties give us? Describe the difference between God sending an infirmity and God permitting an infirmity. Why is this distinction important to keep in mind, especially when talking to others who are suffering or when we are suffering ourselves?

8. Though we are guilty when we sin, and though we often regret our mistakes, what does God do with our sins and mistakes? Can you think of an example in your own life to illustrate what God does?

9. Why does God overrule some events, but permits others to happen? Does this also explain why we, or others, do not always experience immediately all the punishment we deserve after we sin?

10. What lesson does Finney teach from the sins of Satan, Judas, and Joseph's brothers? How can you apply this lesson when sins are committed against you, or when you recognize that you have sinned against God and others?

11. *All Events, Ruinous to The Sinner*

1. Why does increasing knowledge of what a person ought to do increase their moral obligation to do what they know they ought to do? What are some of the consequences of not doing what we know we ought to do?

2. What are some daily events that increase the sinner's knowledge of God and make him more guilty and liable to greater punishment for not turning to God in faith and repentance? How might you teach this to sinners?

3. What arguments might you conceive from reading the Bible and Finney to use when reasoning with someone contemplating suicide to not do so? What are some of the differences between heaven and hell?

4. What is the conscience? What does the conscience do? How might a person harden their conscience so it will no longer act as a reliable guide? How can hardening the conscience lead to the inevitable ruin of a sinner?

5. How can good fortune be a curse? How can good fortune be a blessing?

6. What are some of the consequences for the sinner when he rejects every merciful effort made by God and others to lead him to saving faith?

7. What are some of the consequences for the sinner when he rejects every chastisement from God which God designs to lead him to repentance?

8. What are some of the things that Finney calls "the voice of God" to the sinner? In what ways do you recognize "the voice of God" to you?

9. What are the consequences when the sinner ignores the Bible, opportunities to study or read the Bible, Sundays, and opportunities to worship God?

10. Why does Finney appeal to the Bible, reason, experience, and observation when presenting the Gospel and warning sinners to repent instead of just quoting the Bible? How effective do you think Finney's approach has been in these two sermons on Romans 8:28 or other lessons?

12. *All Things for God to Those That Love God*

1. What is a universal proposition? Why does Finney say that Romans 8:28 is a universal proposition? Can you think of any other universal propositions in the Bible? How can these universal propositions encourage you and others?

2. As a moral agent, what does Finney say is a condition that we must fulfill in order to be happy? In what ways does knowledge of God help us fulfill this condition?

3. How does it make you feel to think that all you have done in this life will be revealed to you so you can see how God worked your choices out for good? Do you think God will actually do this, or do you think Finney was mistaken in his view? What scriptures can you think of that will either support or not support Finney's view?

4. Of what value are God's judgments and chastisements?

5. What resulted when God overruled Peter's sins for his benefit? Can you think of any of your sins or poor choices that God has overruled for your good or the good of others? If so, how does that make you feel or think about the future, here and hereafter?

6. According to Finney, in our battles with the devil what hope does God and the Bible give us?

7. In what ways, according to Finney, can we truly know that all things will work out for good for those who love God? What does that tell us about God's attributes?

8. Define and distinguish between blame and regret. What does "*on the whole* regret" mean? Do you think Christians will experience blame and regret throughout eternity? If people will experience blame and regret forever, what does Finney say will be the consequences for those who believe in Jesus Christ and for those who do not?

9. What does Finney teach about God experiencing regret? Do you agree or disagree with Finney? Give reasons for your answer.

10. Why is it impossible to sin benevolently?

13. Religion of the Law and the Gospel

1. How were people saved under the Old Testament dispensation (or Old Covenant) before Jesus Christ was born and came into the world?

2. What are some dangers when some believers think that the gospel sets aside the moral law of God; therefore, they are under no obligation to obey it? What do Antinomians believe? What is a good argument against Antinomianism?

3. What did some of the Perfectionists believe in Finney's day? Do we have any who believe their teachings today? What might you say to them?

4. How do some misinterpret gospel liberty? What is Finney's reply?

5. How does the faith of legalists differ from the faith which people must have in order to be saved? How do some confuse true Christian faith with legalism?

6. What is the difference between works produced by legal considerations and works produced by faith? What are the only two principles on which obedience to any government can rest? How are these two principles manifested in the kingdom of God or in God's government?

7. What is the role of conscience before and after a person comes to saving faith in Jesus Christ as Lord and Savior?

8. What is the only obedience acceptable to God? Why do you think this is so? Define *filial confidence* and describe it in three different relationships. Apply your three examples in a hypothetical presentation to lead someone away from legalism and to gospel faith in Jesus Christ.

9. Why is the religion of the gospel more than a purpose or goal that one might have for the way he lives?

10. How do legalists and true Christians differ in their feelings when they see their duty and contemplate what their duty requires of them and whether or not they will do their duty?

Henry Cowles
Editor of the "Oberlin Evangelist"
1803-1881

*Professor of Church History, Hebrew,
and Old Testament Literature*

Biographical Sketch of Professor Henry Cowles

The Reverend Henry Cowles was born in Norfolk, Connecticut in 1803. He graduated from Yale and was ordained in 1828. He became professor of languages at Oberlin College in September 1835. His heart was in the work, and all he asked was a place to lay out his strength. In 1838, he took the chair of Church History in the seminary, and of Hebrew and Old Testament Literature in 1840. In 1848, in consequence of straitened means on the part of the college, and the necessity of reducing expenses, he resigned his work in the seminary, and took the editorship of the *Oberlin Evangelist*.

When the *Evangelist* ceased publication in 1862, Professor Cowles was about sixty years of age. The habit of communicating his thought to others by writing was strong upon him, and by what seemed a divine leading he entered upon the work of writing commentaries upon the Scriptures. He commenced with parts of the Old Testament, and went on, year after year, adding volume to volume, devoting to it all his energies and all his resources, through a period of seventeen years. In 1881, he issued the last volume, and the result remains with us—a commentary on the entire scriptures, full of practical wisdom and the ripe fruits of scholarship. He died in September of that same year. The interests of the college through all these years filled his heart and hands.

It would be much more satisfactory to give the family life of these men, to look into their homes and observe there the results of Christian character and fidelity. By the side of each one of these men there stood a woman of like spirit and faith, whose life in the community was no less valuable; and children were gathered around them whose work and life it would be pleasant to follow, but this opens too wide a field.

Condensed and edited from, *Oberlin: the Colony and the College, 1833-1883,* by James J. Fairchild, President of Oberlin College, Oberlin, Ohio: E.J. Goodrich, 1883, pages 284-287.

Henry Cowles Commentary on Romans

Romans 7:1, 22-23

Romans 7:1, 22-23—*Know ye not, brethren, (for I speak to them that know the law,) how that the law hath dominion over a man as long as he liveth? For I delight in the law of God after the inward man: But I see another law in my members, warring against the law of my mind, and bringing me into captivity to the law of sin which is in my members.*

The key to this chapter, the clue to its exposition and bearing in the great argument of this epistle, is to be found in the Pharisaic idea of being under law as a system of salvation, *i.e.* as a power to do for sinful man two things:—(a.) To save his soul from sinning; and (b.) From condemnation before God;—*i.e.* to give him both sanctification and justification.—This discussion really starts from chapter 6, verse 14—"For sin shall not have dominion over you, for ye are not under law but under grace." Taking up this point—no more under law in the Pharisaic sense but under grace—Paul goes fundamentally into the first part—the being under law—to show (a.) That if one adopts that religious system, he must needs carry it through—work in it and under it while it remains in force upon him—illustrating this point by the law of marriage (verses 1-3);—next (b.) That by the dead body of Christ, the demand for the old Pharisaic law is dead, and the way is gloriously open for a new and better system—*viz.* of loving allegiance to Christ and the really redeeming, saving power of the gospel (v. 4); Next, (c.) That the old system is utterly powerless as to saving souls from sin, for the law is in its nature good and has only a good intent, yet, working by itself alone, it only reveals moral obligation, and in all sin-loving souls, provokes resistance (verses 5-13);—(d.) That this law meets the approval of man's moral nature [the "*nous*"] and serves to stimulate this moral nature to resist the clamorous demands of the lower nature [the "*sarx*" flesh] but only to the result of being perpetually overcome;—for depravity being universal to the race, the flesh always holds sway over the will and overpowers the voice of the moral nature [the "*nous*"] every time (verses 14-23);—(e). Finally victory comes at last, through Jesus Christ our Lord (verses 24, 25).

Romans 7:1-3—*Know ye not, brethren, (for I speak to them that know the law) how that the law hath dominion over a man as long as he liveth? For the woman which hath a husband is bound by the law to her husband so long as he liveth; but if the husband be dead, she is loosed from the law of her husband. So then if, while her husband liveth, she be married to another man, she shall be called an adulteress: but if her husband be dead, she is free, from that law; so that she is no adulteress, though she be married to another man.*

The remarks above, introductory to chapter seven, should be considered attentively. The reader's thought should be held closely to the scope of Paul's argument—*i.e.* as made with the typical Pharisee of his age, who is "*under law*" in the sense of seeking to find in his observance of it both the power that *sanctifies* and the power that *justifies*. To such Pharisaic

Jews, Paul says—"Brethren; know ye not"—certainly ye must know (for I speak to law-knowing men)—"that the law," (the law which you so much honor) "has dominion over the man" [who seeks salvation under it] "as long as he liveth?" Placing yourselves under law for the purposes of salvation according to your system, ye must make it a life-business, to be prosecuted as long as ye live. Manifestly nothing less than this can suffice. Take this illustration:

The married woman is bound by the marriage law to her husband while living (literally, to her living husband), but if the husband die, she is released from the law of her husband (*i.e.* from the law which binds her to her husband). Wherefore (verse 3), if her husband being still living, she becomes another man's wife, she shall be called an adulteress (literally, she will be doing business as an adulteress—running that business as a profession, and therefore fully deserving that name). But if her husband die, she is free from that law (of marriage) so as not to be an adulteress though married to another man.

Romans 7:22-23—*For I delight in the law of God after the inward man: But I see another law in my members, warring against the law of my mind, and bringing me into captivity to the law of sin which is in my members.*

In these verses the dual personality stands out with even greater distinctness, (if possible), and noticeably, these dual persons appear under new names. The better part of man's moral nature is here "the inner man;" also "the law of my mind" Over against this power is that of the lower nature, called "another law in my members;" also "the law of sin which is in my members;" and further on, "the body of this death."—Here Paul says (verse 22.)—"I am pleased with the law of God"—that is the I [*ego*] which represents the inner man, so called because the outer man is of the flesh, visible to the eye; while the reason and conscience are of man's inner invisible being. The voice of the inner man is in harmony with the law of God, approving the right.—But I see another law in my members [my flesh] which always puts itself in hostile array, doing battle against the law of my reason and conscience, [*nous*] and always enslaving me (making me a captive of war) under the law of sin which is in my members (flesh).—

This is the same conflict, put in military terms—the same irrepressible antagonism between the higher and the lower elements of man's being. Noticeably here, as throughout this chapter, the lower is always the conqueror; the higher is beaten in every conflict.

---

*Cowles, Henry, *The Longer Epistles of Paul*, New York: D. Appleton & Company, 1880, pages 70-73, 81. [Henceforth, Cowles, page #.]

Romans 7:4

Wherefore, my brethren, ye also are become dead to the law by the body of Christ; that ye should be married to another, even to him who is raised from the dead, that we should bring forth fruit unto God.

This doctrine of the law of marriage, *viz,* that the death of either party severs the bond, is perfectly clear; yet we may suppose it had a pertinence in Paul's argument quite apart from its clearness,—*viz,* in the striking analogy which it suggests between the death of the husband and the death of Christ. As the husband's dead body sunders the marriage bond and sets the wife free, so Christ's dead body frees us (all who so will) from being in the Pharisaic sense "under law" as our reliance for salvation. In this sense we become dead to the law by means of the dead body of Christ.—Of course Christ's dead body carries with it and fully signifies his incarnation, death, atonement, resurrection—all those sublime and mighty moral forces which lie in the gospel scheme. These moral forces open to us an entirely new method of salvation, and therefore at one master stroke deliver us from the old law (as used for Pharisaic righteousness) and invite us to a new marriage with the risen Christ, under which we "shall bring forth fruit unto God"—this fruit-bearing having reference to the passage (6: 22); "ye have your fruit unto holiness, and the end everlasting life."—Thus we are married not to a dead Christ but to a Christ living, yea risen from the dead ; while around his death are clustering evermore those grand moral forces in which lie the power that redeems us from sin and from its condemning curse.—Cowles, page 73.

Romans 7:9-11

For I was alive without the law once: but when the commandment came, sin revived, and I died. And the commandment, which was ordained to life, I found to be unto death. For sin, taking occasion by the commandment, deceived me, and by it slew me.

Here a new objection is sprung upon this discussion, which of course brings up a new question to be put and answered. What Paul has said of the law has seemed to imply that it is not only powerless to save the soul from sinning, but worse yet;—is even provoking men to greater transgression—What then shall we say of it? Is the law sin? Is it a bad, pernicious thing, a positive power unto wickedness and truly responsible for the sins of men? Never let this be said!

How then does Paul explain himself? On this wise;—(1.) The law gives me a deeper, truer knowledge of sin. For indeed I should have had no just sense of sin but for the law. To be yet more particular, I should not even have thought of lust as a sin, if the law had not said to me—"Thou shall not covet."—(2.) The law stirred up my selfish heart to resist its demands. In this sense it took occasion by its specific commands to work in me all sorts of lust—all sinful passions. I would not brook control; I could not endure that authority which forbad me the indulgence of my propensities. But this was through no fault in the law; it was wholly through fault in myself.—(3.) Notice that *apart from law*, in the absence of its authority—sin, in this particular aspect of it, was dead;—at least its impulses lay dormant; no exciting cause roused them into activity. In fact before the law came to act upon me I was alive with hope; I had a very comfortable opinion of myself;—but when the commandment came, sin sprang into life and activity; I died, in the sense that my hopes vanished. I saw in myself sins I had not dreamed of before. —That is no strange fact of human experience. It needs no great amount of genuine conviction of sin under a clear perception of God's law to throw the human soul into the agony of despair.—So much good the law wrought for me. The commandment which God gave as a means unto life, I have found to be in my case unto death. It seemed to ring out the death-knell of doom for my guilty soul. Then verse 11 repeats the points made in verse 8 with slight variations. In the same sense here as there "sin takes occasion by the commandment"—sin being here as there the overmastering proclivity toward self-indulgence, despite of God's authority—the imperial demands of lust in the depraved, unsubdued heart of man. This sin-power in the soul took occasion by the commandment to *deceive*, and then to *kill* him;—to deceive first, in the sense of making it seem almost right to resist God's prohibition of self-indulgence—moreover putting the reasons for resisting God's authority in strangely fascinating forms and so bewitching the soul into deeper and more mad rebellion. This again is a terrible fact in the experience of many a human soul under its first clear apprehensions of God's law as forbidding long cherished sin. "And by it slew me"—for my fond but blind hopes of being in a sort right before God went down with a crash before these appalling revelations of my own wickedness of heart.—Thus Paul shows that the law working conviction of sin in his soul, had done him most valuable service.—Cowles, pages 75-76.

Romans 7:24-25

O wretched man that I am! who shall deliver me from the body of this death? I thank God through Jesus Christ our Lord. So then with the mind I myself serve the law of God; but with the flesh the law of sin.

Suddenly Paul's description culminates in one outburst of agony—"O wretched man! Who shall deliver me—who can ever deliver me from the body of this death!—from this power of the flesh, this all-conquering sin-power of my lower nature; which always enslaves—against which, so long as only law stands for my help, I struggle forever in vain!

Here light breaks gloriously upon his darkness; help drops down from on high, and his out-poured thanksgivings bear witness to his inexpressible relief and triumph.—"Thanks be to God through Jesus Christ our Lord!" The great Deliverer of human souls from their sin-bondage has come at last!

Then as the conclusion of this chapter's discussion,—"I myself with the mind [the *nous*] serve the law of God—endorsing, approving it;—but with the flesh [the *sarx*], the law of sin—the flesh always carrying the day against the mind till God's help in Christ appears.

We must now give attention briefly to the long mooted question—whether in this passage (verses 14-25.) Paul is speaking of Christian experience, and particularly of his own then present experience as a Christian.

This question must certainly be answered *in the negative*; for the four following reasons—each strong in itself; all combined sufficient to annihilate that mischievous interpretation forever.

1. *The whole scope of the context forbids its reference to Christian experience.*

The thought of the context should be traced even from Romans 6: 14: "Sin shall not have dominion over you; for ye are not under law, but under grace"—not "under law" specially as a *sanctifying power* because it is utterly inadequate for this purpose.—Then in Romans 7: 4, and onward, we have the same argument still in hand—the law good, excellent in itself, but rather provoking more sin than itself subduing sin and producing holy obedience;—and then to make his argument demonstrably clear, he outlines in this passage the life and death-struggle between the higher and the lower nature in the unrenewed man, with no other help toward virtue except the law. Man's better elements (reason and conscience) approve the law of God and have its help in their moral efforts; but even so, are entirely unavailing. Throughout it is vital to Paul's entire argument that this struggle be that of the unregenerate man, with the law only and no gospel present for the help of his better nature; but this help from the law, all too weak for the victory.

2. The conflict so vividly portrayed throughout this passage is beyond all question between the flesh and the mind (the "*sarx*" and the "*nous*")—*i.e.* the lower appetites and passions, having their seat mainly in the flesh on the one hand; and on the other, the higher elements—those of "the inner man;" his nobler qualities as a moral being. The element always present in all Christian experience *viz.* "the Spirit of God," is not once alluded to—is not even thought of throughout this entire passage. This fact alone is perfectly decisive against the theory that this is Christian experience. For there never can be any Christian experience without the

presence of the Spirit of God. The *"pneuma"*—the "Holy Ghost"—is a present element, a living power, in all Christian experience. The Christian life cannot even begin without the Holy Ghost; can never be carried forward, when once begun, without the Spirit. So Paul teaches in this very connection : "Ye are not in the flesh but in the Spirit, if so be that the Spirit of God dwell in you. Now if any man have not the Spirit of Christ, (*i.e.* dwelling within him) he is none of his." Or read Paul (as in Galatians 5: 16-24) and mark how in all Christian experience the conflict is not (as here) between "flesh" and "mind," but between the flesh and the Spirit: "Walk in the Spirit, and ye shall not fulfil the lusts of the flesh. For the flesh lusteth against the Spirit and the Spirit against the flesh; *and these are contrary the one to the other;*"—between these all the antagonism of really Christian experience lies.—The utter absence of the Spirit in this experience drawn out in Romans 7, ought to have shown it forever impossible that this can be the regenerate, Christian man—with no Holy Ghost in his heart and none of his power in the soul.—This is all unknown to the scriptures—is an utter impossibility!—When in Romans 8, Paul comes to expand his views of the glorious *victory* for which he thanks God in the close of this chapter, he shows how thoroughly he recognizes this victory as coming through the presence of the Spirit and how certainly he ascribes it to the law of the spirit of life in Christ Jesus that he is made free from the law of sin and death.

3. The present tense here (as said above) is not *historical* but is *rhetorical*. It does not delineate Paul's own personal experience at that time, nor indeed specially *at* any time, but it makes himself a *supposed case*—a case for the illustration of a great law of sinning human nature. Here I call the reader's attention to the fact that Paul uses the Greek tongue with great accuracy. In quite a number of passages he does refer to his experience in his pre-christian life—before his conversion; but never in the present tense—never in any other than the proper historic past. See Acts 22: 3, 4, 19, 20—"I was brought up in this city; was taught in the law of the fathers; was zealous toward God. I persecuted this sect; and imprisoned and beat them *etc.*"—all with perfect accuracy, in the really past, historic tense. So Acts 26: 9-15—"I verily thought with myself that I ought." See also Philippians 3: 4-7—"I was circumcised the eighth day;" "what things

were gain to me, I counted loss for Christ." Thus Paul knew how to speak of his ungodly experience, of the life he lived before his conversion, using sensibly the right historic tenses.—From this we must certainly infer that this passage (verses 14-25), running regularly in the present tense, was not, could not be, his experience *before* his conversion. That is, he is not reciting it *as such*. With equal certainty it was not his experience in any part of his *Christian* life—because as here put there is no Holy Ghost in it, and no victory over sin in a single instance—nothing but being overcome in every struggle. This present tense is therefore nothing but a supposed case of a soul—without the gospel and without the Holy Ghost.

4. Finally, throughout this delineation (verses 14-25) sin absolutely triumphs in every conflict. It conquers every time. Is this a *Christian* experience? Alas, if it be, a sinner's experience can be no worse! There is no salvation in this sort of Christian experience; no victory over sin whatever. Whatever grace there may be here is powerless; indeed (as already said) so powerless that the passage contains not the slightest allusion to any grace whatever in the struggle. But, be if carefully noted, Paul has already spoken of the really Christian experience on this point; *viz*, in Romans 6: 14-22. "For sin shall not have dominion over you" (how utterly unlike this conflict!) "for ye are not under law but under grace."—"But now, being made free from sin, ye have your fruit unto holiness, and the end, everlasting life." This is a totally different experience from what we have in Romans chapter 7. So also as we shall see throughout Romans chapter 8. The real Christian experience is there—the Spirit of God; the life-giving, the sin-conquering power.

Therefore, let the notion that Romans chapter 7, gives Christian experience be forever exploded. It has been a terrible delusion, encouraging multitudes of unconverted men in the belief that because their own experience was quite well drawn out there; they at least belonged to one class of Paul's Christian people—as good as Paul himself during at least one stage of his Christian life! —Cowles, pages 82-85.

Principles of Peace — Finney's Lessons on Romans

Romans 8:1-8

This chapter throughout stands over against chapter 7, in closest antithetical relations; *that* giving us the inefficiency of the law to save human souls from sin and consequently from condemnation: this, on the other side, giving us the perfect efficiency of the gospel scheme, especially through its glorious power of the Spirit. Here Paul catalogues the blessings which come to believers in Christ through the Holy Ghost. We shall find it a wonderfully rich group of blessings—No more condemnation upon those in Christ, walking no longer after the flesh but after the Spirit (verses 1, 2), God having achieved through His Son what the law never could do (verses 3, 4); changing the whole heart and life from loving and serving flesh to the spiritual mind which is life and peace (verses 5-8); results wrought by the indwelling presence of Christ and His Spirit (verses 9-11); which should bind Christians morally to live no more after the flesh, but to follow the Spirit as sons of God, and. so heirs of glory (verses 12-17); a glory great beyond compare (verse 18)—toward which glory the whole creation looks with longing hope (verses 19-25); the Spirit helping toward hope by inspiring our prayers (verses 26, 27); confidence in God's love as built upon His eternal purpose (verses 28-30); God *for* us should inspire our faith and hope for every blessing (verses 31-34); nothing can separate us from Christ's love (verses 35-39).

Romans 8:1-2—*There is therefore now no condemnation to them which are in Christ Jesus, who walk not after the flesh, but after the Spirit. For the law of the Spirit of life in Christ Jesus hath made me free from the law of sin and death.*

"No condemnation"—for be it carefully observed, Paul has said and shown that being justified by faith we have peace with God through our Lord Jesus Christ (Romans 5:1), so that to those who are in Christ there is no more condemnation before and under God's law. It only remained to show here that the conscious self-condemnation, resulting from present sin, has ceased in the case of those who walk no longer after the flesh but after the Spirit. They are free, for the law of the spirit that works life has lifted them out from the bondage of slavery under the law that wrought sin and death.—The "law" is used here as above (Romans 7: 21,23, 25), in the sense of a well defined *power*, acting efficiently and constantly—the law of sin to produce sinning, and the law of life and grace, to beget holiness. In verse 2, therefore, Paul teaches that the Spirit of God delivers the soul from the power of sin and death.—The reader should note the full assumption here that the state of "no condemnation" presupposes not only free pardon—actual justification before the law—but deliverance from reigning sin also—the real saving of human souls from its present dominion. This great fact cannot be too thoroughly understood, or too deeply impressed.—In verse 2, the improved text has "thee" instead of "me."

These verses should not be passed without special attention to the agency ascribed to Christ (as well as to that ascribed to the Spirit)—the blessing being limited to those who are *in Christ Jesus*.—In verse 2, the true relation (to other words) of the clause—"*in Christ Jesus*," should be carefully noted. Our King James Version of the Bible will naturally (but incorrectly) be understood to connect it to the words "spirit of life." It should rather qualify "*made free*"—thus: "For the law of the spirit of life hath made thee—being in Christ Jesus—free from the law of sin and death. Or the two verses might be translated thus:—"There is no condemnation to those in Christ Jesus. *For in Christ Jesus* the law of the spirit of life hath made thee free from the law of sin and death.—Thus verse 2 gives a reason for the fact stated in verse 1. Both alike speak of those who are *in Christ Jesus*.

Romans 8:3-4—*For what the law could not do, in that it was weak through the flesh, God sending his own Son in the likeness of sinful flesh, and for sin, condemned sin in the flesh: That the righteousness of the law might be fulfilled in us, who walk not after the flesh, but after the Spirit.*

It happens not infrequently that Paul's especially important passages are especially difficult of construction—a fact due apparently to the deep, impetuous emotions which they excited in his mind. These verses are a case in point. They need to be studied very carefully and with the closest attention to the drift and demands of the context in order to obtain any well grounded satisfaction as to their precise significance

Manifestly, Paul wishes to show how it comes to pass that the law of tho spirit of life in Christ has made thee free from the law of sin. We know this to be his object, not only by the previous context but also by the following—as we shall see.

To put in plainest light both the grammatical construction and the full significance of verse 3, we may paraphrase thus;—For as to that result, impossible for the law because it was weak through the flesh, God having sent his own Son in flesh like man's flesh of sin and *for* sin (i. e. for the sake of overcoming sin) has condemned sin (sealing its death-warrant and triumphing over it) in the incarnate flesh of his Son ;—(verse 4.) to the end that the righteous demands of the law might be fulfilled in and by us (in our renewed life)—in the case of us all who walk not after the flesh but after the Spirit.

The first clause—"what the law could not do"—is literally—the thing impossible of law—*i.e.* impossible for law to do. Some critics construct it with some verb understood, having the sense, "effect, accomplish." But the introduction of new words should be avoided if possible. Other critics, more wisely, take it for a nominative independent, and suppose that Paul puts what he had to say about this result, impossible to mere law, into the next verb "condemned"—this verb being chosen here with some reference to the same word in verse 1. and a sort of play upon that "no condemnation." There is no condemnation to those who so walk (as in verse 1), because, though the law could not break that awful power of sin in the flesh, yet God, by sending His Son to become incarnate, has perfectly smitten that power, condemned it so utterly that now all the righteous claims of moral law on human souls may be amply met in the case of those who walk after the Spirit and not after the flesh.

That victory over sin is impossible to mere law because the power of sin in human flesh is too strong for it, is the great doctrine of chapter 7. On the other hand the great doctrine of chapter 8, is that what law could not do, the Spirit of God has well and thoroughly done—and done it in connection with the mission of God's own Son, made incarnate in human flesh.—Noticeably, Paul does not say that the Son was sent in man's sinful flesh, but only in a flesh which *resembled* this flesh of sin. It was human but not sinful—human in all points but the sin.

The precise sense and relation of the words "and for sin," before "condemned" are points of some critical difficulty. Our authorized King James Version assumes that this "and" connects the verb "condemned" with the participle "sending;" but this is harsh. I have chosen to connect it with the word" sin'" which in Paul's Greek stands immediately before it—thus; Having sent His Son in a likeness of flesh of sin and for sin—*i.e.* He sent His Son both under the form of man's sinful flesh and for the sake of conquering this sin.

The critics would readily agree to read—"condemned the sin which is in human flesh"—if Paul had put the article after the word "sin," giving the phrase this sense—*the* sin which is in human flesh;—but he did not. Therefore it seems better to connect "in the flesh"—with "condemned," to indicate that it was by the incarnation of the Son that this victory over sin was wrought.

In verse 4, "the righteousness of the law" must certainly be the subjective, ethical righteousness of a right heart and life. This is the proper sense of Paul's word (*dikaioma*) in such a connection (*e.g.* in Romans 2: 26).

Paul's choice of his Greek negative before "walk after the flesh" is significant—it having this shade of thought They *being supposed* not to walk after *etc.*—*i.e.* on condition that they walk not after the flesh but after the Spirit.

Finally, let it be said emphatically that the current of thought throughout this passage is not upon justification by faith in the sense of pardon for sin; nor upon any sort of "imputed righteousness;" but is upon the deliverance of human souls from the presence and dominion of sin as aa reigning power in their flesh—their depraved nature—a deliverance achieved in consequence of Christ's incarnation in human flesh—and specially through the agencies of the Holy Ghost.

Romans 8:5-8—*For they that are after the flesh do mind the things of the flesh; but they that are after the Spirit, the things of the Spirit. For to be carnally minded is death: but to be spiritually minded is life and peace. Because the carnal mind is enmity against God: for it is not subject to the law of God, neither indeed can be. So then they that are in the flesh cannot please God.*

These verses have one object and one only—*viz:* to show what is meant by walking after the flesh and after the Spirit respectively; how they are squarely opposed to each other—the former against God and unto death; and the latter, for God, after God, and unto life.

They who live according to (or after) flesh, giving mind and heart, thought and affection, to things of flesh, care for those things supremely; give to them their hearts' love, and seek their happiness therein.—Over against this, those who receive the Spirit of God into their heart love the things of that Spirit; seek and love purity, obedience, God's worship and service—a state of heart and course of life totally opposite to living after the flesh.—Then (in verse 6) the minding of the flesh is death—in its tendencies and in its certain results; while the minding of the Spirit is life and peace.—This must be so (verse 7) because the minding of the flesh is enmity against God—precisely this; it is rebellion against His authority; it is hostile to God, in every element and feature for it does not subject itself to the law of God and never can. God's law demands a totally different heart and life in the strongest contrast with this. Then (verse 8) they who are in the flesh,—living in it, choosing to follow its impulses and be governed by its behests—"cannot please God." Nothing can be more demonstrably certain than this. There is nothing in this character that can please God; God would have His moral creatures hold the flesh under the control of right and reason. Every impulse toward sinful indulgence; all that is of the flesh as a sin-power—He would have them withstand utterly and supplant it by the force of a stronger affection—the love of God and the spirit of obedience to His will.—Cowles, pages 85-90.

Romans 8:14-17

For as many as are led by the Spirit of God, they are the sons of God. For ye have not received the spirit of bondage again to fear; but ye have received the Spirit of adoption, whereby we cry, Abba, Father. The Spirit itself beareth witness with our spirit, that we are the children of God: And if children, then heirs; heirs of God, and joint heirs with Christ; if so be that we suffer with him, that we may be also glorified together.

For all those who are led by the Spirit of God—those and none other, and all those without exception—are sons of God. Being led by the Spirit makes them sons. And the Spirit which they thus receive from God is not one of bondage—this negative form of statement being chosen for its greater strength. The son-spirit is not at all a spirit of bondage but of adoption, of filial confidence under which they spontaneously cry, "Father, Father." The Spirit of God himself witnesses conjointly with our own son-feeling that we are children of God. He inspires this feeling; He makes it more and more strong in our heart. It is no small part of His official work to breathe into our souls this child-confidence and prompt those outgoings of loving trust which voice themselves in the cry, "Father, Father."—The word "Abba" is the Aramean (original Hebrew) word for father, coupled here with the Greek word, perhaps to suggest that in every tongue and every nation, the children of God seize the word "father" as the best expression of their humble, trustful, loving heart toward God.—"If children, then heirs"—according to the universal law—inheritance being evermore the prerogative of sonship.—"Fellow heirs with Christ," inheriting the wealth of God even as He does and because we are in Him.—If indeed we suffer with Him, then shall we surely share with Him in His final glory—a truth often assumed or expressed by our Lord (Luke 12: 32, and 22: 28-30.) and repeated by His apostles.—Cowles, pages 91-92.

Romans 8:26-27

Likewise the Spirit also helpeth our infirmities: for we know not what we should pray for as we ought: but the Spirit itself maketh intercession for us with groanings which cannot be uttered. And he that searcheth the hearts knoweth what is the mind of the Spirit, because he maketh intercession for the saints according to the will of God.

This "likewise" compares the help given us by the Spirit to the inspirations of hope brought to view in the two previous verses; or possibly it may look further back in the chapter to other agencies of the Spirit.—"Helpeth our infirmities"—certainly in the sense of helping us *under our infirmities*; giving us fresh strength because we are weak and to enable us to bear burdens too great for our unaided strength.—Especially he helps us in prayer; first, to apprehend more truly what we need under present exigencies; and next, to pour forth our longing desires with groanings which no words can utter. This twofold help is clearly indicated here. "What to pray for as we ought"—means what our present circumstances call for and what therefore we have present occasion to ask. It is a precious truth that in our ignorance on this point, the Spirit of all light comes to our relief with suggestions wiser and better adapted to our case than our unaided wisdom could reach.

Next, this interceding for us is best explained, not as an intercession before God—this agency being elsewhere ascribed to our great Mediator and High Priest—the Son of God; but as an inspiration which acts upon our sensibilities and calls forth intense longings of desire." That is to say, the sphere of his action is not before the throne of God but within the human soul. Our conscious experience testifies that this is done by heightening immensely our sense of the preciousness of the blessings we need, and also by fresh and clear views of God's waiting readiness to "give us exceedingly above all we can ask or think."

God who searches all hearts knows the mind—*i.e.* the prayerful, longing state of mind—produced in us by the Spirit, because His spiritual impulses in our souls (His intercessions for and in the saints) are always in harmony with God's thought ["according to God."] The Father will always comprehend perfectly the prayer which His own Spirit begets and inspires, for it never can be any thing else or other than in and with His will.

The great truth imbedded in these verses takes us into the deep experiences of true prayer. The divine Spirit helps all really praying souls, both in the line of knowing what to ask, and of asking for larger blessings, with more intense longings and with more assured faith.—With the Spirit of God so freely and so abundantly promised—energizing our souls unto and in our prayer; suggesting what we shall ask for; inspiring desires unutterable and faith unfaltering;—what may not prayer accomplish!

Moreover, let it be noted that though Paul very often speaks of the Holy Spirit's dwelling within the souls of God's people as in a temple, yet He has nowhere else explained so fully what His special agencies are, particularly in the matter of prayer and of direct communion with God. This passage therefore has preeminent value and should have a large place in our conceptions of the positive agencies of the Spirit in Christian experience and toward the Christian life.—Cowles, pages 96-97.

Romans 8:28-30

And we know that all things work together for good to them that love God, to them who are the called according to his purpose. For whom he did foreknow, he also did predestinate to be conformed to the image of his Son, that he might be the first born among many brethren. Moreover, whom he did predestinate, them he also called: and whom he called, them he also justified: and whom he justified, them he also glorified.

"Working together" in the sense of cooperating, combining their influences and agencies to this result.—"We know," suggests that this is a matter of universal Christian experience and consciousness.—Remarkably this co-working for good gathers strength from both the preceding and the following context; from the preceding, for with such privileges of prevailing prayer in the Holy Ghost, how can anything that bears upon us in the line of either God's providence or His grace, fail to work for our good?—From the following context also; for those whom God has called according to His purpose, He has surely committed himself to carry through triumphantly to the glorious consummation of their purity and bliss in heaven.—Foreknowing, foreordering, calling, justifying, glorifying,—succeed each other in their natural order with no derangement, no break, no failure in the ultimate result. What God thus sets His heart upon accomplishing will never fail! This is a sufficient reason why all things must combine their agencies unto the good of all who love God, being His called ones—called with most distinct purpose to bring forth their final glorification.

Noticeably, the people upon whom all things shall combine for their good are described here, not primarily as "the called ones," but by a descriptive trait of much safer application—*viz.* "them that love God."—Who His "called ones" are, God himself would know perfectly; but men might mistake if that were the only criterion. But loving God falls within the pale of personal experience. "Them that love God" have the witness of it deep in their own heart—certainly so if this love has become a positive element in their character, and if it moves them perpetually to "*do his commandments*." "He that keepeth my commandments, he it is that loveth me,"

"Predestinated"—*to what?*—Not, to be borne from earth to heaven, primarily, merely, or chiefly—as some seem to suppose;—but *to be transformed morally into the image of Christ the Son*; to be saved from sin and made like Christ in spirit and life—a fact that should never be overlooked. Hence the proof of one's own personal election must always lie in this conformity of heart and life to the image of Christ, and will be in measure *as this* conformity; no more, no less.

It is worthy of notice that when Paul had occasion to say that Jesus would have many brethren like himself, even a multitude of redeemed souls, morally washed from their pollutions and wrought into His own pure moral image, He should say it in this particular way:—"That he might be the first-born among many brethren;"—which puts Christ wholly in the foreground; makes emphatic the fact of His infinite supremacy; and pertinently throws His people behind him as filling the subordinate place of "brethren" under their Great Chief.

Perhaps a word is due upon the point very distinctly assumed here—*viz.* that foreknowledge comes in the order of nature before "predestination." The order of the five successive steps—"foreknow," "predestine," "call," "justify," "glorify"—is plainly not accidental but of design;—is not a chance arrangement, but a well considered method, following throughout an order of nature. It is therefore legitimate to infer that foreknowledge is here before predestination, because it belongs here in the order of God's thought and act.—Noticeably Peter has the same doctrine;—"elect according to the foreknowledge of God the Father" (1 Peter 1:2).

On this subject I can only take time to suggest briefly the following points:

1. This order of nature in the divine mind *provides a sphere for human freedom*; *i.e.* for the really free agency of beings created to be morally free and therefore legitimately responsible for their free moral activities.

2. This is not equivalent to saying that personal election turns upon God's foreseeing what free moral agents would do *without and apart from* His own spiritual influence; but,

3. It may supposably open the way for election to turn upon what free moral agents are foreseen to do *under God's influence*.

4. As to the reprobate, the scriptures are entirely definite and emphatic in the doctrine that reprobation assumes them to have been tried morally with proffered truth, promise, mercy—but to have been found wanting and therefore rejected, disapproved, shut off from salvation; "given over to a reprobate mind because they did not like to retain God in their knowledge" (Rom. 1: 28).

Of course this reasoning assumes that what occurs here in time interprets to us what was God's thought and plan in the past eternity, and what was the ultimate ground and reason for it.—Cowles, pages 97-99.

Romans 9:30-33

What shall we say then? That the Gentiles, which followed not after righteousness, have attained to righteousness, even the righteousness which is of faith. But Israel, which followed after the law of righteousness, hath not attained to the law of righteousness. Wherefore? Because they sought it not by faith, but as it were by the works of the law. For they stumbled at that stumbling stone; As it is written, Behold, I lay in Sion a stumbling stone and rock of offence: and whosoever believeth on him shall not be ashamed.

What then, is the conclusion to which we come? This:—that the Gentiles who as a body had not sought righteousness, in the sense of the Pharisees, had yet attained to righteousness before God by faith in Jesus Christ—illustrations of which appear repeatedly in the history of Paul's gospel labors (*e.g.* Acts 13:44-48, and 17:4, and 18:4-6, and 28:23-28).

But Israel, the Jews—long following after the righteousness of the law in the Pharisaic sense—had come utterly short of attaining righteousness, because they sought it not by faith in Christ, but only by punctilious and proud works of law. Alas! they stumbled over the Messiah—thought of as a stone upon which unbelievers in Him must stumble and fall to their destruction. (So Isaiah 8:14,15, and 28:16).—How this very frequent symbol is used by our Lord may be seen in Matthew 21:42-44, and Luke 20:15-18. "Jesus saith unto them, Did ye never read in the Scriptures, The stone which the builders rejected, the same is become the head of the corner: this. is the Lord's doing, and it is marvellous in our eyes? Therefore say I unto you, The kingdom of God shall be taken from you, and given to a nation bringing forth the fruits thereof, And whosoever shall fall on this stone shall be broken: but on whomsoever it shall fall, it will grind him to powder."—Cowles, page 125..

www.ingramcontent.com/pod-product-compliance
Lightning Source LLC
Chambersburg PA
CBHW031239290426
44109CB00012B/364